Innovations in Corruption Studies

edited by

Alena Ledeneva, Roxana Bratu and
Philipp Köker

Modern Humanities Research Association
for the
UCL School of Slavonic and East European Studies
2017

Published by

The Modern Humanities Research Association
Salisbury House
Station Road
Cambridge CB1 2LA
United Kingdom
for the
UCL School of Slavonic and East European Studies

This collection also appeared as Volume 95:1 (2017) of
The Slavonic and East European Review

First published 2017

ISBN 978-1-78188-631-1

CONTENTS

Introduction

Corruption Studies for the Twenty-First Century: Paradigm Shifts and Innovative Approaches

ALENA LEDENEVA, ROXANA BRATU
and PHILIPP KÖKER

THE key question currently driving innovations in corruption studies is why anti-corruption reforms do not work. The explanatory factors for the disappointing outcomes of anti-corruption interventions over the last twenty-five years include those associated with: 1) understanding and modelling of corrupt practices; 2) measurement and monitoring; and 3) policy design and implementation.

This special issue emerges from the international seminar series on innovations in corruption studies in Europe and beyond held by the School of Slavonic and East European Studies (SSEES), University College London, between October 2015 and March 2016. The purpose of the series, which brought together researchers of the project 'Anticorruption Policies Revisited: Global Trends and European Responses to the Challenges of Corruption' (ANTICORRP), was to highlight innovations in the field of corruption studies regarding theory, methodology, analysis and policy. The articles in this issue represent a sample of the wider academic debates but focus on integrating expertise relating to Central and Eastern Europe into a comparative framework. The outcome reflects the openness of the authors to work across area and discipline and to ensure cross-fertilization between area studies and the social sciences in general. Such network-based research has been enabled by funding from the European Commission.[1]

The authors wish to thank the European Commission and the SSEES Centre for European Politics, Security and Integration for their financial support of the series, and all participants in the seminars for their constructive comments, useful suggestions and insightful contributions to the general discussion. The authors likewise gratefully acknowledge the assistance of the anonymous *SEER* reviewers, *SEER* Deputy Editor Dr Barbara Wyllie, General Editor Professor Martyn Rady and the *SEER* Editorial Board.

[1] Grant No. 290529, 'Anticorruption Policies Revisited: Global Trends and European Responses to the Challenges of Corruption'.

Wider ANTICORRP findings include a historical analysis of corrupt practices,[2] how they are reflected in the media,[3] how they surface in measurement,[4] how they relate both to good governance and to organized crime[5] and how they differ locally, regionally and globally.[6] In this special issue, we interpret 'corruption studies' narrowly, meaning academic discourse, separate from government policy, media or activist discourses. Rather, we focus on the challenges in corruption studies and the emergence of cross-discipline and cross-area analyses in order to accommodate the complexity and context-bound nature of corruption.

1. The challenges of defining and modelling corruption

One of the earlier academic definitions postulates that corruption is 'the intentional misperformance or neglect of a recognized duty, or the unwarranted exercise of power, with the motive of gaining some advantage more or less personal'.[7] Subsequent definitions have echoed this understanding, defining corruption as 'behavior which deviates from the formal duties of a public role because of private [...] pecuniary or status gains; or violates rules against the exercise of certain types of

---

[2]   Mette Frisk Jensen and James Kennedy (eds), 'Two literature reviews on the pre-modern and modern categories of cases respectively', ANTICORRP Deliverable D2.1, August 2013 <http://anticorrp.eu/publications/fighting-corruption-in-modernity-a-literature-review/> [accessed 24 October 2016].

[3]   Paolo Mancini (ed.), 'A comparative research on the print press coverage of corruption', ANTICORRP Deliverable D6.1, June 2016 <http://anticorrp.eu/publications/a-comparative-research-on-the-print-press-coverage-of-corruption/> [accessed 24 October 2016].

[4]   Alina Mungiu-Pippidi (ed.), 'A comparative assessment of regional trends and aspects related to control of corruption', ANTICORRP Deliverable D3.2.1, February 2014 <http://anticorrp.eu/publications/a-comparative-assessment-of-regional-trends-and-aspects-related-to-control-of-corruption/> [accessed 24 October 2016]; Jana Warkotsch (ed.), 'Case study reports on control of corruption and EU funds', ANTICORRP Deliverable D8.2, February 2016 <http://anticorrp.eu/publications/eight-case-study-reports-on-control-of-corruption-and-eu-funds/> [accessed 24 October 2016].

[5]   Salvatore Sberna and Alberto Vannucci (eds), 'Integrated report on the link between political corruption and organised crime', ANTICORRP Deliverable D9.1, February 2015 <http://anticorrp.eu/publications/integrated-report/> [accessed 24 October 2016].

[6]   Davide Torsello (ed.), 'Comparative country reports on institutional performance', ANTICORRP Deliverable D4.1, June 2014 <http://anticorrp.eu/publications/d4-1-report-on-institutional-performance-and-corruption/> [accessed 24 October 2016]; Lena Wängnerud, 'Case studies on gender and corruption: The link between gender and corruption in Europe', ANTICORRP Deliverable D5.3, October 2015 <http://anticorrp.eu/publications/case-studies-on-gender-and-corruption/> [accessed 24 October 2016].

[7]   Robert C. Brooks, 'The Nature of Political Corruption', in Arnold J. Heidenheimer (ed.), *Political Corruption: Readings in Comparative Analysis*, London, 1970, pp. 56–64.

private-regarding influence',[8] or simply the 'the abuse of public office for private gain'.[9] Irrespective of length, the conceptualizations of corruption are typically based on three constituents: a public official (A), acting for personal gain, violates the norms of public office and harms the interests of the public (P) in order to benefit a third party (C) who rewards A for access to goods or services that C would not otherwise have.[10] The formulations may vary (see Table 1), but the principle remains.[11] For most purposes, the definition of corruption employed by the ANTICORRP project is also based on the 'particularistic (non-universal) allocation of public goods due to abuse of influence',[12] underlining the emphasis on public-sector activity.

Table 1. Definitions of corruption

'TURN'	OF		FOR	
Betrayal	Public	Office/duty	Private	Gain
Diversion	Common	Good/trust	Personal	Interest
Ab(mis)use	Communal	Funds/resources	Individual	Benefit
Manipulation	Administrative	Barriers/influence	Unauthorized	Advantage
Exploitation	Institutional	Position/power	Group	Profit
Bending	Formal	Rules/regulations	Informal	Goal

The problem, however, with multi-faceted and context-bound practices of corruption is that they cannot be captured in a universal definition or formula. Thus, corruption tends to be used as an umbrella term for a wide range of complex phenomena. The more abstract a definition of corruption we achieve — such as 'abuse of public office for private gain' — the further

[8] Joseph S. Nye, 'Corruption and Political Development: A Cost-Benefit Analysis', *American Political Science Review*, 61, 1967, pp. 417–27.

[9] Daniel Kaufmann, 'Corruption: The Facts', *Foreign Policy*, 107, Summer 1997, pp. 114–31. Transparency International uses an essentially similar definition of corruption as 'the abuse of entrusted power for private gain'; this, in contrast to other definitions, is also applicable to private-sector corruption (Transparency International Annual Report, 2011 <http://www.transparency.org/whatwedo/publication/annual_report_2011>).

[10] Mark Philp, 'Corruption Definition and Measurement', in Charles Sampford, Arthur Shacklock, Carmel Connors and Fredrik Galtung (eds), *Measuring Corruption*, Farnham and Burlington, VT, 2006, pp. 45–79.

[11] Alena Ledeneva, 'Corruption in Postcommunist Societies: A Re-examination', *Perspectives on European Politics and Society*, 10, 2009, 1, pp. 69–86.

[12] Valts Kalniņš, 'Latvia: Mixed Regime with a Promise', *Anti-Corruption Policies Revisited: D3.28. Background paper on Latvia*, edited by Alina Mungiu-Pippidi, February 2014, p. 5 <http://anticorrp.eu/wp-content/uploads/2014/03/Latvia-Background-Report_final.pdf> [accessed 24 October 2016].

we are from understanding the complex, context-bound and fluid nature of corrupt practices. However, contextual complexity has to be downplayed to enable research and measurement, often based on the 'you know it when you see it' principle. The variation in forms of corruption is often grasped through the perception of experts or participants, as in Transparency International's Corruption Perception Index (TI CPI), and through the construction of aggregated indices. Thus, the measure used by the Political Risk Services' International Country Risk Guide (ICRG) — the third largest source of data within the TI CPI — is 'more concerned with actual or potential corruption in the form of excessive patronage, nepotism, job reservations, "favor-for-favors", secret party funding, and suspiciously close ties between politics and business'.[13] Re-integrating context into defining, modelling and comparing data on corruption constitutes an important dimension of innovation in this special issue.

1.1. The challenge of measurement and monitoring

Whereas the history of corruption is centuries old, the endeavour to measure corruption is fairly contemporary. Since the invention of the methodologies based on perceptions of corruption, much comparative research follows the assumption that corruption and its various aspects can be quantified and measured. It is presumed that such measurement can be performed not only within specific settings but also across contexts. Current attempts to measure corruption or corruption-perception can generally be divided into three main groups:[14] 1) surveys of households/individuals and organizations concerning their experience of corruption; 2) expert surveys regarding the perceived level of corruption in a specific country; and 3) composite indices that combine surveys of experts, civil servants and/or politicians.

The challenge of measurement relates to validity and reliability. Most scholars agree that it is neither possible nor practical to measure the actual volume of corruption as such. Quantifiable indicators that seek to measure the perceptions of corruption by a specific group of people and the policies implemented in order to curb corruption are considered approximations at best. Even if the social construction of 'perception'

---

[13] Political Risk Services Group, 'International Country Risk Guide Methodology', November 2012 <http://www.prsgroup.com/wp-content/uploads/2012/11/icrgmethodology.pdf> [accessed 24 October 2016].
[14] For a more detailed discussion, see Stephen Knack, 'Measuring Corruption: A Critique of Indicators in Eastern Europe and Central Asia', *Journal of Public Policy*, 27, 2007, 3, pp. 255–91.

is left out of the discussion, the mere assumption that a complex and multi-faceted phenomenon could be assessed in one figure by averaging people's perceptions of different types of corruption must be questioned. Quantitively, the corrupt practices included in the most prominent indices are far from unrelated and this may bias indices. Qualitative research into corrupt practices has established the so-called 'equalizing effect' of a number of practices legitimized by the fact that others are engaged in substantially similar exchanges.[15]

A further and potentially even greater challenge to using composite indices in corruption research lies in the fact that the agencies and non-governmental organizations (NGOs) compiling them are rarely fully transparent about their construction. As Stephen Knack points out, the definition of corruption underlying the index is often not made explicit, neither is the exact methodology.[16] Composite indices exacerbate this problem as they combine the results of several surveys. Sources on corruption are also frequently interdependent so that previous studies influence analyses and respondents' answers in following years. The degree to which sources lack independence is impossible to determine, which further reduces the usefulness of indices. Lastly, the majority of corruption indicators lack comparability over time (none of the Transparency International pre-2012 indices have been set for comparison across countries in the same year).

Trends within academic discourses, however, seem to replicate the importance of numbers. For example, a short history of the sociology of corruption emphasizes the demise of counter-intuitive approaches and the rise of numerical comparisons.[17] As the fundamental principles of modern scientific inquiry, measurability and universalism have shaped the 'global corruption paradigm'. It emerged in the 1990s, largely as a result of the collapse of Communism in Europe. Other factors include the 'end of history' argument, whereby the centrally planned economic models have proved unviable; an increase in the number of democracies with free media; globalization, which has brought countries and individuals into closer contact; the heightened role of international organizations such as the World Bank, the International Monetary Fund and the Organisation

[15] Monika Bauhr, 'Need or Greed Corruption', in *Good Government: The Relevance of Political Science*, edited by S. Holmberg and B. Rothstein, Cheltenham, 2014.

[16] Knack, 'Measuring Corruption'.

[17] Fran Osrecki, 'A Short History of the Sociology of Corruption: the Demise of Counter-Intuitivity and the Rise of Numerical Comparisons', *The American Sociologist*, June 2016, pp. 1–23.

for Economic Co-operation and Development; and the growing role of NGOs and of Transparency International Corruption Perception Index (TI CPI). The centrality of corruption as the world's Number One Enemy in the era after Communism and before terrorism, and the 'end of history' outcome of privatization and restructuring of economic institutions in post-Communist countries, have created a perfect setup for thinking 'big' in anti-corruption policy.[18]

1.2. The challenge of policy design and implementation

The increasingly high profile of indices such as TI's CPI influences policy at international level and persuades politicians at national level to implement anti-corruption policies. Institutional frameworks are reformed with the expectation that the changes will lead to an improved standing for the respective country in the existing ranks, indices and indicators.[19]

This three-stage process (defining — measuring — controlling) highlights a key problem in studying and containing corruption. Policy-interventions are often based on the assumption that corruption can be defined and measured, and that research results can then be translated into anti-corruption policy. There is an increasing number of examples of governmental reforms that were informed by corruption indices and stimulated by a desire to reduce perceived corruption — that is, to lead to an improvement in indicators, rather than in substance.[20] As a consequence, some scholars now argue against the use of corruption indices for political or social purposes.[21]

The complexity of the context and such characteristics as a country's level of economic development, political history, institutional legacies, ethnic make-up and socio-cultural traditions, are often ignored in policy design in favour of a 'can do', 'one-size-fits all' approach. The importance of context is often confused with the contested view that some cultures are more predisposed to corruption than others, which locks them into dependence on corrupt practices. Experimental evidence in behavioural economics dispels this myth and instead highlights the importance of

---

[18] Victorio Tanzi, 'Corruption Around the World', *IMF Staff Papers*, 45, December 1998, 4, pp. 1–23.

[19] Ledeneva, 'Corruption in Postcommunist Societies'.

[20] See examples outlined by Susan Rose-Ackerman, *Corruption and Government*, Cambridge and New York, 1999.

[21] Fredrik Galtung, 'Measuring the Immeasurable: Boundaries and Functions of (Macro)corruption Indices', in Sampford, Shackback, Connors and Galtung (eds), *Measuring Corruption*, pp. 101–32.

context.[22] Failures in the field of democratization — another area where earlier contextualized approaches gave way in the 1990s to the so-called 'no predisposition' outlook — also highlight the importance of a return to context and complexity in order to ensure the successful implementation of reforms.[23]

To overcome further challenges created by global, technological and digital developments, more nuanced approaches are needed, both in the academic study of corruption and in policy responses. Alina Mungiu-Pippidi argues that successful anti-corruption reforms tend to rely on the assessment of a country's development stage.[24] Policy should then be informed by respective local norms and implemented with cooperation at grassroots level — even making specific non-governmental actors responsible for the reforms' success. Such an approach marks a significant departure from the top-down approaches generally advocated and recommended by international agencies. The idea of integrating context-bound complexity into the measuring and monitoring of anti-corruption policies is also reflected in the 'paradigm shift' in modelling corruption outlined in the next section.

2. Policy paradigms: learning from failed anti-corruption reforms

While scholars have tried to account for the failure of anti-corruption reforms from different theoretical perspectives, many of them have stayed short of scrutinizing the assumptions of the 'corruption paradigm'. Followers of a principal-agent perspective agree that the scarcity of resources cannot explain the failure of anti-corruption reforms.[25] Rather, the lack of principals — be they government officials, civil society activists, NGOs or ordinary citizens — who are willing to enforce both new and existing policies appears to lie at the root of the problem.[26] This consensus

[22] Nina Mazar, On Amir and Dan Ariely, 'The Dishonesty of Honest People: A Theory of Self-Concept Maintenance', Journal of Marketing Research, 45, 2008, 6, pp. 633–44.

[23] Thomas Carothers, 'The End of the Transition Paradigm', Journal of Democracy, 13, 2002, 1, pp. 5–21.

[24] Alina Mungiu-Pippidi, 'Corruption: Diagnosis and Treatment', Journal of Democracy, 17, 2006, 3, pp. 86–99.

[25] Robert Klitgaard, Controlling Corruption, Oakland, CA, 1988; Susan Rose-Ackerman, Corruption: A Study in Political Economy, New York, 1978.

[26] Stephen P. Riley, 'The Political Economy of Anti-Corruption Strategies in Africa', European Journal of Development Research, 10, 1998, 1, pp. 129–59; Mark Robinson. 'Corruption and Development: An Introduction', European Journal of Development Research, 10, 1998, 1, pp. 1–14; Michael Johnston, Syndromes of Corruption: Wealth, Power and Democracy, Cambridge and New York, 2005; Inge Amundsen, 'Political Corruption and the Role of Donors (in Uganda)', Chr. Michelsen Institute Commissioned Report, Royal Norwegian Embassy, Kampala, 2006.

echoes the common assertion that anti-corruption reforms will not succeed if there is no strong political will.[27] The collective action perspective holds that people will choose to act corruptly as long as they expect that most other people will also act corruptly. Even if they realize that this is detrimental to the collective and see it as morally unacceptable, people will continue to engage in corrupt practices to equalize their chances.[28] In such settings, the cost of non-corrupt behaviour will rise since the actions of individuals will have no effect on the general situation.[29] Consequently, where corruption is part of expected behaviour, implementation of any anti-corruption reform turns into a collective action problem. Let us look into this paradigm shift in more detail.

2.1 Principal-agent model

The principal-agent model[30] situates the analysis of corruption at the interaction between principals (as bearers of the public interest) and agents (who might prefer corrupt transactions as long as the benefits of such transactions outweigh the costs). This is based on two key assumptions: 1) that there is a conflict of interests between principals and agents and 2) that agents are better informed than principals, leading to information asymmetry.[31] When a principal delegates a task to an agent, the agent gains an opportunity to pursue his or her own self-interest and to betray the principal's trust. The principal-agent model rests on the assumption that the principal is 'principled' and will take on the role of controlling corruption.[32] If the principal is corrupt and does not act in the interest

---

[27] Derick W. Brinkerhoff, 'Assessing Political Will for Anti-Corruption Efforts: An Analytical Framework', *Public Administration and Development*, 20, 2000, 3, pp. 239–52; Michael Johnston and Sahr J. Kpundeh, 'Building a Clean Machine: Anti-Corruption Coalitions and Sustainable Reform', *Policy Research Working Paper No. 3466*, World Bank, Washington, D.C., 2004; Robert Williams and Alan Doig, *A Good Idea Gone Wrong? Anti-Corruption Commissions in the Twenty-First Century*, Bergen, 2004.

[28] Rasma Karklins, *The System Made Me Do It: Corruption in Post-Communist Societies*, Armonk, NY and London, 2005.

[29] Donatella della Porta and Alberto Vannucci, *Corrupt Exchanges: Actors, Resources, and Mechanisms of Political Corruption*, New York, 1999; Anna Persson, Bo Rothstein and Jan Teorell, 'Why Anticorruption Reform Fails: Systemic Corruption as a Collective Action Problem', *Governance*, 26, 2013, 3, pp. 449–71.

[30] Best illustrated by the work of Susan Rose-Ackerman, *Corruption: A Study in Political Economy*, and Robert Klitgaard, *Controlling Corruption*.

[31] Ibid.

[32] Fredrik Galtung and Jeremy Pope, 'The Global Coalition against Corruption: Evaluating Transparency International', in Andreas Schedler, Larry Diamond and Marc F. Plattner (eds), *The Self-Restraining State: Power and Accountability in New Democracies*, Boulder, CO, 1999; James E. Rauch and Peter B. Evans. 'Bureaucratic Structure and Bureaucratic Performance in Less Developed Countries', *Journal of Public Economics*,

of the public good (as in the case of state capture or legal corruption, for example), the principal-agent framework becomes impractical as an analytical tool since there is no actor willing to monitor and punish corrupt behaviour.[33]

In the classic case — which refers to situations of bureaucratic corruption — the ruler is the principal and the bureaucracy is the agent.[34] 'Informational asymmetry' occurs when the ruler cannot perfectly observe what happens in the field since they are remote and do not possess the same information that the agents have. For example, tax collectors are better informed about the revenue potential of a particular tax base than is the head of the Treasury. This creates the opportunity for bribery.

However, recent thinking suggests that it is not only the bureaucrats who need to be controlled, but also the ruling elite. In this case — which refers mainly to situations of political corruption — rulers are modelled as agents and citizens as principals.[35] High-ranking government officials may institute or manipulate policy and legislation in favour of particular interest groups in exchange for rent or kickbacks. This model resembles the classic principal-agent framework in every respect with the exception that, instead of assuming the presence of benevolent principals 'at the top', it takes for granted another attribute — namely, the presence of benevolent principals 'at the bottom', in the form of ordinary citizens.[36]

Regardless of how the principal-agent relationship is modelled, the policy implications that follow from this framework hold that, in order to reduce corruption, the principal should aim at reducing the agent's incentives to engage in corrupt behaviour. Such incentives can most effectively be sustained through control instruments that decrease the level

75, 2000, 1, pp. 49–71; Jens Christopher Andvig and Odd-Helge Fjeldstad, 'Corruption: A Review of Contemporary Research', *Report R*, 7, 2001; Mungiu-Pippidi, 'Corruption: Diagnosis and Treatment'.

[33] Andvig and Fjeldstad, 'Corruption: A Review of Contemporary Research'.

[34] Gary S. Becker and George J. Stigler, 'Law Enforcement, Malfeasance and Compensation of Enforcers', *Journal of Legal Studies*, 3, 1974, 1, pp. 1–18; Caroline Van Rijckeghem and Beatrice Weder, 'Bureaucratic Corruption and the Rate of Temptation: Do Wages in the Civil Service Affect Corruption, and by How Much?', *Journal of Development Economics*, 65, 2001, 2, pp. 307–31.

[35] Torsten Persson and Guido Tabellini, *Political Economics: Explaining Economic Policy*, Cambridge, MA, 2000; Alícia Adserà, Carles Boix and Mark Payne, 'Are You Being Served? Political Accountability and Quality of Government', *Journal of Law, Economics and Organization*, 19, 2003, 2, pp. 445–90; Timothy Besley, *Principled Agents: The Political Economy of Good Government*, Oxford and New York, 2006.

[36] Roger B. Myerson, 'Effectiveness of Electoral Systems for Reducing Government Corruption – A Game-Theoretic Analysis', *Games and Economic Behavior*, 5, 1993, 1, pp. 118–32.

of discretion among agents, limit the monopoly of agents, and increase the level of accountability in the system. This may in turn be condensed to Klitgaard's formula: 'corruption equals monopoly power plus discretion minus accountability' (C=M+D-A).[37] The P-A approach to understanding corruption has shaped mainstream anti-corruption policies proposed by the World Bank, the International Monetary Fund and other international organizations.

Formal institutions are not, however, the only players that can influence decisions over whether or not to get involved in corrupt behaviour. As the overall failure of anti-corruption reforms in Africa suggests, the above formula works considerably better in theory than in practice. It rests on the assumption that it is possible to identify 'principled principals' who will not be driven by the kind of rational utility-maximizing calculations that drive the rent-seeking actions of agents. Moreover, this approach cannot explain why in a given institutional setting, different individuals behave differently. To complicate things still further, the principal may not be consistent in motivation or behaviour, whereas corrupt officials can be differentiated on the basis of 'quantitative morality'. The principal-agent approach also assumes that there is a way of designing and implementing new institutions that will not be sabotaged by corruption. It is here that collective action theory becomes relevant as an alternative analytical tool.

2.2. Collective action model

The collective action model questions the underlying assumption that every society holds at least one group of actors willing/able to act like 'principals', to create proper incentives and to enforce control mechanisms for the 'agents'. It starts from the assumption that all actors — rulers, bureaucrats and citizens alike — are rational maximizers of their own self-interest. However, within the framework of collective action theory, rationality is understood to be context-bound in the sense that it is highly dependent on shared expectations about how other individuals will act.[38] Contrary to the principal-agent theory, the collective action theory defies the view

[37] Klitgaard, *Controlling Corruption*.

[38] Elinor Ostrom, 'A Behavioral Approach to the Rational Choice Theory of Collective Action', *American Political Science Review*, 92, 1998, 1, pp. 1–22; Robert J. Aumann and Jacques H. Dreze, 'When all is said and done, how should you play and what should you expect?', *Discussion Paper 2005/21*, Center for the Study of Rationality at Hebrew University, Jerusalem, 2005; Ernst Fehr and Urs Fischbacher, 'The Economics of Strong Reciprocity', in Herbert Gintis, Samuel Bowles, Robert Boyd and Ernst Fehr (eds), *Moral Sentiments and Material Interests*, Cambridge, MA, 2005.

that universal policies can equip agents with strategies that are most rational to pursue.[39] Rather, it argues that the rewards of corrupt behaviour incentivize any rational actor to opt for such behaviour, and that individual strategies depend critically on how many other individuals in the same society are expected to engage in similar behaviour.[40] Consequently, in a context in which corruption is the expected norm, there will simply be no actors willing to take on the role of controlling corruption.

In a context in which corruption is the expected behaviour[41] the implementation of anti-corruption reforms turns into a collective action problem of the second order.[42] In such settings, monitoring devices and punishment regimes are likely to be largely ineffective since there will be no actors willing to implement them. Even if most people morally disapprove of corruption and are fully aware of its negative consequences for society, few rational actors should have an interest in establishing and enforcing reforms.[43] Hence, any anti-corruption policy based on such assumptions is not sustainable.

The conceptualization of systemic corruption as a collective action problem rather than as a principal-agent problem has significant policy implications. Following its logic the solution to curb corruption is to design policies that change actors' beliefs about what 'all' other actors are likely to do in such a way that most actors trust others to play fairly.[44] As argued by Larry Diamond, endemic corruption is not some flaw that can

[39] Mungiu-Pippidi, *The Quest for Good Governance*; Bo Rothstein and Marcus Tannenberg, *Making Development Work: The Quality of Government Approach*, Expertgruppen för biståndsanalys (EBA), Stockholm, 2015.

[40] Toke S. Aidt, 'Economic Analysis of Corruption: A Survey', *Economic Journal*, 113, 2003, 491, pp. F632–52; Olivier Cadot, 'Corruption as a Gamble', *Journal of Public Economics*, 33, 1987, 2, pp. 223–44; Ajit Mishra, 'Persistence of Corruption: Some Theoretical Perspectives', *World Development*, 34, 2006, 2, pp. 349–58.

[41] Åse B. Grødeland, Tatyana Y. Koshechkina and William L. Miller, 'Foolish to Give and Yet More Foolish Not to Take: In-Depth Interviews with Post-Communist Citizens on Their Everyday Use of Bribes and Contacts', *Europe-Asia Studies*, 50, 1998, 4, pp. 651–77; William L. Miller, Åse B. Grødeland and Tatyana Y. Koshechkina, *A Culture of Corruption?*, Budapest, 2001.

[42] Elinor Ostrom, *Governing the Commons: The Evolution of Institutions for Collective Action*, Cambridge and New York, 1990.

[43] Dino Falaschetti and Gary Miller, 'Constraining the Leviathan: Moral Hazard and Credible Commitment in Constitutional Design', *Journal of Theoretical Politics*, 13, 2001, 4, pp. 389–411; Bo Rothstein, *The Quality of Government: Corruption, Social Trust and Inequality in International Perspective*, Chicago, IL, 2011.

[44] Paul Collier, 'How to Reduce Corruption', *African Development Review*, 12, 2000, 2, pp. 191–205; Douglass C. North, John Wallis and Barry R. Weingast, *Violence and Social Orders: A Conceptual Framework for Interpreting Recorded Human History*, Cambridge and New York, 2009.

be corrected with a technical fix or a political push. [45] It is the way that the system works, embedded in the norms and expectations of political and social life. Reducing it to less destructive levels — and keeping it there — requires revolutionary change in institutions. [46]

2.3. The third way

Heather Marquette and Caryn Peiffer argued recently that both the principal-agent and collective action approaches to understanding corruption provide valuable insights and should be applied depending on the context. [47] They also pointed out that, while both approaches see corruption in wholly negative terms, people who live in systemically corrupt settings may perceive it as a productive strategy. This 'problem-solving' understanding of corruption — which means that in some situations it may be the only means of satisfying basic needs — highlights how corruption can play a productive function in the context of weak or ineffective state institutions.

In order to overcome the simplistic models dominating contemporary thinking about corruption, we should turn our attention to its complexities and the limits of the binaries predominant in political science: corrupt/non-corrupt, good/bad, ethical/non-ethical. The conceptualization of corruption through its opposites — good governance, integrity — has marked an important departure from universalist anti-corruption policies, but has in turn underpinned dualist perspectives on bad, poor or unethical forms of governance: rigged elections, [48] the failure of politicians and state officials to deliver funded infrastructure, [49] an unattractive climate for foreign direct investment, [50] fraud and extortion in the health sector. [51] Labelling entire contexts as corrupt, and assuming that corruption plays a role that is *a priori* dysfunctional, can be detrimental for understanding the full range of consequences, including the latent functions that may

[45] Larry Diamond, 'A Quarter-Century of Promoting Democracy', *Journal of Democracy*, 18, 2007, 4, pp. 118–20.

[46] Mungiu-Pippidi, 'Corruption: Diagnosis and Treatment'.

[47] Heather Marquette and Caryn Peiffer, 'Corruption and Collective Action', *DLP/U4 Research Paper 32*, Developmental Leadership Program, University of Birmingham, 2015.

[48] Bernd Beber and Alexandra Scacco, 'What the Numbers Say: A Digit-Based Test for Election Fraud', *Political Analysis*, 20, 2012, 3, pp. 211–34.

[49] Miriam A. Golden and Lucio Picci, 'Proposal for a New Measure of Corruption, Illustrated with Italian Data', *Economics and Politics*, 17, 2005, pp. 37–75.

[50] Aparna Mathur and Kartikeya-Singh, 'Foreign Direct Investment, Corruption and Democracy', *Applied Economics*, 45, 2013, 8, pp. 991–1002.

[51] Taryn Vian, 'Review of Corruption in the Health Sector: Theory, Methods and Interventions', *Health Policy and Planning*, 23, 2008, 2, pp. 83–94.

be enabled by corrupt behaviour, and identifying possible drivers for change.[52]

Experiments in behavioural economics undermine the common assumption that people can be divided into corrupt or non-corrupt, and instead point to the key importance of context. Quite simply, it cannot be assumed that an individual always acts with integrity. For example: a public official who embezzles stationery and uses a ministry car for personal shopping may also believe that s/he is person of integrity when it comes to the moral fight against the abuse of public office.[53] By the same token, an individual may steer clear of corrupt practices not so much because of their moral standing, but because they are excluded from certain networks of trust.[54]

The norms of bending the rules are defined much more by social circles and context than by geographical borders or personal values. Experiments by behavioural economists testing personal integrity have found no country variation. Moreover, the 'matrix' tests assessing people's predisposition to game the system by lying point to the key importance of context (not necessarily the same as 'country'), peer-pressure and what has come to be called 'quantitative morality,' whereby people cheat, but within limits and as appropriate, so that they can preserve their positive self-image.[55] Scholars of regional corruption have also found national surveys of corruption to be misleading.[56] National stereotypes such as 'Russia is a kleptocracy' or 'Switzerland's informal norm is to follow the formal rules' seem to be supported by the country ratings in the TI Corruption Perception Index. However, given the complexity of corrupt behaviour and its embeddedness in context, a more appropriate answer to the question of whether some countries are more corrupt than others should remain context-bound, reflecting upon the ambivalent nature of corruption (being both a problem and a solution). Capturing ambivalence in measurement requires methodologies for complex, hard to categorize, realities.

---

[52] Jonathan Rose and Paul Heywood, 'Political Science Approaches to Integrity and Corruption', *Human Affairs*, 23, 2013, 2, pp. 148–59; Cheyanne Scharbatke-Church and Diana Chigas, 'Taking the Blinders Off. Questioning How Development Assistance is Used to Combat Corruption', *Occasional Paper*, Institute for Human Security, The Fletcher School of Law and Diplomacy, Tufts University, June 2016.

[53] Mark Philp, 'Corruption Definition and Measurement'.

[54] Namawu Alhassan-Alolo, 'Gender and Corruption: Testing the New Consensus', *Public Administration and Development*, 27, 2007, 2, pp. 227–37.

[55] Mazar, Amir and Ariely, 'The Dishonesty of Honest People'.

[56] Nicholas Charron, Victor Lapuente and Bo Rothstein (eds), *Quality of Government and Corruption from a European Perspective: A Comparative Study of Good Government in EU Regions*, Cheltenham, 2013.

Future conceptions of corruption will have to transcend the binary oppositions between subjective and objective, public and private,[57] formal and informal, legal and illegal,[58] good and bad, prey and victim.[59] Understanding the inherent ambivalence of corrupt behaviour, the blurring of the boundaries and the grey zones in which it resides, its drivers and implications, presents a major challenge for corruption studies. Paradoxical concepts such as legal corruption, legislative corruption, state capture and business capture point in the direction of the unfitting nature of dichotomies for grasping the complexity of corrupt behaviour.

3. Innovative ideas in this volume

The contributions to this volume present new ideas on how to approach corruption studies in ways that address and help to overcome current deficiencies. In his analysis of existing approaches, Paul Heywood reflects on the studies of corruption over the last twenty-five years and calls for disaggregation. He questions oversimplified conceptualizations, dualistic typologies, the focus on nation-states as units of analysis and the insufficient differentiation of modalities of corruption. Heywood argues that mainstream academic research and policy-makers have devoted surprisingly little attention to unpacking the concept of corruption, leading to solutions that are doomed to fail since they are based solely on institutional reconfiguration. He asserts that corruption is better understood as a spectrum containing a number of different types of

[57] According to Rose-Ackerman, the very idea of a sharp distinction between public and private life seems alien to many people ('Corruption and Government').

[58] The relative nature of the 'legality' line (whereby an identical act, depending on the state of legislation, can be either corrupt or non-corrupt, and it is presumed that where acts are not illegal, they are not corrupt) has been illustrated in the context of tax-avoidance practices of offshore businesses and ethical concerns expressed in the media and by governments in the 2014 scandals around Starbucks, Amazon and other global giants, who have paid up settlements, despite their arguably legal operations. The entry into force in 1999 of the Organisation for Economic Co-operation and Development's Convention on Combating Bribery of Foreign Public Officials in International Business Transactions brought the non-corrupt act of bribing officials abroad into the realm of corruption in many countries. The UK Anti-Bribery Act of 2010 placed responsibility for the use of intermediaries in corrupt transactions on the beneficiaries of these transactions. See also, The Panama Papers <https://www.occrp.org/en/panamapapers/>.

[59] The example 'One does not condemn a Jew for bribing his way out of a concentration camp' (Rose-Ackerman, 'Corruption and Government', p. 9) illustrates the point that only the formal transgression by the official is corrupt: thus, only the guard is corrupt, not the prisoner. Moreover, the guard is corrupt only because he enriches himself in the process. Had he simply broken the rules and let the prisoner escape, the action would not be corrupt according to the definition. Thus we are on the territory of double standards, applied to the holders of formal office but not to others.

activities, not as dichotomies of 'petty vs. grand corruption', 'need vs. greed corruption' or 'systemic vs. individual' corruption. A thorough understanding and analysis of corruption is furthermore hindered by the fact that most research — including prominent corruption-perception indicators — and policy responses are focused on nation-states and government action. Heywood points out that globalization, too, has had its impact on corruption and the lack of focus on private sector action means that tax havens, tax evasion, capital flight and the offshore financial world have not been in the focus of regulation and advocacy. From this perspective it follows that, in order to move forward, anti-corruption research and advocacy must differentiate not only between types but also between levels of corruption. Such an approach would allow for examining the interdependencies between transnational developments (macro-level) and how nation-states operate in practice (meso-level) as well as ways in which corruption is experienced and practised within specific contexts (micro-level).

In a similar vein of disaggregation, Claudia Baez-Camargo and Alena Ledeneva provide an innovative examination of the crossover between the public and the private sphere based on the workings of informal governance in Mexico, Russia and Tanzania. Their argument questions the public/ private division at the heart of the most widely used conceptualizations of corruption. Their research findings question the capability-building approach in policy. Rather than focusing on obstacles to anti-corruption reforms, institutional design or leadership commitment to anti-corruption, they explore functioning patterns of informal governance that work so effectively that the anti-corruption reforms do not hit their targets. The instruments of informal power allow authorities to stay in power and to give citizens access to services and resources. The authors demonstrate the grey zones between the public and the private spheres and identify practical norms that enable the seemingly effortless crossover between the two. The three modalities of informal governance are termed *co-optation*, *control* and *camouflage* and refer to instruments utilized, respectively: 1) to re-distribute resources and tie strategically-relevant actors to the regime; 2) to manage people through personalized loyalties and extra-legal pressure; and 3) to manipulate façades of formal (democratic) institutions in order to serve private interests. Baez-Camargo and Ledeneva find that the resilience of corrupt behaviours is associated with the underresearched aspects of informal governance's normative and motivational ambivalence. Their findings call for a new generation of anti-corruption strategies grounded in political, social and economic realities rather than a transfer of models that have worked elsewhere.

Mihály Fazekas and Luciana Cingolani's contribution to this issue highlights the immense potential of innovative 'Big Data' approaches in research and policy evaluation, including the field of corruption studies. Taking as their starting point the lack of systematic evidence on networks between politicians and businesspeople and their effect on public procurement, the authors seek to measure the magnitude of high-level institutionalized corruption in government procurement by using micro-level data on some three million contracts awarded in twenty-nine European countries between 2009 and 2014. They test competing hypotheses on the effect of laws on political and party financing in controlling corruption in procurement and in counteracting high-level institutionalized corruption. On the one hand, more stringent political financing regulations can make it harder for companies to donate to political parties in return for government contracts. On the other hand, there is evidence that incumbents strategically modify political finance regulations for their own benefit, simultaneously depriving political opponents of access to valuable resources. Thus, restrictions on political financing may also be associated with an increase in high-level corruption.

Relying on statistical models, Fazekas and Cingolani find that the introduction of (additional) restrictions in the financing of political parties does not measurably curb the risk of high-level corruption. On the contrary, it increases the risk — irrespective of whether financing regulation is taken into account as a whole or according to its constituent parts. The authors also argue that, if laws are changed shortly before national elections, this can lead to a decrease in corruption levels after the elections. As such, their findings cannot provide a definitive assessment of the effectiveness of laws governing the financing of political parties, yet they point to a number of subsequent opportunities for research, for example in the area of policy implementation, the time needed for achieving regulatory impact, and the effect of institutional inter-dependencies.

Roxana Bratu, Dimitri Sotiropoulos and Maya Stoyanova test the transfer of anti-corruption policies in a context-sensitive comparative study of Bulgaria, Greece and Romania. They shed light on the complex interaction between the emergence of corruption as a major social problem and the implementation of anti-corruption policies. Comparing the Bulgarian, Greek and Romanian contexts, they analyse the way in which similar anti-corruption policies have produced different outcomes.

Their multi-methods framework combines qualitative interviews with the analysis of official documents and ample secondary data. All three countries have experienced vilification by the EU due to widespread and pervasive corrupt practices that were subsequently targeted by the imposition of blanket policies relying on Western-centric definitions of corruption. However, as activists and academics have pointed out, such one-size-fits-all approaches have not been successful in reducing corruption since they have ignored country-specific historical and cultural factors. The authors employ a social-constructionist view to uncover a number of trends in anti-corruption policy-formation. While some of these trends appear at first glance to be contradictory, Bratu, Sotiropoulous and Stoyanova show how they are nonetheless interconnected by examining the emergence, role and practice of anti-corruption in their respective contexts. Thereby, a particular focus is placed on the ways in which 'grand corruption' is conceptualized, institutionalized and tackled. They argue that anti-corruption measures are not merely a technical solution to an equally technical problem, but also an agency in the production of contemporary political culture.

To illustrate their argument, Bratu, Sotiropoulous and Stoyanova devise a schema to describe anti-corruption policy in each country in terms of evolution, institutions, implementation and politicization. Greece is presented as a case of 'unreflective accommodation' where anti-corruption is primarily implemented on the basis of de-contextualized international advice. Bulgaria shows a 'reactive legitimation' of anti-corruption where the problem is acknowledged but a significant implementation gap exists. Romania exhibits a 'proactive assimilation' of practices and thus emerges as the most promising case. Although imperfect, anti-corruption policies have in Romania become the top priority for policy-makers and prosecutors and illustrate the potential of 'proactiveness' that may serve as a template for other countries.

The combination of proactive leadership and a bottom-up, context-bound approach seems to be effective in tackling corporate corruption. The article by Stanislav Shekshnia, Alena Ledeneva and Elena Denisova-Schmidt seeks to identify agency for change in systemically corrupt environments. Building on a study of 110 company owners and directors, they search for political will among corporate leaders, test a new ethnographic approach to managing corruption at the level of the firm, and evaluate the effectiveness of a variety of mitigation strategies. Taking Russia as an example of a systemically corrupt environment, the article endeavours to offer insights for practitioners on how to 'manage' corruption, that is, how to devise and implement strategies that effectively mitigate corruption-related risks. Using a sequential multi-step research design, the authors first engage in exploratory analysis to identify and validate the prevalence of corrupt practices mentioned in academic literature and media reporting. The findings then provide the basis for in-depth interviews. Shekshnia, Ledeneva and Denisova-Schmidt identify four prevailing attitudes towards corruption held by Russian business leaders: toleration (held by a majority of respondents), exploitation, avoidance and management of corruption (synonymous with proactive leadership).

The authors assert that anti-corruption strategies at the level of the firm must target specific non-compliant practices. They propose a simple, yet comprehensive four-step approach that allows business leaders to identify suitable targets. They stress that while target practices are best identified bottom-up, willing corporate leaders implement mitigation strategies top-down. Systemically corrupt environments are generally conducive to tolerance and passive attitudes towards corruption among business leaders, yet preventive and controlling leadership action via formal hierarchies as well as informal networks can nevertheless provide for effective 'management' of corruption despite the pressures of the corrupt environment. The article concludes by recommending 'action points' for senior business leaders in systemically corrupt environments which can also be used for leadership training.

4. Conclusion

The contributors to this special issue of the *Slavonic and East European Review* share the belief that, despite great advances in corruption studies over the last three decades, there is still a lot to learn about corruption and anti-corruption policies. All the articles present specific contributions to academic debates and policy discourse about corruption and anti-corruption measures, questioning established practices and thereby pushing the boundaries of theoretical perspectives. That is not to say that this volume claims to present a final answer to the questions it addresses. The authors differ in their theoretical and methodological approaches, highlighting the variety of perspectives from which corruption and informal practices may be studied, explained and understood. It is not necessary for scholars and policy-makers to agree on a single conceptualization or measurement of corruption. It is more important that they are able to come up with context-sensitive policies that accommodate and adjust to the complexity of local environments.

The ANTICORRP project has proved successful in expanding research networks and producing novel policy recommendations. Questions nevertheless remain regarding the failure of anti-corruption policies and how to deal with corruption as a complex, dynamic and often contradictory phenomenon. Some promising new avenues respond to the puzzles in anti-corruption research and policy. For instance, how can we analyse practices of 'camouflage' where selective law-enforcement and misuse of the law are masked among the law's regular exercise and application? Corruption, where it is part of the system, is driven by a number of factors that are difficult to disentangle, but which include social pressure to engage in corruption and citizens' fear of the criminal justice system. Anticorruption activists also point out that classic anti-corruption programming misses some key elements that drive corruption. The majority of anti-corruption measures focus primarily on the enablers of corruption (lack of oversight and citizen knowledge) and respond by creating capacity for oversight and funds for the anti-corruption sector.[60] Yet such policies miss out on those contextual situations in which corruption can be seen as a mechanism of last resort to ameliorate structural disadvantages. There emerges a new generation of policies based on new indicators, oblique, or indirect approaches,[61] 'nudge' thinking[62] and collective-action logic[63] that make it possible to integrate context into analysis. Thus, in their as yet unpublished research Allan Sikk and Philipp Köker show how the turnover of electoral candidates in Central and Eastern Europe is associated with variations in corruption perceptions.[64] A rich new line of investigation developed by Roxana Bratu and Iveta Kazoka uncovers the complexity of this phenomenon by looking at the metaphorical representations of corruption in the media.[65]

---

[60] Cheyanne Scharbatke-Church and Diana Chigas, 'Facilitation in the Criminal Justice System: A Systems Analysis of Corruption in the Police and Courts in Northern Uganda', *Occasional Paper*, Series 1, Number 2, September 2016, Institute for Human Security, The Fletcher School of Law and Diplomacy, Tufts University.

[61] John Kay, *Obliquity: Why our Goals are Best Achieved Indirectly*, London, 2011.

[62] Richard H. Thaler and Cass R. Sunstein, *Nudge: Improving Decisions About Health, Wealth and Happiness*, London, 2008.

[63] Heather Marquette and Caryn Peiffer, 'Corruption and Collective Action'.

[64] Allan Sikk and Philipp Köker, 'Rejuvenation or Renomination? Corruption and Candidate Turnover in Central and Eastern Europe', unpublished paper prepared for presentation at the Annual Meeting of the American Political Science Association, Philadelphia, 1–4 September 2016.

[65] Roxana Bratu and Iveta Kazoka, *Narratives of Evil: Localized Understandings of Corruption* <http://anticorrp.eu/publications/narratives-of-evil-localized-understandings-of-corruption/> [accessed 24 October 2016].

Further research into policies capable of accommodating complexity is being supported by the British Academy and the UK Department for International Development Anti-Corruption Evidence (ACE) Partnership.[66] Comparative research into informal governance, unwritten rules and informal practices will be conducted in East Africa and Central Asia. The Horizon 2020 INFORM project, 'Closing the Gap between Formal and Informal Institutions in the Balkans'[67] and the UCL-based study of social and cultural complexity, Global Informality Project,[68] focus on the role of informality in corrupt environments. While we may not (yet) be fully equipped in terms of conceptual tools, measurement instruments and policy-thinking to accommodate the complexity of contexts in which corruption is grounded, this special issue aims to present at least a selection of new avenues and thereby feed into the on-going discussion of the new generations of anti-corruption policies.

---

[66] British Academy and UK Department for International Development, Anti-Corruption Evidence Partnership <http://www.britac.ac.uk/anti-corruption> [accessed 24 October 2016].

[67] See <http://www.formal-informal.eu> [accessed 24 October 2016].

[68] 'The Global Informality Project — The First Online Multimedia Resource on Informality' <http://in-formality.com> [accessed 24 October 2016].

1

Rethinking Corruption:
Hocus-Pocus, Locus and Focus

PAUL M. HEYWOOD

Introduction

Academic research on corruption and how to combat it has vastly increased over the last twenty-five years. However, the jury remains out on whether such an increase in productivity has had any meaningful effect in terms of actually reducing corruption. Indeed, some evidence suggests that global concerns about corruption are on the increase,[1] even if we have no reliable way of measuring precisely the extent of the problem.[2] The apparent mismatch between the attention focused on corruption and our collective capacity to make a practical difference naturally raises questions about what might be going wrong. This article identifies three reasons for such a discrepancy: the way in which corruption has been conceptualized in much mainstream academic research, resulting in 'magic bullet' solutions based on institutional reconfiguration (hocus-pocus); the tendency of much research and anti-corruption advocacy to concentrate on nation-states as the primary unit of analysis (locus); and the lack of sufficient disaggregation of different types and modalities of corruption beyond crude binary divisions that do not recognize the complexities of an increasingly transnational world (focus). Another way of presenting the argument is that approaches to studying and fighting corruption have been characterized by social theories developed in the mid-twentieth century being used to underpin practical remedies developed in the late twentieth century, but applied to a twenty-first century context that no longer matches the initial propositions.

1   Pew Research Center 2014 <http://www.pewresearch.org/fact-tank/2014/12/04/global-worries-about-corruption-are-on-the-rise/> [accessed 3 March 2016].

²   See Paul M. Heywood and Jonathan Rose, '"Close but no Cigar": The Measurement of Corruption', *Journal of Public Policy*, 34, 2014, 3, pp. 507–29; Paul M. Heywood, 'Measuring Corruption', in Heywood (ed.), *The Routledge Handbook of Political Corruption*, London, 2015, pp. 137–53.

Many of the examples used to illustrate and support the argument in this article are drawn from the experience of the post-Communist world, reflecting the signal importance of the end of the Cold War and the consequent reordering of the financial world order in stimulating the massive increase in the attention paid to corruption.[3] As noted by Abed and Gupta,

> The breakup of the former Soviet Union [...] brought on one of the most profound and far-reaching transformations of the twentieth century. The disintegration of the command structures in the old regimes triggered some of the most chaotic economic, political, and social changes in modern history. Absence of the rule of law and accountable systems of governance led to rent seeking, corruption, and outright thievery.[4]

The quasi-triumphalist belief that capitalism had 'won' contributed to the aggressive implementation of the so-called Washington consensus, characterized by what became the global hegemony of neoliberal, market-focused policy prescriptions best summarized by the twin axes of privatization and deregulation.[5] This post-Keynesian turn had a huge influence on how corruption was understood and the remedies proposed to address it.

Hocus-pocus: thinking differently about how to understand (anti-)corruption

There has been no shortage of attempts to define corruption.[6] In this article, I do not want to engage directly with that debate. The widely-accepted generic definition that corruption is 'the abuse of entrusted power for private gain', as popularized by Transparency International, is less than ideal, but nonetheless serves to capture the essence of what we instinctively understand by the term — even if it still leaves open the question of what

---

[3] For a good discussion, see Amy Linch, 'Introduction: Postcommunism in a New Key: Bottom Up and Inside Out', in Jan Kubik and Amy Linch (eds), *Postcommunism from Within*, New York and London, 2013, pp. 18–39, and also part four, 'Corruption', pp. 310–400.

[4] George T. Abed and Sanjeev Gupta, 'The Economics of Corruption: An Overview', in Abed and Gupta (eds), *Governance, Corruption and Economic Performance*, Washington, D.C., 2002, pp. 1–16.

[5] See Janine R. Wedel, 'High Priests and the Gospel of Anti-Corruption', *Challenge*, 58, 2015, 1, p. 8. The Washington consensus was originally developed in relation to Latin America, but soon came to assume a much broader focus.

[6] For excellent recent overviews of the core debates, see Mark Philp, 'The Definition of Political Corruption', and Oskar Kurer, 'Definitions of Corruption', in Heywood (ed.), *The Routledge Handbook of Political Corruption*, pp. 17–29 and 30–41.

exactly constitutes abuse and who decides. My emphasis here is more on arguments about why corruption occurs and what needs to be done to prevent it, rather than trying to establish a definitive account of what it precisely entails.

Over recent decades, the dominant approach to understanding corruption has adopted a principal-agent (P-A) lens influenced by neo-institutional economics; that is, corruption occurs when the interests of the principal and the agent diverge, there is informational asymmetry between them that favours the agent, and the principal can determine the pay-off rules of the relationship they enter into.[7] This broad approach, with various modifications and adaptations, has underpinned much of the work that looks at the impact of corruption on economic growth — the key driver behind the increased concern about corruption since the end of the Cold War.[8] P-A analysis thus influenced the reform proposals that characterized mainstream thinking about anti-corruption, reflected most notably in Klitgaard's (in)famous 'corruption formula': 'corruption equals monopoly power plus discretion minus accountability' (C=M+D-A).[9] The P-A approach to understanding corruption is also evident in the highly influential work of other scholars, notably Rose-Ackerman[10] and Bardhan,[11] that helped inform and shape mainstream anti-corruption policies proposed by the World Bank, the International Monetary Fund and other international organizations.

What followed from this understanding of corruption being primarily a P-A problem was the belief that it could be reduced by establishing institutions that would promote 'good governance', understood in strongly normative terms. These reformed institutions would change the incentive structures facing key actors, and would be supported by more effective monitoring and control mechanisms: that is, they would reduce monopoly and discretion, and increase accountability. In essence, the good governance approach rests on the belief that it is possible to identify 'principled principals', who will be somehow impervious to the kind of rational utility-maximizing calculations that drive the rent-seeking actions of agents. Such a notion

[7] Nico Groenendijk, 'A Principal-Agent Model of Corruption', *Crime, Law and Social Change*, 27, 1997, 3, pp. 207–29.

[8] See, as a representative example, Vito Tanzi, *Corruption Around the World*, IMF Staff Papers, 45, 1998, 4, available at <https://www.imf.org/external/pubs/ft/staffp/1998/12-98/pdf/tanzi.pdf>.

[9] Robert Klitgaard, *Controlling Corruption*, Berkeley, CA, 1988, p. 75.

[10] Susan Rose-Ackerman, *Corruption and Government*, Cambridge, 1999.

[11] Pranab Bardhan, 'Corruption and Development: A Review of Issues', *Journal of Economic Literature*, 35, 1997, 3, pp. 1320–46.

seems to run counter to the behavioural assumptions about motivation on which the argument rests. Moreover, this approach cannot explain why in a given institutional setting, different individuals behave differently. It also assumes that there is some way of designing and implementing new institutions that is not itself subject to subversion by corruption.

An alternative perspective, associated primarily with Mungiu-Pippidi,[12] and with Persson, Rothstein and Teorell,[13] seeks to understand corruption more as a collective action issue, critically dependent on citizens' assessments of how others will behave in any given situation. Such an approach reflects the model developed by Ostrom[14] in relation to common pool resources. Thus, according to Persson et al., in situations where corruption is so widespread as to be near systemic, individuals may well conclude that it makes little sense for them not to act corruptly when everyone else is doing so:

> Insofar as corrupt behaviour is the expected behaviour, everyone should be expected to act corruptly, including both the group of actors to whom the principal-agent framework refers to as 'agents' and the group of actors referred to as 'principals.'[15]

A similar idea was neatly encapsulated some years earlier by Grødeland, Koshechkina and Miller in the title of their article on corruption in post-Communist Europe: 'foolish to give and yet more foolish not to take.'[16]

More recently, Marquette and Peiffer[17] have provided a comprehensive assessment of the principal-agent and collective action approaches to corruption, arguing that the issue should not be understood in either-or terms. Instead, each perspective has something valuable to offer, depending on context. Moreover, they add a further perspective to the P-A/CA debate, pointing out that whilst both approaches see corruption in

---

[12] Alina Mungiu-Pippidi, *Contextual Choices in Fighting Corruption: Lessons Learned*, Oslo, 2011, pp. xiv, 7.

[13] Anna Persson, Bo Rothstein and Jan Teorell, 'Why Anti-Corruption Reforms Fail: Systemic Corruption as a Collective Action Problem', *Governance*, 25, 2013, 3, pp. 449–71.

[14] Elinor Ostrom, *Governing the Commons: The Evolution of Institutions for Collective Action*, Cambridge, 1990.

[15] Persson, et al., 'Why Anti-Corruption Reforms Fail', p. 457.

[16] Åse B. Grødeland, Tatyana Y. Koshechkina and William L. Miller, 'Foolish to Give and Yet More Foolish Not to Take: In-Depth Interviews with Post-Communist Citizens on Their Everyday Use of Bribes and Contacts', *Europe-Asia Studies*, 50, 1998, 4, pp. 651–77.

[17] Heather Marquette and Caryn Peiffer, *Corruption and Collective Action*, DLP/U4 Research Paper 32, 2015 <http://publications.dlprog.org/CorruptionandCollectiveAction.pdf> [accessed 3 March 2016].

wholly negative terms, for citizens who live in systemically corrupt settings it may in fact be a positive solution. This 'problem-solving' understanding of corruption — in which lived experience means that it may be the only means of accessing basic needs — stresses how corruption can therefore serve as a positive function for citizens (*and* political leaders) who need to operate and survive in the context of weak or ineffective state institutions.

Some of these attempts to overcome the dualism of P-A/CA approaches in understanding citizen responses to corruption have a striking parallel in the earlier work of Kuran on 'preference falsification', that is 'the act of misrepresenting one's wants under perceived social pressure'.[18] Early versions of the theory of preference falsification sought to explain the practical functioning of how many East European citizens experienced 'living a lie' under Communism, professing support in public for the regime they lived under, but privately despising it.[19] From a social theory perspective, Kuran wanted to explain why it was not possible for scholars to predict the point at which the Communist edifice would collapse in spite of the long-lived widespread opposition to it from within.[20] His approach sought to overcome the division between structural and rational choice approaches to explaining revolution by highlighting that preference falsification was both a source of stability for Communist regimes and also a reason for their rapid disintegration. In Communist regimes that routinely demanded support from citizens, individuals faced a personal trade-off between internal and external costs: that is, the psychological cost of preference falsification in expressing support versus the assumed cost of siding with opposition to the regime. As opposition was seen to grow, so the internal trade-off shifted for ever more individuals, resulting in the emergence of a 'revolutionary bandwagon'. However, for any given individual, it is impossible to know at what tipping point preference falsification gives way to action, meaning that the timing and speed of the overall snowball effect is inherently unpredictable. Kuran expresses this in terms of the relationship between an individual (i), the level of opposition (S), private preferences (x^i), and the revolutionary threshold (T^i): a person's internal payoff varies positively with their private preferences, which in

[18] Timur Kuran, *Private Truths, Public Lies: The Social Consequences of Preference Falsification*, Cambridge, MA, 1995, p. ix. Preference falsification differs from the classic Marxian notion of false consciousness, in that its subjects are fully aware of the falsification they are engaging in and knowingly hide their true feelings.

[19] This lived contradiction was brilliantly captured in the fictional account of life in post-war Hungary by Tibor Fischer in *Under the Frog*, Edinburgh, 1992.

[20] Timur Kuran, 'Now Out of Never: The Element of Surprise in the East European Revolution of 1989', *World Politics*, 44, 1991, 1, pp. 7–48.

turn are influenced by what they see around them, and so as x^i rises as a function of a growth in S, so T^i falls.

As Kuran argues, preference falsification is routine in all types of regime, not just non-democracies.[21] The argument has a clear resonance with the reluctance of individuals in a host of settings to take a stand against corruption even when they are strongly opposed to it: a fear of potential consequences can easily lead someone ostensibly to support activity they know is wrong. However, unlike collective action approaches that essentially account for non-action, preference falsification also helps explain why in some circumstances, people *do* take a dramatic stand against corruption, as happened in the 'Arab Spring'. Just as in the case of the collapse of Communism, it was impossible to predict the timing of the popular risings that characterized the Arab Spring, when rejection of corruption became a leitmotiv of protestors across the region. In regard to Kuran's formula, in this case it could be argued that the individual payoff for many citizens reached the point at which private preferences outweighed preference falsification, particularly once they saw others taking a stand: their individual revolutionary threshold was crossed and they joined the protestors.

Whilst not on the scale of the Arab Spring, popular protests against corruption[22] have become widespread globally, with major demonstrations taking place, for instance in India (2011), Argentina (2012), Lithuania (2012), Brazil (2013), Bulgaria (2013), Ghana (2014), Kuwait (2014), Mexico (2014), Thailand (2014), Ukraine (2014), Guatemala (2015), Honduras (2015), Iraq (2015) and Lebanon (2015).[23] Although there may seem little ostensible relationship between academic debates about theories of corruption on the one hand, and raw street protests on the other, they do share a significant common feature: in virtually all these cases, 'corruption' is presented as an undifferentiated target, operating as a sort of catch-all term to encompass negative behaviours.

In practice, of course, there are all kinds of implicit differentiations at work in both the academic literature and amongst the protestors. The latter are often broad-ranging in their demands for change, but insofar as they

---

[21] Kuran, *Private Truths*, p. xi.

[22] In addition, the global demonstrations of 15 October 2011 under the slogan 'United for #GlobalChange' were partly, if not explicitly, driven by concern over corruption. The other examples cited here had a primary focus on anti-corruption.

[23] Similarly, the so-called 'colour revolutions' of the early 2000s — notably in Georgia (2003) and Ukraine (2004) — were prompted in part by anti-corruption sentiments, even if the proximate stimulus was usually disputed elections. See Donnacha Ó Beacháin and Abel Polese (eds), *The Colour Revolutions in the Former Soviet Republics*, Abingdon and New York, 2010.

have a focus on corruption it is usually governmental, with political leaders at all levels (local, provincial, national) seen as crooks, thieves and general ne'er-do-wells.[24] In part, this reflects how the discourse around corruption has developed in recent decades. As Krastev has argued, following the collapse of Communism in Eastern Europe, corruption came to serve as a universal explanation for all failings:

> Corruption is the most powerful policy narrative in the time of transition. [...] Blaming corruption for the post-communist citizen is the only way to express his disappointment with the present political elites [...]. Talking about corruption is the way post-communist public talks about politics, economy, about past and future.[25]

In similar vein, Bratsis observed:

> Regardless of the interpretive frame [...], the specter of corruption is a constant [...], corruption seems to refer to underlying tensions, antagonisms, and traumas that, regardless of one's conceptual toolbox and political tendencies, cannot be ignored or passed over.[26]

That such arguments continue to have currency is evidenced, for instance, by the South African advocacy group, Corruption Watch, posting a feature piece in October 2015 with the title, 'Corruption Affects Everything and Everybody'.[27] Indeed, it has become almost a commonplace to refer to corruption in such all-encompassing terms, perhaps best reflected in the near apocalyptic pronouncement of the then World Bank President, Paul Wolfowitz, who in 2005 described corruption as the greatest evil facing the world since Communism.[28]

It is understandable that anti-corruption activists and campaigners should want to raise awareness of the serious problems generated by corruption, but there is a clear risk that in over-extending the use of the

---

[24] World Protests 2006–13 <http://policydialogue.org/files/publications/World_Protests_2006-2013-Executive_Summary.pdf>.

[25] Ivan Krastev, 'Corruption, Anticorruption Sentiments and the Rule of Law', in *Shifting Obsessions: Three Essays on the Politics of Anticorruption*, Budapest, 2004, p. 43.

[26] Peter Bratsis, 'The Construction of Corruption, or Rules of Separation and Illusions of Purity in Bourgeois Societies', *Social Text*, 77, 21, 2003, 4, p. 9.

[27] Corruption Watch <http://www.corruptionwatch.org.za/corruption-affects-everything-and-everybody/>.

[28] Cited in Jeevan Vasagar, 'Kenya gets $25m loan from World Bank despite corruption row', *The Guardian*, 26 January 2006 <http://www.theguardian.com/world/2006/jan/26/kenya.jeevanvasagar>.

term, the effect is actually to so void the term of real meaning that it will ultimately de-sensitize people.[29] Some forty years ago, Aaron Wildavsky published an influential article with the title 'If Planning is Everything, Maybe it's Nothing'.[30] Wildavsky's focus was on the developing world, and it is striking how apposite his analysis remains, if we substitute 'anti-corruption' for 'planning':

> Where planning [anti-corruption] does not measure up to expectations, which is almost everywhere, planners [designers of anti-corruption measures] are handy targets. They have been too ambitious or they have not been ambitious enough. They have perverted their calling by entering into politics or they have been insensitive to the political dimensions of their task. They ignore national cultural mores at their peril or they capitulate to blind forces of irrationality. [...] If they are supposed to doctor sick societies, the patient never seems to get well.[31]

Such seemingly contradictory calls will strike a chord amongst many who have observed anti-corruption efforts over recent years. Indeed, it could be argued that corruption, like planning in Wildavsky's original conception, has become 'a way of restating in other language problems we do not how to solve';[32] in turn most anti-corruption efforts are bound to fail unless we can find more effective ways of unpacking the problem we are seeking to address.

A starting point for such unpacking would be to move away from an undifferentiated conception of corruption. Even if we accept the generic definition of corruption as being the abuse of power for private gain, in practical terms that still leaves a vast array of different activities that fall within that remit. Indeed, so vast are the differences — ranging from a traffic officer extorting a bribe from an innocent motorist to a government minister selling decision-making to private interests — that it is unhelpful in operational terms to describe all such actions simply as corruption. We need to be able to make a meaningful differentiation between these (and other) types of activity, even if they fall within the same spectrum. Just

[29] Writing about post-Communist Russia, Varese has commented that where corruption is an all-pervasive norm, the very notion of corruption becomes meaningless. Federico Varese, 'Pervasive Corruption in Economic Crime in Russia', in A. Ledeneva and M. Kurkchiyan (eds), *Economic Crime in Russia*, London, 2000, pp. 99–100.
[30] Aaron Wildavsky, 'If Planning is Everything, Maybe it's Nothing', *Policy Sciences*, 4 1973, pp. 127–53.
[31] Ibid., p. 127.
[32] Ibid., p. 149.

as we routinely differentiate within other wide-ranging spectrums (for instance, between different frequencies in the electromagnetic spectrum, or between different severities in the Autistic spectrum), so we should expect to identify different types of corruption. As Bussell has argued,

> If we are serious about understanding the dynamics of corruption both theoretically and empirically, then a more meaningful conversation about the ways in which we operationalize the concept is necessary for pushing forward our knowledge.[33]

To be sure, there have been various attempts to identify such differentiations. One such recent approach is that of Bauhr,[34] who draws a core distinction between 'need' and 'greed' corruption. The former builds on coercion and extortion (for instance, forcing citizens to pay bribes to access services they should have a right to access), and the latter on collusion (for instance, government ministries selling favourable legislation to private interests). Bauhr points out how this distinction challenges the idea that corruption will necessarily give rise to collective action responses borne of popular outrage. Much 'greed' corruption is 'unobtrusive' and can remain invisible for long periods. As others have done, Bauhr questions the idea that relying on principals willing to enforce anti-corruption legislation is a credible approach to tackling the issue; instead, anti-corruption efforts would do better to address how corruption is experienced and seen in different societies and adjust their focus accordingly.

Other dichotomous classifications include 'petty' versus 'grand' corruption[35] (sometimes referred to as 'bureaucratic' versus 'political' corruption),[36] or 'systemic' versus 'individual' corruption. A more detailed schema was developed by Alatas,[37] whose typology drew a core distinction between 'extortive' and 'transactive' corruption, but with several sub-types identified within each strand (including, for instance, defensive, investive, nepotistic, supportive, autogenic) in order to provide a more

---

[33] Jennifer Bussell, 'Typologies of Corruption: A Pragmatic Approach', in Susan Rose-Ackerman and Paul Lagunes (eds), *Greed, Corruption and the Modern State*, Cheltenham, 2015, pp. 23–24.

[34] Monika Bauhr, 'Need or Greed Corruption?', in Soren Holmberg and Bo Rothstein (eds), *Good Government: The Relevance of Political Science*, Cheltenham, 2012, pp. 68–86.

[35] Susan Rose-Ackerman, *Corruption and Government*, Cambridge, 1999, pp. 27, 91.

[36] Inge Amundsen, *Political Corruption: An Introduction to the Issues*, Chr. Michelsen Institute Working Paper 7, Bergen, 1999, p. 3.

[37] Syed Hussain Alatas, *Corruption: its Nature, Causes and Consequences*, Aldershot and Brookfield, VT, 1990, ch. 1.

nuanced categorization. Johnston[38] has distinguished between different 'syndromes' of corruption, focusing on influence markets, elite cartels, oligarchs and clans, and official moguls; he outlines different political and economic opportunities, as well as the nature of institutions, in each of these syndromes.

Whilst these categorizations offer important insights, it is noteworthy that a great many of the most widely-cited and influential analyses of corruption make no reference to any such attempt to distinguish between different types — nor even to identify what is understood by corruption itself. In much of the existing literature, therefore, we are faced with a lack of fit between attempts to conceptualize and describe corruption on the one hand, and empirical accounts of the causes or impact of corruption on the other. Bussell notes that

> analyses of corruption are problematic for the purposes of cumulating knowledge on at least two levels. First, it is difficult to tell if analysts are using the same initial concept of corruption to inform their theoretical perspective. [...] Second, even in those cases where analysts specify their concept of corruption, the operationalization of that concept is likely to differ dramatically across different empirical analyses.[39]

Bussell herself suggests distinguishing between types of corruption according to how they relate to different types of state resources and in particular who has indirect influence and direct control over government policies, public licenses and contracts, government jobs and public goods and services.[40] This is a promising approach, but does not address a further issue that is explored in more detail below: that is, what 'counts' as corruption changes over time and space. As Neild points out, 'the nature of the activities that are held to be corrupt has changed with time and has differed from one part of the world to another, in step with the rules governing society'.[41]

Locus: thinking more deeply about where corruption takes place
My argument here is that differentiation between different types of corruption is a necessary, but nor sufficient, step if we are to find more effective ways to combat it in its various manifestations. In addition to that

---

[38] Michael Johnston, *Syndromes of Corruption*, Cambridge, 2005.
[39] Bussell, 'Typologies of Corruption', p. 24.
[40] Ibid., pp. 37–41.
[41] Robert Neild, *Public Corruption: The Dark Side of Social Evolution*, London, 2002, p. 5.

differentiation, we need to develop a more realistic understanding of the different levels and locations in which different types of corruption take place. It is striking that much of the academic literature on corruption focuses on nation-states as the primary unit of analysis. In particular, there is no shortage of work that seeks to link corruption with a host of variables that are measured at the level of nation-states, including such things as levels of GDP, foreign direct investment, human rights, judicial effectiveness, press freedom, political institutions, the number of women in government, bureaucratic rewards and so forth.[42] In these studies, sometimes corruption is the dependent variable, and sometimes the independent variable; rarely, though, is corruption defined in anything other than the most generic terms. It is arguable that this lack of conceptual specification is a key contributory factor in the sometimes contradictory findings from such research: notably, according to some authors, corruption can (in certain circumstances) have a positive effect on economic development, whereas according to others it has only negative effects; some argue that corruption flourishes under 'big' government, whereas others point to the Nordic states as evidence to the contrary. Even laboratory based experiments, which have become increasingly popular amongst economists who study corruption, have led to 'some puzzling, contradictory results'.[43]

One thing that nearly all these studies have in common is that their account of corruption, whether as dependent or independent variable, derives from some form of global index: most often, Transparency International's Corruption Perceptions Index, or the World Bank's Control of Corruption Index, but also the Global Corruption Barometer, the Business Environment and Enterprise Performance Survey, Freedom House reports and others. There has been a veritable explosion of such indices and rankings in recent years, described as a 'frenzy' by Cooley, with eighty-three new indices established since 1990.[44] One stimulus for this frenzy, according to Cooley,[45] was the desire to measure what was believed to be the ineluctable march of progress in post-Communist states towards

[42] For good discussions of the growth and contradictions of such studies, see Bo Rothstein, *The Quality of Government*, Chicago, IL, 2011, ch. 2; Mlada Bukovansky, 'Corruption Rankings', in Alexander Cooley and Jack Snyder (eds), *Ranking the World*, Cambridge, 2015.

[43] Sheheryar Banuri and Catherine Eckel, *Experiments in Culture and Corruption: A Review*, World Bank Policy Research Working Paper 6064, 2012, p. 2.

[44] Alexander Cooley, 'The Emerging Politics of International Rankings and Ratings', in Cooley and Snyder (eds), *Ranking the World*, p. 9.

[45] Ibid., pp. 7–8.

market-based liberal democracy. The new indices were designed to track that process, at the same time as underlining the superiority of Western institutional arrangements for delivering positive performance across a whole range of indicators.

The Corruption Perceptions Index and the Control of Corruption Index are well-established and have assumed an important place in the ever greater focus on 'the quiet exercise of power through indicators',[46] with global rankings increasingly driving policy-making both nationally and internationally.[47] However, there is now an extensive literature on the many problems — both conceptual and methodological — involved in attempts to measure corruption (and many other indicators of government quality), which relate primarily to a mismatch between concepts and their measurement, an over-reliance on proxy indicators and Western-focused elite bias.[48] There is no need to rehearse those arguments in any detail here, but it is important to note, as Cooley observes, that

> [a]t the most basic level, rankings provide specialized information about the performance of states on a number of issues. Rankings and ratings [...] reduce complex phenomena into quantifiable indicators that can be used to assess the performance of states.[49]

Leaving aside the question of how a single indicator can conceivably capture a concept as complex as corruption, the key point to underline here is the emphasis on states and, by extension, state activity. It is individual countries that are the focus of the most widely-cited indices.

This focus on individual countries in both measurement and ranking could be seen as somewhat ironic, given that '[t]he practice of global corruption rankings has been a central part of the construction of the corruption issue as a global, rather than comparative, country-specific, issue'.[50] By the 'global' nature of the problem of corruption, however, is meant that it is an issue that afflicts nations across the world, amenable to being identified and measured *within* state borders. Hence the rankings by country. Moreover, it is a problem that reflects *state* activity, meaning the

[46] Kevin E. Davis, Benedict Kingsbury and Sally Engle Merry, 'The Local-Global Life of Indicators: Law, Power and Resistance', in Engle Merry, Davis and Kingsbury (eds), *The Quiet Power of Indicators*, Cambridge, 2015, p 1.

[47] Cooley, 'The Emerging Politics', p. 18.

[48] Heywood and Rose, 'Close but No Cigar'; Heywood, 'Measuring Corruption'; Bukovansky, 'Corruption Rankings'.

[49] Cooley, 'The Emerging Politics', p. 14.

[50] Bukovansky, 'Corruption Rankings', p. 71.

institutions and activities of governments rather than the private sector. Hence the focus on institutional reforms to engender 'good governance', as discussed above.

There are two main problems with this approach to analysing corruption. First, it reflects an ever more unrealistic understanding of how corruption works in practice; second, it reflects an ever more unrealistic understanding of how contemporary states are organized and function. Profound changes in the nature and organization of the contemporary state mean that many of our traditional concepts and categories in regard to power and authority — perhaps most notably, the separation between public and private sectors and the autonomy of state action — need to be revised. There is burgeoning literature on the post-Cold War new world order and what might be termed the 'post-modern state' in which national borders have become increasingly irrelevant owing in large measure to new technologies that have changed how states operate.[51] Often described (not without controversy) as 'globalization', one of the key changes has been greater integration of national economies into the international economy through trade, foreign direct investment, capital flows, migration, the spread of technology and military presence. To be sure, these changes have been uneven and their full impact is still to be worked out, but it is undoubtedly the case that traditional notions of national sovereignty (and all that goes with that idea) are being refocused and reformulated.

Whatever the merits or otherwise of debates about globalization, what is clear is that some forms of corruption have seen significant changes in recent years. As Shelley argues,

> In recent decades, globalization has catalysed a sea change in the level of corruption. Money can easily be moved internationally, to major banking centers and offshore locales, via wire transfers. [...] In the new globalized economic order, worldwide corruption undermines states and permits the siphoning off of large amounts of national revenue with dizzying speed.[52]

Of particular importance in this respect has been financial market liberalization, which has wrought profound changes in the nature of and the players within the sector, with new fields emerging based on financial

---

[51] Robert Cooper, *The Post-Modern State and the World Order*, London, 2000. See also, Rob Atkinson, 'Globalisation, New Technology and Economic Transformation', in Olaf Cramme and Patrick Diamond (eds), *Social Justice in a Global Age*, Oxford, 2009, pp. 154–75.

[52] Louise I. Shelley, *Dirty Entanglements: Corruption, Crime and Terrorism*, Cambridge, 2014, pp. 66, 68.

mathematical modelling and algorithms that are dependent on access to cheap computing power.[53] The growth of new forms of ever more complex securities and derivatives, designed in part to stay ahead of regulatory frameworks, was accompanied by a changing attitude towards risk and speculation, which was in large part responsible for the global financial crisis that emerged in 2007–08. In turn, such developments have contributed to an erosion of trust in the financial sector, in particular, and also to the broader citizen disillusionment that has been reflected in the protests referred to above. As Hosking has observed,[54] trust is a vital element within the web of interdependence that characterizes contemporary societies, and the growing reliance on regulation as opposed to reputation as a primary mechanism for integrity management can undermine generalized social trust and contribute to conditions conducive to corrupt exchanges.[55]

It could be argued that it suits the interests of countries in the developed world, most of which do well in the global rankings, to focus on corruption within individual states. That way, they avoid having to confront the extent to which they are complicit in facilitating the growth in worldwide corruption. According to Bukovansky,

> focusing international attention on corruption as a characteristic of developing country governments can obscure the broader permissive context of the international financial architecture, through which activities such as offshore tax havens and money laundering operate to sustain corrupt payment systems, not to mention the facilitation of 'state capture' by financial interests.[56]

What is not open to question, however, is that some forms of financial corruption in the developing world have been assisted by opportunities for money laundering that are linked to lax enforcement of regulations in key centres such as London, New York and Singapore.[57]

---

[53] Nick Vanston, 'Trust and Reputation in Financial Services', *Driver Review DR30*, Foresight, Government Office for Science, 2012.

[54] Geoffrey Hosking, *Trust: A History*, Oxford, 2014.

[55] European Bank for Reconstruction and Development, *Life in Transition: After the Crisis*, London, 2011. See chapter 4, 'Corruption and trust', pp. 36–47.

[56] Bukovansky, 'Corruption Rankings', p. 64.

[57] TI-UK, *Don't Look, Won't Find: Weaknesses in the Supervision of the UK's Anti-Money Laundering Rules*, 2015; Global Witness, *Banks and Dirty Money: How the Financial System Enables State Looting at a Devastating Human Cost*, London, 2015; *Corruption and Money Laundering* <https://www.globalwitness.org/campaigns/corruption-and-money-laundering/#more>.

In an important recent study, Findley, Nielson and Sharman[58] focus on 'shell companies' that cannot be traced back to their real owners and therefore enable crimes like corruption, sanctions-busting, tax evasion and illegal trade in drugs and weapons. They make the telling point that although regulatory efforts underpin most attempts to combat these issues, notably via the inter-governmental Financial Action Task Force (FATF), a focus on the state misses the central role of service providers:

> It turns out that governments are not the main locus of compliance with international financial transparency standards. Rather, firms such as the GT Group, which provide incorporation services for clients seeking to set up new businesses, are the primary points where international standards mandating that shell companies can be traced back to their real owners are either followed or violated.[59]

The activities of shell companies, and their role in enabling corruption, highlights how the capacity of states to regulate activity is being transformed in an increasingly transnational financial world, in which the architecture of compliance mechanisms is itself open to manipulation by private interests.[60] Such developments, that create new opportunities for corrupt rulers in particular, underline the extent to which boundaries between public and private sectors are becoming increasingly blurred.

Some analysts have spoken of what amounts to the privatization of public power. Wedel's recent study of the so-called 'shadow elite'[61] has argued that in many areas the functional separation between public and private has effectively been superseded. Wedel developed her analysis on the basis of post-Cold War developments in Poland, before extending it to look at Russia and the USA. She identifies the rise of so-called 'flexians', who operate within new forms of social network and manoeuvre seamlessly between a range of different roles: government advisors, think tank employees, business consultants, media pundits and so forth. As a

---

[58] Michael G. Findley, Daniel L. Nielson and J. C. Sharman, *Global Shell Games*, Cambridge, 2014.

[59] Ibid., pp. 2–3.

[60] On the increasingly complex nature of the relationship between major corporations and nation states, see Stephen D. Cohen, *Multinational Corporations and Foreign Direct Investment*, Oxford, 2007. See also, Parag Khanna, 'These 25 Companies are More Powerful Than Many Countries', *Foreign Policy*, March/April 2016, available at <http://foreignpolicy.com/2016/03/15/these-25-companies-are-more-powerful-than-many-countries-multinational-corporate-wealth-power/>.

[61] Janine Wedel, *Shadow Elite: How the World's New Power Brokers Undermine Democracy*, New York, 2010.

result, 'private players are afforded fresh opportunities to make governing
and policy decisions without meaningful government involvement.
Whether for profit or to advance an agenda, they can privatize policy
beyond the reach of traditional monitoring systems'.[62] This has been
especially apparent, for instance, during US-led reconstruction efforts in
Afghanistan, where 'private contractors not only carry out public functions
but oversee, supervise and manage other contractors who perform such
functions'.[63] Wedel contends that transnational political and financial
elites have become ever more inter-linked, leading to the emergence of
what has been termed elsewhere a financial-political complex[64] and
reinforcing the ineffectiveness of regulation in the banking and financial
sector in particular. As Johnston reflects, '[i]n some respects, international
boundaries between the public and private sectors, and between political
and economic power, are weakening or vanishing as rapidly as international
borders'.[65]

This blurring of traditional spheres in the 'post-modern' state matters
greatly for our understanding of corruption. As Wedel herself notes,
analytic concepts such as 'corruption' and 'conflict of interest' struggle
to capture the operational complexity of how 'flexians' function.[66] Yet,
in much of the existing work, corruption is routinely understood as
necessarily involving state officials: 'the private wealth-seeking behaviour
of someone who represents the state and the public authority, or as the
misuse of public goods by public officials for private ends.'[67] Such an
emphasis cannot capture the reality of much contemporary corruption,
especially in some parts of the world: 'limiting corruption exclusively
to the state sector is difficult in most developing and post-Communist
countries, as there is an absence of clear boundaries between state office
and private business.'[68] Even if there is growing recognition amongst some
analysts of the need to extend our understanding of corruption beyond

---

[62] Ibid., p. 75.

[63] Lawrence B. Wilkerson, '"Shadow Elite": War and the Deadly Privatization of Public
Power', *Huffington Post*, 21 March 2010 <http://www.huffingtonpost.com/lawrence-b-
wilkerson/shadow-elite-war-and-the_b_428209.html>.

[64] Sy Harding, 'Beware the Financial-Political Complex', *Forbes*, 16 July 2012
<http://www.forbes.com/sites/greatspeculations/2012/07/16/beware-the-financial-political-
complex/#494484fc2bef>.

[65] Michael Johnston, 'Reflection and Reassessment', in P. M. Heywood (ed.) *The
Routledge Handbook of Political Corruption*, p. 280.

[66] Wedel, *Shadow Elite*, p. 12.

[67] Amundsen, *Political Corruption*, p. 2.

[68] Shelley, *Dirty Entanglements*, p. 66.

just the public sector, in practice many of the indices and rankings that measure corruption and have been used to assess both its determinants and its impact focus *specifically* on state or public sector activity. Thus, TI's Corruption Perceptions Index 'measures the perceived levels of *public sector* corruption',[69] and the World Bank's Control of Corruption indicator 'captures perceptions of the extent to which *public power is exercised for private gain*'.[70] One consequence of this focus is that the anti-corruption discourse — at least until very recently — has made virtually no mention of such issues as tax havens, tax evasion, capital flight, or the offshore financial world.[71]

It is therefore highly ironic that some of the leading measures of corruption have themselves contributed to the blurring of the distinction between public and private:

> The last two decades have seen the rapid rise of private actors playing governance functions such as setting standards, resolving disputes, and framing appropriate international responses to common challenges. [...] For example, though senior officials at Transparency International deny their role as a source of global regulation, TI has been the central actor in the spawning of a new transnational anti-corruption advocacy network.[72]

The lack of attention paid to changes in the nature and organization of contemporary states as a result of processes linked to globalization, and the increasingly transnational nature of corruption, seriously undermines those approaches that see corruption as a country-specific issue linked to the public sector. By extension, attempts to develop anti-corruption strategies that build upon such an understanding are almost bound to fall short, insofar as they tend to focus on institutional fixes that are either too generic or else wrongly targeted. In particular, the notion of 'good governance' that has underpinned many anti-corruption initiatives fails to reflect the reality of how contemporary states function in practice, even those that look like Denmark; as Mungiu-Pippidi points out, 'anti-corruption efforts cannot be effective unless they are contextual'.[73] That

---

[69] Transparency International, *The Corruption Perceptions Index* (emphasis added), available at <http://www.transparency.org/cpi2014> [accessed 3 March 2016].

[70] World Bank, *Worldwide Governance Indicators* (emphasis added), available at <http://info.worldbank.org/governance/wgi/index.aspx#doc-sources> [accessed 3 March 2016].

[71] Bukovansky, 'Corruption Rankings', p. 75.

[72] Cooley, 'The Emerging Politics', p. 17.

[73] Alina Mungiu-Pippidi, *The Quest for Good Governance*, Cambridge, 2015, p. 129.

means paying more attention to the complex dynamic between historical development paths and institutional architecture within individual states: 'by copying the formal institutions of present-day Sweden or Denmark, "one-best-way" transfer models presume that the actual path those countries took to get where they are does not matter.'[74]

There have been a number of recent studies that have sought to explore the long-term historical origins that underpin success and failure of states in terms of developing 'clean' or effective governance. Many of these stress the importance of institutional design and political choices. However, by definition, such studies generally concentrate on the internal architecture of given states, emphasizing, for instance, the nature of the rules of the political game and the nature of institutions (extractive or inclusive),[75] (in)equality in the distribution of income and assets,[76] the pursuit of power and military competition,[77] and so forth. Whilst they reinforce the need to pay attention to historical context and the role of agency, these types of study inevitably pay less attention to the impact of globalizing trends on the nature and operation of contemporary states. Indeed, Mungiu-Pippidi suggests that:

> while globalization has turned corruption into a global phenomenon in need of a global response, the battlefield upon which this war is won or lost remains national. [...] [T]his war cannot be fought and won internationally, although it might help if we conceptualize international anticorruption assistance as the empowerment of domestic forces.[78]

In regard to many manifestations of corruption, this is undoubtedly true. However, when dealing with the kind of transnational flows of corrupt money outlined above, as well as the emergence of transnational networks of elites, then national-level responses are not only likely to miss their target, but are also potentially vulnerable to precisely the kind of collective action difficulties highlighted in response to the principal-agent approach.[79]

The reference to Denmark is from her influential article, 'Becoming Denmark: Historical Designs of Corruption Control', *Social Research*, 80, 2013, 4, pp. 1259–86.

[74] Mungiu-Pippidi, *Quest for Good Governance*, p. 99.

[75] Daron Acemoglu and James A. Robinson, *Why Nations Fail: The Origins of Power, Prosperity and Poverty*, London, 2012.

[76] Jong-sung You, *Democracy, Inequality and Corruption: Korea, Taiwan and the Philippines Compared*, Cambridge, 2015.

[77] Neild, *Public Corruption*.

[78] Mungiu-Pippidi, *Quest for Good Governance*, p. 210.

[79] See ibid, pp. 183–85.

Focus: adjusting the lens

Hocus-pocus and locus-driven considerations indicate that if we are to address corruption for the purposes of effective policy, we need to disaggregate it into different types, as well as between the different levels and locations in which it occurs. In particular, we need a better understanding of how different forms of corruption operate in practice in specific settings. A useful starting point might be to distinguish between macro-, meso- and micro-level approaches, although it should also be acknowledged that these different levels do not operate as mutually exclusively spheres and developments in one can influence those in another. At the macro-level, the focus should be on the developing international geo-political and financial architecture outlined in the previous section, to see how it has influenced and shaped the emergence of new transnational corruption networks. Some important work has already started to be done in this area, such as that by Shelley and by Findley, Nielson and Sharman, referred to above. Not only do we need more studies in such a vein, but we also need to see them inform anti-corruption initiatives more directly. National level responses remain as primary battlefields, but concerted international efforts to address the ease with which corrupt money can flow across borders are also essential. Indeed, it is instructive in this regard to consider how the 1977 Foreign Corrupt Practices Act in the USA, a national-level response to concern over US companies engaging in bribery, came to act as a catalyst for subsequent efforts by both the OECD and United Nations to reconstruct corruption as a global problem.[80] Without similar international policy responses to tax havens, secrecy jurisdictions and other forms of complicity in money laundering operations, national level initiatives to prevent corrupt financial transfers risk being hamstrung. In fact, it is arguable that the development of transnational corruption networks, with their links to both international crime and to terrorism, represent the most urgent challenge the anti-corruption movement faces.

At the meso-level, we need to focus on corruption at the level of the nation-state, but also to move beyond mechanistic approaches to using indices and rankings — particularly those that provide a single rating per country — as dependent and independent variables. That is not because such approaches have no value; on the contrary, we have learned a lot in recent years about the causes and consequences of corruption, understood

---

[80] See Elitza Katzarova, 'The World is Broken: The Social Construction of a Global Corruption Problem', unpublished PhD dissertation, School of International Studies, University of Trento, 2015.

grosso modo, and those parts of the world where it is endemic as opposed to sporadic or isolated. For all the disagreements about precise causal mechanisms, we can assert — with caveats — that corruption (especially bribery) is more deeply embedded in less developed parts of the world; that it tends to be linked with less effective and poorer performing political and administrative institutions; and that it is also associated with poorer outcomes on most measures of quality of life, though not necessarily overall levels of inequality. But there is probably little more that we can usefully learn in this vein. Instead, what we need to understand in more detail is how and why it takes particular forms in different countries, and how its specific manifestations have developed in given settings. That is, within individual countries, we need to understand better the relationship between historical development paths, institutional configurations, socio-economic organization and particular corruption issues.

There is already some important work that has started to address such questions, and it is notable that much of it does not deal with corruption per se, so much as forms of governance,[81] as evidenced in the above-cited work by Acemoglu and Robinson, or in Rothstein's recent work on the quality of government.[82] In this book, Rothstein focuses on particular trajectories that have affected the quality of government (understood in his terms as referring primarily to impartiality in the exercise of power) to demonstrate that we need to understand how and why (in)efficient institutions become established in spite of what large-*n* analyses might lead us to expect about the relationship between democracy and economic growth. One of his chapters provides a striking case study of how Jamaica and Singapore have followed dramatically different trajectories in spite of strong similarities in their post-independence starting points in the early 1960s.[83] In similar vein, Mungiu-Pippidi looks at different historical paths to corruption control approaches in a range of countries, focusing on the competing claims of structural, institutional and equilibrium models and exploring in depth several contemporary 'achievers': Chile, Uruguay, Estonia, Botswana, Taiwan and South Korea.[84] What emerges from these

---

[81] Following the World Bank definition of 'governance' as entailing: i) the form of political regime; ii) the process by which authority is exercised in the management of a country's economic and social resources for development; iii) the capacity of governments to design, formulate and implement policies and discharge functions. See World Bank, *Governance: The World Bank's* Experience, Washington, D.C., 1994, p. xiv.

[82] Rothstein, *Quality of Government*.

[83] Ibid., ch. 9, pp. 193–206.

[84] Mungiu-Pippidi, *Quest for Good Governance*, chs 3–5, pp. 57–160.

various studies is that we need to explore combinations of issues, and interdependencies between them, not least because 'control of government in a society has to be understood as a complex balancing act rather than as a group of separate factors determining corruption'.[85]

In practical terms, this means we also need to understand the interdependencies between the transnational developments highlighted in the previous section, and the reality of how nation-states are organized in practice. Increasingly, we are likely to witness the emergence of multiple challenges to the formal models of governance within a given state, both from national and from transnational actors — in particular, challenges driven by demographic factors ('youth bulge', un- and under-employment), political crises (declining trust in the political class and institutions, exacerbated by issues such as migration flows into Europe), economic uncertainties (market volatility linked to geopolitical tensions) and their interaction with the rent-seeking opportunities that have expanded through globalization.[86] We therefore need more nuanced, detailed and sophisticated analyses of what local practices are understood as being corrupt, how they change over time, and what their organization looks like in given states.

Some twenty years ago, Cartier-Bresson explored the emergence of institutionalized socio-economic networks of corruption.[87] Such networks offer a system of hybrid co-ordination for the exchange of goods and services, which may be economic, political, social, symbolic and so on. Equally, networks establish standards — usually non-monetary and non-material — that manage such exchanges and engender values systems that are not reducible to market relationships. Cartier-Bresson stressed the need to explore how different organizational forms foster particular types of corruption and encourage individuals to join corruption networks rather than abide by the law. In a somewhat similar vein, though from a different disciplinary perspective, Ledeneva has explored informal networks in Russia. In a series of important studies over recent years,[88] she has

---

[85] Ibid., p. 129.

[86] See Jack Goldstone, Eric P. Kaufmann and Monica Duffy Toft (eds), *Political Demography: How Population Changes are Reshaping International Security and National Politics*, Oxford, 2012; David Held, 'Climate Change, Migration and the Cosmopolitan Dilemma', *Global Policy*, 7, 2016, 2, pp. 237–46.

[87] Jean Cartier-Bresson, 'Corruption Networks, Transaction Security and Illegal Social Exchange', in Paul Heywood (ed.), *Political Corruption*, Oxford, 1997.

[88] Alena Ledeneva, *Russia's Economy of Favours*, Cambridge, 1998; Alena Ledeneva, *How Russia Really Works: The Informal Practices That Shaped Post-Soviet Politics and Business*, Ithaca, NY, 2006; Alena Ledeneva, *Can Russia Modernise? Sistema, Power*

explored methods of informal governance to describe how power networks substitute the role of formalized vertical structures in the provision of public goods like security, justice and health. Describing 'sistema' as the reality of how things get done in post-socialist Russia, Ledeneva identifies different kinds of network that have built up around Vladimir Putin, including an inner circle, core contacts, useful friends and mediated contacts. The key point is that informal governance and networks undermine the core characteristics of a democratic state: in particular, the rule of law and properly functioning autonomous state institutions. Moreover, globalization has reinforced informality by opening up new opportunities and increasing the opportunity costs of trying to operate outside the 'sistema'. As Ledeneva indicates, the kinds of institutional reform derived from principal-agent understandings of corruption would be highly unlikely to achieve any purchase within the contemporary Russian state.

The meso-level approach draws more attention to specific sectors, in order to understand better the modalities of corruption and corruption-related risks in key areas. Although there have been some attempts to explore the link between particular sectors and corruption (notably, for example, public administration, the energy sector, the judiciary, defence and security and so forth), these have often taken the form of seeking to account for the extent or overall level of corruption within a given polity. What is needed now is a more detailed understanding of how and why corruption takes place within these sectors: what it looks like in practice, what particular characteristics it has, and how we can better identify risks. It is remarkable that in the latest version of Matthew C. Stephenson's compendious bibliography on corruption and anti-corruption, which runs to some 337 pages, just twenty entries specifically reference corruption and infrastructure, ten reference corruption and construction, and sixty-one reference corruption and procurement, despite these being prime locations of corrupt exchanges.[89] Items on other key sectors such as parliament, bureaucracy, health, education and utilities number in the tens, and there are just five entries that deal specifically with private sector involvement in corruption. Studies of the media and corruption focus overwhelmingly

---

Networks and Informal Governance, Cambridge and New York, 2013.

[89] Matthew C. Stephenson, 'Bibliography on Corruption and Anti-Corruption', February 2016 version at <http://www.law.harvard.edu/faculty/mstephenson/2016PDFs/ Stephenson%20Corruption%20Bibliography%20Feb%202016.pdf> [accessed 3 March 2016]. The bibliography, which is regularly updated, currently contains something in the order of 4,000 items. Several hundreds of these relate to 'growth', 'bribes/ry' or 'development'.

on its watchdog role in revealing scandals, but there is a dearth of work on corruption *within* the media, or its role in shaping understandings and framing debates about corruption,[90] or on the relationships between media owners and other key players in the post-modern state.

This brings us to the third, micro-level, approach that can deepen our understanding of how corruption operates in the contemporary world. Here, the focus should be on how and why individuals engage in various different kinds of corruption, moving beyond the basic incentives-based model of instrumental rationality that has underpinned much economic analysis.[91] We need a better understanding of how corruption is experienced and understood within specific contexts, what motivations and strategies lie behind an individual's decision to engage in a corrupt act, and how corrupt networks develop and sustain themselves. There have been some promising developments in the literature and again much of it is focused on the post-Communist states. A relatively early example is the study by Miller, Grødeland and Koshechkina, which looked at how ordinary citizens cope with government in Ukraine, Bulgaria, Slovakia and the Czech Republic, exploring the quality of democracy in these four countries and how it impacted on individuals' day-to-day dealings with officials.[92] Their study — based on focus group discussions and in-depth interviews with members of the public and junior officials, supported by large scale surveys — underlines the complexity of that relationship, and of the motivations that underlie individual actions.

A more explicitly qualitative approach has been adopted by Torsello and his colleagues, using ethnographic approaches to analysing corruption within public administration in a range of countries, including Hungary, Bosnia, Russia and Kosovo. This work emphasizes the importance of

[90] A notable exception is the recent work by Paolo Mancini under the auspice of the European Union Framework 7 programme, ANTICORRP (Anticorruption Policies Revisited), looking at how corruption is reflected in the media, what trends emerge in corruption coverage and how they are related with national and international strategies against corruption. See <http://anticorrp.eu/work_packages/wp6/> [accessed 7 March 2016].

[91] For a recent example of the continued prevalence of such an approach, see Benjamin A. Olken and Rohine Pande, 'Corruption in Developing Countries', *Annual Review of Economics*, 4, 2012, pp. 479–509: 'we find fairly robust evidence that corrupt behavior can be modeled in line with a few general economic principles: corrupt officials respond to monitoring and punishments as one would expect from basic incentive theory, and standard market forces influence the level of bribes.' For an alternative approach, see Ajit Mishra, *Incentives, Norms and the Persistence of Corruption*, Dundee Discussion Papers in Economics, No. 161, University of Dundee, 2004.

[92] William L. Miller, Åse B. Grødeland and Tatyana Y. Koshechkina, *A Culture of Corruption?*, Budapest, 2001.

looking at a variety of explanations to understand how corruption becomes embedded at societal level, exploring how the process of signification of corruption is shaped and influenced by cultural perceptions of integrity:

> because there are different local explanations to corruption and its related phenomena (clientelism, nepotism, trade of influence, abuse of office, illegal gift-exchanges and so on), corruption is extremely resistant to eradication and ultimately it is adaptable to institutional development and reform. [...] [H]ow the benefits of corruption are understood differs significantly according to the social and cultural norms and values that instruct citizens to perceive the real salience of corruption in their everyday life.[93]

The micro-level emphasis on the individual values and motivations that underpin the decision by citizens either to engage in or to resist corruption is complemented in the work of Zinnbauer, who looks at 'ambient accountability'. That is, he seeks to understand how people shape, use and engage with the built environment and public places and explores design interventions that can help citizens identify and exercise their rights.[94]

In addition to these kinds of analyses, we also need more carefully targeted quantitative and experimental approaches. In particular, social psychological research would be valuable to help understand the interactions that help influence individual decisions to engage in corrupt exchanges. In a recent article that bemoans the lack of social psychological research on corruption, in marked contrast to the rich body of work on deviance and rule-breaking more generally, Zaloznaya[95] calls for the application of interactionist social psychology to three micro-sociological questions: what are the collective roots (rituals, traditions, institutions) of beliefs that are favourable to corruption; what are the communicative processes through which individuals acquire their definitions of (in)appropriate behavioural patterns; and what are the particular contextual cues that evoke different

[93] Davide Torsello, Maria Giulia Pezzi, Elena Denisova-Schmidt, Nita Luci, Zaira Tiziana LoFranco, Muhittin Acar and Claudia Baez-Camargo, 'Outcomes of Ethnographic Research Conducted in Italy, Hungary, Bosnia, Turkey, Kosovo, Russia, Tanzania, Mexico' (ANTICORRP Deliverable WP4.2) 2015, available at <http://anticorrp.eu/publications/outcomes-of-ethnographic-research/>. See also, Davide Torsello (ed.), *Corruption in Public Administration*, Cheltenham and Northampton, MA, 2016.

[94] Dieter Zinnbauer, '"Ambient Accountability": Fighting Corruption When and Where it Happens', *SSRN*, 2012, available at <http://papers.ssrn.com/sol3/papers.cfm?abstract_id=2168063>.

[95] Marina Zaloznaya, 'The Social Psychology of Corruption: Why It Does Not Exist and Why It Should', *Social Compass*, 8, 2014, 2, pp. 187–202.

beliefs about corruption. Whilst recognizing the practical challenges of such research, Zaloznaya is withering about the assumptions of strategic instrumentality that underpin so many current approaches to analysing corruption, arguing that:

> It is precisely in the contexts that lack Western-style bureaucracies, have flexible boundaries between public and private domains, and rich legacies of gift and exchange economies, that dominant neoliberal approaches to corruption tend to yield inaccurate and culturally insensitive conclusions.[96]

Whilst symbolic interactionism is hardly likely to resolve the kinds of issues outlined in this article, it may — in collaboration with a range of other insights and approaches drawn from a range of different disciplinary traditions — help us to develop a more nuanced, complex and realistic way of both understanding and combating different forms of corruption at an appropriate scale and level.

Conclusion

This article has argued that three main reasons explain the mismatch between the academic attention devoted to corruption over the last quarter-century and its limited practical impact. First, the dominance of economistic analyses of the role of incentives in decision-making has given rise to proposed institutional fixes that are too abstracted from reality to gain purchase. That dominance was partly prompted by a misplaced assumption that market-based liberal democracies would become the modal regime type following the collapse of Communism. Second, an emphasis on the nation state as the primary unit of analysis has not kept pace with significant changes in how some forms of corruption operate in practice, nor with the changing nature of states themselves. Third, different types of corruption are insufficiently disaggregated according not just to kind and form, but also to the locations in which they occur (sectoral, organizational, geographical), the actors involved, and the dependencies that enable them. This reflects an overuse of the term 'corruption' in both academic literature and policy recommendations; insufficient attention is paid to what exactly is being addressed and ultimately, the notion of corruption, without adjectives, is a poor guide both to analysis and to policy prescription.

Although it is widely recognized in the literature that corruption is not just one thing, such recognition has often not been translated into research

---

[96] Zaloznaya, 'Social Psychology of Corruption', p. 188.

design. In particular, many recent large-*n* studies have in practice used an undifferentiated concept of corruption to serve as either a dependent or independent variable, seeking to explain a host of specific failings across a very wide canvas. Moreover, where there have been attempts to disaggregate corruption, these have often proposed bipartite, rather than graded, classifications (grand/petty, political/bureaucratic, need/greed and so forth). In practice, corruption is a *much* more complex phenomenon than such dichotomous approaches can conceivably capture. Indeed, it follows from the arguments outlined in this article that the notion of corruption incorporates at least four significant dimensions that should inform analysis, two of which relate to focus and two to locus (see Figure 1).

First, we should be much clearer when discussing corruption what specific type we mean: there are important differences, for instance, between kleptocracy, bribery, influence-peddling and so forth, not just in how they operate, but also in which actors and what kinds of resource exchange are involved. Too often in the research on corruption, there is a rhetorical acknowledgement of these different types followed by unreflective conflation of them in practice through reliance on aggregate indicators.[97] Second, we should specify in what particular sector the corruption in question takes place and, therefore, which constellations of actors are involved — as well as any relevant interactions and dependencies that serve as enablers. Third, we need to be more aware of the level at which any specific type of corruption is operating, whether it be a complex transnational network allowing shell companies to launder huge sums of money, for instance, or a network of local law-enforcement agents taking advantage of their position to secure non-monetary favours. Fourth, we should look more closely at the direction of corruption, in terms of the role of culture in relation to values, attitudes, norms, roles, rituals, framing mechanisms and how they help shape particular manifestations of what behaviours are understood as corrupt in different contexts.

Interacting with these four dimensions are two further considerations that should have a significant impact on how we analyse different forms of corruption and develop strategies to combat them. First, in any given jurisdiction, we need to assess the extent to which public services are managed and delivered on a more universalistic or a more particularistic

---

[97] I recently received an email from a PhD student (based at another institution) in relation to the Corruption Perceptions Index prior to 2012: 'I was hoping you could answer a question for me. As the nature of the CPI does not allow year to year comparisons and TI itself says it is inappropriate as time series data, why is it that all academic studies use the data in this manner when looking at the effects of corruption on economic growth or investment or so on?'

Figure 1. Four dimensions of corruption

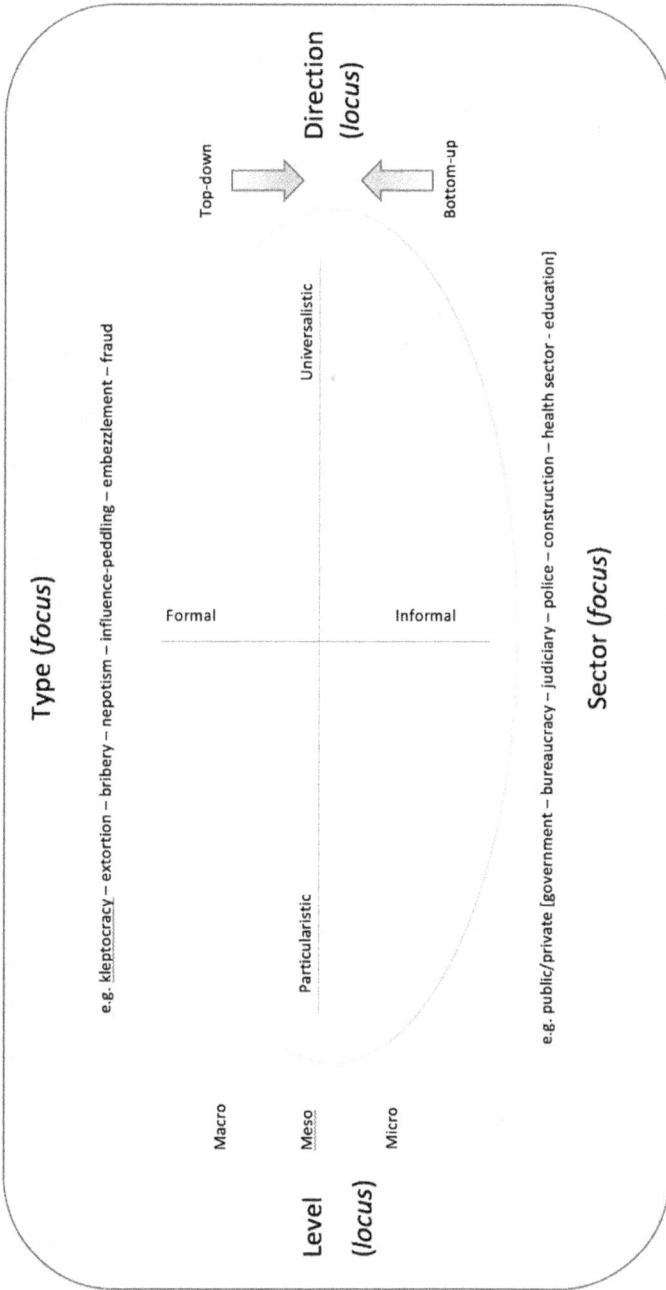

Type (focus)

e.g. kleptocracy – extortion – bribery – nepotism – influence-peddling – embezzlement – fraud

Formal

Informal

Particularistic

Universalistic

Direction (locus)

Top-down

Bottom-up

Sector (focus)

e.g. public/private [government – bureaucracy – judiciary – police – construction – health sector - education]

Macro

Meso

Micro

Level (locus)

basis, recognizing variation in different sectors is possible. Second, we need to assess the extent to which regimes are organized and operate in line with formal or informal practices, and how that has been shaped by the various developments associated with globalization. In short, whenever we are confronted with any analysis that refers to 'corruption' — particularly when corruption is defined as the abuse of entrusted power for private gain — we should ask: what kind of corruption is it; where is it taking place; who is involved; what are their motivations; who/what is needed to allow it to take place; what level does it operate at; what sectors are implicated; what are the key interdependencies; how does it relate to the broader social context? Without clear answers to these kinds of question, it will remain difficult to develop interventions that have an impact on the lived reality of specific instances of actual corrupt practices, as opposed to generic observations about which places are more corrupt than others.

2

Where Does Informality Stop and Corruption Begin? Informal Governance and the Public/Private Crossover in Mexico, Russia and Tanzania

CLAUDIA BAEZ-CAMARGO & ALENA LEDENEVA

Despite significant investment and anti-corruption capacity building in the past decades, 'most systematically corrupt countries are considered to be just as corrupt now as they were before the anti-corruption interventions'.[1] Statements like this are indicative of the frustration shared by practitioners and scholars alike at the apparent lack of success in controlling corruption worldwide and point to the need to rethink our understanding of the factors that fuel corruption and make it so hard to abate. In this article we propose a novel analytical lens through which to understand the root causes of corruption. Our arguments emerge out of the study of commonplace practices shaping political, economic and social outcomes in Mexico, Russia and Tanzania. The comparative analysis of these three seemingly dissimilar cases revealed striking similarities in rudimentary patterns of informal governance, which in turn can be linked to specific incentives to engage in corrupt behaviours.

On this basis, we propose to integrate notions of informality and informal practices into the discussion of corruption and aim to uncover the ways in which they are embedded in social and political behaviours. Given the tacit nature of the informal order embodied by the practices of informal governance in groups, organizations, elites and societies, it is perhaps not surprising that until now the literature on informal governance has been somewhat limited.[2] Therefore, we embark on a challenging yet effective

[1] H. Marquette and C. Peiffer, 'Corruption and Collective Action', U4 Research Paper, 32, University of Birmingham, 2015.
[2] T. Christiansen and S. Piattoni, *Informal Governance in the European Union*, Cheltenham and Northampton MA, 2003; T. Christiansen and C. Neuhold, *International Handbook of Informal Governance*, Cheltenham, 2012; A. V. Ledeneva, 'Russia's Practical

quest to assemble ethnographies of informal governance expressed in 'vernacular knowledge' and to identify similarities and differences across our three cases.[3] We discover rudimentary patterns of informal governance that perform a valued role for those actively engaged in them and establish that such patterns operate at most levels. Acknowledging the functionality of informal practices goes a long way in accounting for their resilience. The vernacular evidence we have gathered reveals the instrumental value of informal governance practices employed by authoritarian elites to ensure regime survival, which sheds light on the mechanisms underpinning the strong correlation observed between high levels of corruption and non-democratic regimes.[4]

The comparative analysis of informal governance is based on our respective experience of conducting extensive research in Mexico, Russia and Tanzania. Since we discovered remarkable similarities in the informal practices prevalent in our three countries, we have been working on possible ways of conceptualizing and framing informal governance norms and practices. Thus, while the ideas presented here do not stem from a rigorous comparative research design, nonetheless the parallels found are compelling enough to warrant theorization and further testing. With the prospect of opening new avenues for developing innovative approaches to anti-corruption policy-making, we hereby propose a comparative framework for further research on informal governance and corruption.[5]

Our conceptual framework highlights the underlying factors generating and perpetuating collective action dilemmas in contexts where a 'principled principal' is conspicuously absent.[6] Our inductive approach allows us to discover how informal governance mechanisms shape or impede the

Norms and Informal Governance: The Origins of Endemic Corruption', *Social Research*, 80, 2013, 4, pp. 1135–62.

[3] Jan Kubik and Amy Linch, *Postcommunism from Within: Social Justice, Mobilization, and Hegemony*, New York and London, 2013, pp. 57, 63.

[4] Susan Rose-Ackerman, *Corruption and Government*, Cambridge, 1999; Rajeev K. Goel and Michael A. Nelson, 'Economic Freedom Versus Political Freedom: Cross-Country Influences On Corruption', *Australian Economic Papers*, 44, 2005, 2, pp. 121–33.

[5] We will further test the ideas presented here in a wider set of countries in a comparative research project funded by the British Academy/DFID Anti-Corruption Evidence Programme where the authors are Principal and Co-Investigators. The case study countries in this project are Kenya, Kazakhstan, Kyrgyzstan, Rwanda, Tanzania and Uganda. For more information and updates on this research project, please see <http://www.britac.ac.uk/node/4660>.

[6] E. Ostrom, *Governing the Commons: The Evolution of Institutions for Collective Action*, Cambridge, 1990; A. Persson, B. Rothstein and J. Teorell, 'Why Anticorruption Reforms Fail — Systemic Corruption as a Collective Action Problem', *Governance*, 26, 2013, 3, pp. 449–71.

performance of formal institutions, thus accounting for the so-called implementation gap. In spite of cultural, historical and regional diversity, the three countries we have studied share a characteristic that is stubbornly persistent outside of the developed world: the failure to control corruption notwithstanding the adoption of exemplary legal frameworks that incorporate many of the internationally recognized best anti-corruption practices. Figure 1 illustrates the difference between the formal quality of anticorruption legislation and actual implementation in our three countries as captured by the Global Integrity Scorecard.[7]

Figure 1. Indicators of the effectiveness of anti-corruption laws in Mexico, Russia and Tanzania

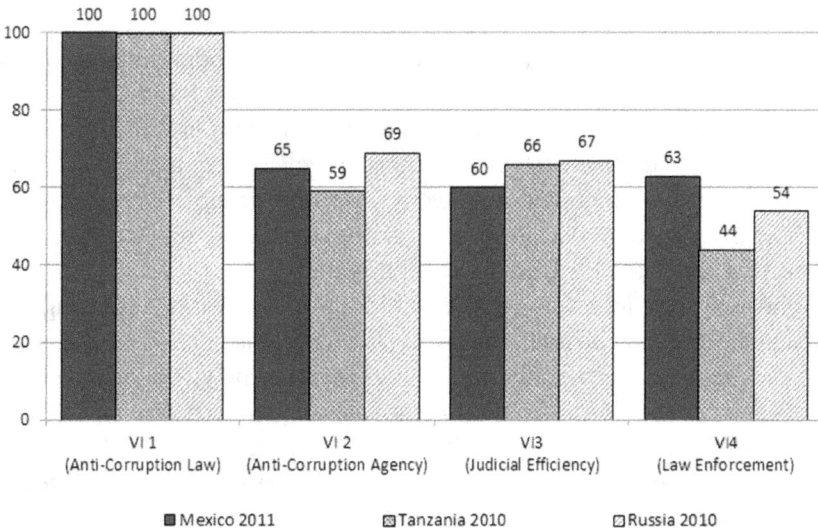

Such a discrepancy does not imply that these countries lack order or effective governance altogether. Rather, the evidence points to the essential role that informal norms and practices play in cases where corruption is widespread. In other words, as Anders found for the case of Malawi, 'beneath the layer of statutes, regulations and bureaucratic hierarchies

[7] Global Integrity's scorecard summarizes key findings from that organization's annual reports in which countries are evaluated, amongst other things, on the basis of the quality of their anti-corruption legal frameworks and the extent to which such legal frameworks are actually implemented and enforced. See <http://www.globalintegrity.org/research/reports/global-integrity-report/> [accessed 27 July 2016].

there is a complex web of interpersonal relationships amounting to a parallel structure within the civil service'.[8] We think that understanding the logics upon which such informal parallel structures function, and analysing them in comparative contexts, is key to overcoming limitations of conventional anti-corruption remedies.

Furthermore, while such logics may be grounded in informal norms and practices, they are not purely 'cultural'. Rather, we underscore that they are resilient because they perform critical functions for the political elites, private interests and ordinary citizens. In fact, we find that the instruments of informal governance perform both allocative and regulatory functions that are not dissimilar to those of formal governance, whereby they both re-distribute official power and resources, on the one hand, and regulate access to and exclusion from the benefits of such redistribution, on the other.

Our conceptual framework includes three major modalities of informal governance, which we have termed *co-optation, control* and *camouflage*. These modalities are instruments utilized by networks of actors spanning the public-private divide to sustain informal governance regimes whereby resources are redistributed in favour of some groups at the expense of others, ensuring discipline among the recipients of resources and protecting the networks from external threats.

The research focus is on the workings of networks including the particular interests of their members, the relationships between donors and recipients and other alliances bound together by virtue of unwritten rights and obligations.[9] The prominent role we give to power networks is supported by evidence gathered in our previous research which suggests that these powerful elite networks channel informal flows of influence, resources and sanctions.[10]

[8] G. Anders, 'Like Chameleons: Civil Servants and Corruption in Malawi', *Bulletin de l'APAD*, 23–24, 2002 <http://apad.revues.org/137> [accessed 29 July 2016].

[9] By network, we mean a 'pattern of interdependence among social actors in which at least a portion of the links are framed in terms of something other than superior–subordinate relations'. Laurence J. O'Toole Jr. and Kenneth J. Meier, 'Desperately Seeking Selznick: Cooptation and the Dark Side of Public Management in Networks', *Public Administration Review*, 64, 2004, 6, pp. 681–93 (p. 682).

[10] C. Baez-Camargo, 'Using Power and Influence Analysis to Address Corruption Risks: The Case of the Ugandan Drug Supply Chain', *U4 Brief*, 2012 <http://www.u4.no/publications/using-power-and-influence-analysis-to-address-corruption-risks-the-case-of-the-ugandan-drug-supply-chain/>; C. Baez-Camargo and R. Sambaiga, 'Between Condemnation and Resignation: A Study on Attitudes Towards Corruption in the Public Health Sector in Tanzania', in Davide Torsello (ed.), *Corruption in Public Administration: An Ethnographic Approach*, Cheltenham and Northampton, MA, 2016; A. Ledeneva,

Power networks are criss-crossing, overlapping groupings of individuals linked to a person in the position of power. Such networks operate across organizations and are therefore more suited analytically to capture the complexities of informal governance as compared to the formal institutions of the state. Whereas formal organizations are meant to work on the basis of universalistic and impersonal rules, power networks operate according to particularistic and personalist criteria.[11]

The three modalities of informal governance are highly interdependent, all being based, directly or indirectly, upon the covert redistribution of resources. Whereas co-optation is associated with recruitment to the power network, control is about ensuring discipline among the network members, while camouflage is needed to protect the network.

Co-optation

For the purposes of our analysis, we use the term co-optation to refer to the practices of building 'capacity to tie strategically-relevant actors to the regime elite'.[12] What is significant about the practices of co-optation we have identified is that they not only represent a mechanism of recruitment into networks, but also involve an informal redistribution of resources in favour of the recruited. The criteria for such recruitment and the non-transparency of the redistribution are both linked to corrupt behaviours.[13]

While informal practices of co-optation serve the purpose of network recruitment and maintenance rather effectively, they operate according to

Russia's Economy of Favours: Blat, Networking and Informal Exchange, New York and Cambridge, 1998.

[11] We thank our colleague Giga Zedania for pointing out this important distinction. See also, A. Ledeneva, *Can Russia Modernise? Sistema, Power Networks and Informal Governance*, Cambridge and New York, 2013.

[12] J. Gerschewski, 'The Three Pillars of Stability: Legitimation, Repression, and Cooptation in Autocratic Regimes', *Democratization*, 20, 2013, 1, pp. 13–38.

[13] The term co-optation is by no means new in the social sciences and has been conceptualized in various manners. In the sociological literature, and in particular in the theory of organizations, the co-optative process has been viewed as a mechanism of adjustment aimed at guaranteeing stability for an authority in the face of a threat. See P. Selznick, 'Foundations of the Theory of Organization', *American Sociological Review*, 13, 1948, 1, pp. 25–35. Acemoglu and Robinson categorize policy decisions as co-optation to the extent that these may be understood as a strategy to avoid upheaval (as in the extension of a franchise): D. Acemoglu and J. Robinson, *Economic Origins of Dictatorship and Democracy*, New York and Cambridge, 2005. For Bertocchi and Spagat (2001) the co-optation strategy implies the creation of a new, privileged group that separates itself from its group of origin: G. Bertocchi and M. Spagat, 'The Politics of Co-optation', *Journal of Comparative Economics*, 29, 2001, pp. 591–607. We opt for a broad definition since we find that the practices of co-optation have multiple manifestations and can be adopted by multiple social groups, not just political elites.

a logic that is different from that of the formal institutions of the Weberian state. The distribution of positions of power and authority effected through co-optation generates and supports relationships based on strong bonds of trust, reciprocity and loyalty. Such relationships, upon which the networks rely and to which they respond, are used for informal governance. Thus, in settings where co-optation practices are commonplace, formal accountability is replaced by personal loyalties and informal checks and balances (see section on control).

As the evidence suggests, co-optation practices involve not only networks of political elites but also networks associated to business interests, organized crime and grassroots social groups. Moreover, one could model co-optation practices as operating across at least three dimensions — top-down, horizontal and bottom up — depending on the nature of the networks involved (see Figure 1).

Prebendal co-optation: top-down pattern

We term the first, top-down co-optation mode utilized by political elites 'prebendal' co-optation because it involves the strategic political allocation of public offices to key elites, granting personal access over state resources.[14] In practice, prebendal co-optation entails the redistribution of the resources of the public sector to the private benefit of the ruling political networks and therefore also implies a privatization of public office.[15]

Our findings are consistent with the proposition that prebendal co-optation is a practice widely resorted to because it plays a key role in ensuring regime stability in that it is conducive to ensuring elite cohesion and to strategically securing bases of support for the regime. Such practices have been well documented and even conceptualized among other governance models as 'limited access orders'.[16]

State exploitation by means of appointments of allies and potential opponents into public office has been a common practice among political elites across the three countries we studied. Whether to fill their own

[14] N. Van de Walle, 'The Path from Neopatrimonialism: Democracy and Clientelism in Africa Today', in D. C. Bach and M. Gazibo (eds), *Neopatrimonialism in Africa and Beyond*, Abingdon and New York, 2012, p. 113.

[15] R. A. Joseph, *Democracy and Prebendal Politics in Nigeria*, Cambridge, 1987.

[16] S. Chayes, *Thieves of State: Why Corruption Threatens Global Security*, New York, 2015; D. C. North, 'Limited Access Orders in the Developing World: A New Approach to the Problems of Development', Policy Research Working Paper 4359, World Bank, Washington, D.C., 2007.

pockets or to selectively distribute among their own clientele, the recipients of the co-opting appointment invariably enjoy impunity in exploiting the power and resources associated to public office in exchange for mobilizing support and maintaining loyalty to the regime. This is the unwritten rule of prebendal co-optation: unconditional support for the regime is expected in exchange for impunity from corrupt exploitation of public office.

Prebendal cooptation practices in the three countries, although informal and in principle clandestine, are also commonplaces in their respective societies. They are open secrets which have come to form part of the political culture, as well as folklore, reflected by the euphemisms people use to refer to them. Strikingly, these euphemisms are similar across the three cases and point to the underlying logic of 'feeding'.

Expectations about 'irregularities' in the behaviours of the *políticos* became part of popular Mexican political culture: when a state official obtained an exploitable position in public office, in popular speech this would be referred to as 'to be given a bone' (*le dieron un hueso*) making reference to how the office holder would be able to gnaw on the bone.[17] Similarly, the term 'feeding' (*kormlenie*) was used in Russia to denote the distribution of regional constituencies for private needs. It has evolved into a widely recognized practical norm, captured in Nikolai Karamzin's remark, 'one steals' (*voruyut*);[18] in Soviet times, the so-called 'feeding places' (*kormushki*) for the party nomenklatura, and pilfering or siphoning out state property by workers (*nesuny*). While these practices are often seen as compensatory for the oppressive regimes,[19] in the aftermath of the collapse of the Soviet Union, Russia came to be seen as a *kleptocracy*.[20] It is similarly common in Tanzania for public officials to extract rents from their positions in public office. Even if the popular perception of leadership as an opportunity to accumulate resources and move up the social ladder is not fully articulated, being poor is anecdotally linked to being stupid. On the contrary, being smart and engaging in some form of prebendalism

[17] During the seventy-year-long hegemonic rule of the Mexican Partido Revolucionario Institucional (PRI) personal enrichment of party officials was not only tolerated but even considered a sign of adeptness and suitability for public office — as expressed by a quote of a powerful PRI cadre who said that 'a politician who is poor is a poor politician' (*un político pobre es un pobre político*).

[18] N. M. Karamzin, *Primechaniia k Istorii Gosudarstva Rossiiskogo*, vols 1–4, 1852.

[19] K. M. Simis, *USSR: The Corrupt Society*, New York, 1982.

[20] J. Granville, '"Dermokratizatsiya" and "Prikhvatizatsiya": The Russian Kleptocracy and Rise of Organized Crime', *Demokratizatsiya*, 11, 2003, 3, pp. 449–57; S. Rosefielde, 'Russia: An Abnormal Country', *The European Journal of Comparative Economics*, 2, 2005, 1, pp. 3–16; K. Dawisha, *Putin's Kleptocracy: Who Owns Russia?*, New York, 2014.

is referred to locally as 'eating' (*kula*), and is associated to what Bayart has coined as the 'politics of the belly'.[21]

Apart from satisfying personal needs, prebendal co-optation is an instrument of power sharing: it works by recruiting potential adversaries into the ruling network while also rewarding loyal supporters. In our three cases, prebendal co-optation is enacted through formal and informal appointments made by a strong president. In the Mexican and Tanzanian cases, the president has traditionally been both head of state and leader of the hegemonic party with extraordinary powers: the Partido Revolucionario Institucional (PRI) held power uninterruptedly in Mexico for seventy-one years from 1929 until 2000,[22] while the Chama cha Mapinduzi (CCM) has been in power in Tanzania since independence in 1961–62. In these cases, the influential political networks were embedded in the ruling party, which was recognized as the only viable vehicle to pursue a political career. Both the PRI and CCM have accommodated a ruling elite composed of a number of political factions associated with influential social groups and regional interests. The two parties have played a crucial role promoting elite cohesion since, beyond the staging of regular elections, real competition for power took place among rival factions through internal (and mostly non-transparent) party processes whereby the 'losing' groups could be compensated in the form of appointments to plum positions in government. This was also the case within the Communist Party of the Soviet Union (CPSU) and to some extent is also replicated within present-day Russia's ruling party, United Russia.

Prebendal co-optation has therefore played an important role in maintaining the support and loyalty of influential groups and party factions. For instance, Mexican labour union leaders, many of them notorious for amassing huge personal fortunes, often had substantial powers because of the strategic function they played through the incorporation of their organizations into the ruling party. They traded social stability and votes in exchange for high-level positions and access to wealth. One finds similar arrangements between the ruling United Russia party and regional

[21] In Nigeria, the analogous practice is called 'stomach infrastructure'. J. F. Bayart, *The State in Africa: The Politics of the Belly*, New York, 1993.

[22] Although the PRI has been back in power since 2012, the political context has changed and can no longer be characterized as a hegemonic party regime. Thus, while many of the informal governance patterns that were established and consolidated during the period of PRI hegemony in the twentieth century have continued to be relevant to date, more research is needed to discern exactly how they have been transformed by democratization and alternation in power. The patterns identified in this study should therefore be, for the most part, understood as associated to the hegemonic party era of Mexican politics.

governors, where personalized loyalty is often the key criteria for political appointments, as well as within the Tanzanian CCM where the unwritten rule of impunity has always been respected for allies as long as they have remained politically influential — commanding loyal bases of support and delivering votes for the party.

In Russia, 'sharing' with those above and below implies a 'certain practical sense' with regard to feeding.[23] Although granted some impunity, a Russian official should remain careful not to lose his sense of proportion, and consult with the boss, exercise fairness and above all transparency in sharing kickbacks with bosses, peers and subordinates. Regional 'feeds' are informally, yet zealously, monitored. As a Russian anecdote has it, 'state officials are caught not for stealing but for stealing too much for their rank'.

The pattern is slightly different in Tanzania where influential political figures associated with corruption scandals may be removed from office, sometimes relocated to other positions of public authority and returned to their home constituencies where they are received as heroes,[24] but in any event they are never prosecuted.

Historically, prebendalism has been associated with traditional societies where resource constraints made this method of remunerating public officials attractive, as during the late middle ages in Russia where political elites rewarded disinterested public servants who served their country well with exclusive rights to exploit regional constituencies for private needs.[25] Our cases, however, demonstrate that prebendal co-optation is not only a pre-modern phenomenon. Rather, prebendal co-optation has been resorted to on the part of state officials and beyond as a practical, if semi-legitimate, norm which we nowadays associate with embezzlement and political corruption. Nonetheless, we argue that it continues to serve the same purpose of facilitating elite cohesion and strategically securing bases of support for the regime.

Reciprocal co-optation: horizontal pattern

Co-optation practices often link political networks with other influential groups and in doing so serve the mutual benefit of those involved. For example, political leaders, faced with undertaking far reaching systemic reforms (such as in the post-Soviet transition to market economies),

---

[23] Ledeneva, *Can Russia Modernise?*, p. 103.
[24] G. Hyden and M. Mmuya, 'Power and Policy Slippage in Tanzania: Discussing National Ownership of Development', *Sida Studies*, 21, 2008, pp. 39–39.
[25] V. O. Kliuchevskii, *Kurs Rossiiskoi Istorii*, part 2, vol. 2, Moscow, 1988, p. 316.

recognize the potentially disruptive power of major interest groups and resort to co-optation tactics, whereby these groups are turned into stakeholders by channelling significant resources and linking their self-interest to the success of the privatization project.[26]

In what may be viewed as reciprocal co-optation, we identify practices by means of which political elites not only gather the support of influential non-state actors but also become recruited into exercising public authority to inordinately favour particular interests. This type of co-optation pattern can be characterized as horizontal, to the degree that it turns power networks into symbiotic relationships involving political elites and business interests and, in the case of Mexico, also organized crime.

In this modality, co-optation promotes the interests of both political and business groups. Political elites need the support of major business interests, because the latter can seriously destabilize political regimes and, in the case of competitive authoritarian regimes, are also often key funders of costly electoral campaigns. Business interest groups, for their part, profit from recruiting major political figures to ensure their interests will be protected and promoted by the authorities. Therefore, through reciprocal co-optation political and business elites recruit each other into their networks — consolidating a new network — whereby the support bases of the regime are solidified and business interests capture state functions.

Whereas in Russia in the 1990s one spoke of state capture by large businesses, since the 2000s under Putin's networks-based system of governance, known as *sistema*, it became necessary for businesses to secure 'political protection' (*kryshi*). Informal alliances between state officials and businesses, elected representatives and business interests, as well as informal financial flows linking politicians and business elites are indeed perceived to be mutually beneficial.[27]

In a similar fashion, anti-corruption experts in Tanzania refer to so-called 'king makers', alluding to influential business interests that search out promising individuals among CCM cadres with the prospect of making connections with the right people in exchange for financial support to bolster their political careers. The beneficiaries of such sponsorship are then indebted and expected to equally reciprocate by garnering and allocating substantial benefits to the sponsors.

Similarly, corrupt practices emerge to serve the private interests of state and criminal actors. As aptly documented in a journalistic investigation,

---

[26] Bertocchi and Spagat, 'The Politics of Co-optation', p. 592.
[27] Ledeneva, *Can Russia Modernise?*

mutual protection relationships have developed in Mexico since the 1970s linking certain high-level political figures and drug trafficking leaders.[28] Such relationships have involved the exchange of significant amounts of money (delivered regularly, almost in tax-like fashion) in return for official disregard (and in some cases even facilitation) of the diverse activities of the cartels.

Reciprocal co-optation may result in awarding inordinate numbers of major procurement contacts, extra-legal tax exemptions or other kinds of benefits to business allies, and is therefore associated with corruption in both the procurement process and state capture.[29] A critical implication of such patterns of selective co-optation is that they entail an informal redistribution of state resources and therefore establish and reinforce a fundamental disparity between the beneficiaries of such informal exchanges and those who are excluded.

Grassroots co-optation: bottom-up pattern

Bottom-up co-optation is the reverse of top-down co-optation. At the grassroots level public officials deliver support for the regime in the form of tangible expressions of popular support while granting favours and delivering resources and services to particular constituencies. Co-optation at the grassroots level is a functional practice from the perspective of regime insiders because, as the vast literature on clientelism and patronage has documented,[30] it helps win elections, generates legitimacy for the status quo and avoids social discontent. However, we also find that grassroots networks may pressurize public officers and co-opt them, 'bottom-up' fashion.

Tanzanian voters understand the logic of clientelism well and refer to electoral campaigns as 'harvesting seasons' — the season of exchanging votes for gifts of money, beer, meals and party apparel referred to

---

[28] A. Hernández, *Los Señores Del Narco*, Mexico City, 2010.

[29] See Mihály Fazekas and Luciana Cingolani's article in this issue.

[30] D. W. Brinkerhoff and A. A. Goldsmith, 'Clientelism, Patrimonialism and Democratic Governance: An Overview and Framework for Assessment and Programming', Cambridge MA, 2002; de Walle, 'The Path from Neopatrimonialism'; J. Auyero, P. Lapegna, F. P. Poma, 'Patronage Politics and Contentious Collective Action: A Recursive Relationship', *Latin American Politics and Society*, 51, 2009, pp. 1–3; J. F. Medard, 'The Underdeveloped State in Tropical Africa: Political Clientelism or Neopatrimonialism?', in S. C. Clapham (ed.), *Private Patronage and Public Power: Political Clientelism in the Modern State*, London, 1982, pp. 162, n.192; M. W. Svolik, *The Politics of Authoritarian Rule*, Cambridge, 2012.

colloquially as 'food', 'soda', 'sugar' or 'tea'.[31] Through the playful use of language, people joke that they give politicians *kula* (eat) when they mean *kura* (votes), which implies that they are giving the candidates a chance to eat by electing them. In rural Mexican communities our research revealed the prevalence of more coercive ways to instruct low income indigenous communities to cast their votes for a particular political party by informing their perception of conditional entitlement to federally allocated cash benefits. Multiple practices of vote-selling can be observed in Russia and other post-Communist societies.[32]

From this perspective co-optation is also highly functional. What prevails in our interview data is the respondents' emphasis on the role of informal networks, which may be formed on the basis of different criteria such as kinship, friendship, neighbourhood or profession. Here, the network expects a proactive stance on the part of the group member who is appointed or recruited into a position of public office in solving problems and enabling access to benefits and resources in the interests of the network. The importance of obligations associated with family, ethnic and other forms of social ties in Africa,[33] Russia[34] and in Tanzania specifically, has been well documented.[35] One of the main arguments is that people's identification and relationship with the state and its institutions are significantly weaker than the identification and relationships with such groups, and that transactions follow what scholars call the 'economy of affection' or 'economies of favour'.[36] As a consequence, practices of 'eating'

[31] K. D. Phillips, 'Pater Rules Best: Political Kinship and Party Politics in Tanzania's Presidential Elections', *PoLAR: The Political and Legal Anthropology Review*, 33, 2010, pp. 109–32.

[32] A. Ledeneva, *How Russia Really Works: The Informal Practices That Shaped Post-Soviet Politics and Business*, Ithaca NY, 2006.

[33] J. P. Olivier de Sardan, 'A Moral Economy of Corruption in Africa?', *The Journal of Modern African Studies*, 37, pp. 25; G. Anders, *Civil Servants in Malawi: Cultural Dualism, Moonlighting and Corruption in the Shadow of Good Governance*, Erasmus University Rotterdam, 2005 <http://repub.eur.nl/pub/1944> [accessed 29 July 2016].

[34] Ledeneva, *Russia's Economy of Favours*; S. Rose-Ackerman, *Trust, Honesty, and Corruption: Reflection on the State-Building Process*, John M. Olin Center for Studies in Law, Economics, and Public Policy Working Papers 255, 2001.

[35] G. Hyden, *Beyond Ujamaa in Tanzania: Underdevelopment and an Uncaptured Peasantry*, Berkeley and Los Angeles, CA, 1980; B. Heilman and L. Ndumbaro, 'Corruption, Politics, and Societal Values in Tanzania: An Evaluation of the Mkapa Administration's Anti-Corruption Efforts', *African Journal of Political Science and International Relations*, 7, 2002, 1, pp. 1–19.

[36] B. Z. Osei-Hwedie and K. Osei-Hwedie, 'The Political, Economic, and Cultural Bases of Corruption in Africa', in K. R. H. Sr and B. C. Chikulo (eds), *Corruption and Development in Africa*, London, 2000, pp. 40–56; G. Hyden, 'The Economy of Affection Revisited: African Development Management in Perspective', in Henrik S. Marcussen

are socially understood in such a manner whereby the public official 'eats' not just for him or herself but for the group. An unwritten but strongly expected duty prescribes the provision of the fruits of holding the public office back to the respective constituencies. Therefore, Russian *sistema* is grounded in the practices of kickbacks sharing,[37] while Tanzanian public officials are expected to deliver not on the basis of national policies and priorities but rather as patrons of specific demographic groups.[38]

Our research in rural areas of Mexico suggests that informal practices of bottom up co-optation are not necessarily only founded on fixed attributes such as kinship or ethnicity but can also be employed creatively in constructing informal networks. Implicit is the common understanding among these communities that access to state services and benefits is conditional and requires adopting certain behaviours that will help them secure favourable outcomes. The intended outcome of such behaviours is to co-opt key state officials to ensure access to state resources. These practices involve simple, symbolic gestures, as one example from our field research illustrates: low-income women in remote rural communities organize fancy meals at their own expense for the public officials who come to their communities in order to deliver the cash benefits from a federal poverty relief programme. This action is intended as pre-emptive gift giving, which is expected to create a link of reciprocity with those public officials and to 'informalize' the distribution process to the women's advantage.[39]

In these examples, the co-optation of public officials on the part of grassroots network generates social pressure, whereby the informal network obligations override the duties of the public office, and practices of petty corruption emerge to bridge the conflicting demands. Thus, such informal ties play an ambivalent role in sustaining community dependence, regime stability and its base for support. While presented as ways to compensate for the defects of state institutions, bottom up co-optation of public officials into social networks, based on social ties, amity and reciprocity, also undermines formal accountability mechanisms.

(ed.), *Improved Natural Resource Management — The Role of Formal Organisations and Informal Networks and Institutions*, International Development Studies Occasional Paper, 17, Roskilde, 2014, pp. 53–75; Ledeneva, *Russia's Economy of Favours*; D. Henig and N. Makovicky (eds), *Economies of Favour after Socialism*, Oxford and New York, 2017.

[37] Ledeneva, *Can Russia Modernise?*

[38] Baez-Camargo and Sambaiga, 'Between Condemnation and Resignation'.

[39] C. Baez-Camargo and R. Megchún, 'Old Regime Habits Die Hard: Clientelism, Patronage and the Challenges to Overcoming Corruption in Post-Authoritarian Mexico', in D. Torsello (ed.), *Corruption in Public Administration: An Ethnographic Approach*, Cheltenham and Northampton, MA, 2016.

Control

Although co-optation may be effective in providing a solution to the problems associated with securing support for the regime on the part of influential groups, in practice the gap between the formal responsibilities and the priorities of various power networks can also create clashes of hidden interests and covert conflict. Thus, co-optation goes hand in hand with practices of informal checks and balances that ensure informal order and discipline within networks and embody enforcement mechanisms to manage dissent.

Such control mechanisms can be found in all three cases. They represent the second modality of informal governance emanating from the necessity to enforce the unwritten rule following obligations to which regime insiders and their supporters are bound. In a similar manner as the co-optation practices discussed above, control practices may be applied in a top-down, horizontal or bottom-up manner. Control mechanisms may also be direct or indirect in nature. When viewed in the context of informal control, it turns out that the holders of public office are not independent (within their remit) individuals or 'iron cage' bureaucrats — but rather are bound by personalized loyalties and are held under extra-legal pressure on the part of the networks they belong to.

Top down, direct control: demonstrative punishment and selective law enforcement

The first pattern of informal control practices that we identify is what we may call demonstrative punishment. While the punishment itself can be formal — exercised in a hierarchical, top-down and direct manner — its selective enforcement serves the informal agenda that underpins the prebendal co-optation: it ensures impunity for the exploitation of public office in exchange for unconditional support for and loyalty to the regime on the one hand, and the atmosphere of 'suspended punishment' on the other.[40]

This pattern of control and its selective enforcement for those dissenting from the informal order is essential for the co-optation patterns to work: the same extra-legal rewards used to secure support from key individuals or groups may also be held against them should it be necessary to reinforce discipline and elite cohesion. The normative ambivalence intrinsic in this type of informal control is best expressed in the saying commonly attributed to Brazilian dictator Getulio Vargas: 'for my friends, everything — for my enemies, the law.'[41]

---

[40] Ledeneva, *Russia's Economy of Favours*.
[41] See, for example, G. O'Donnell, *Why the Rule of Law Matters*, in L. Diamond and

It is tempting to think about informal control as a pyramid, by analogy with formal power, because the networks involved in informal governance are somewhat vertically integrated, and somewhat hierarchical, which makes them similarly rigid and brutal 'like a wolves' pack' (in the expression of one respondent).[42] Yet they surface in more subtle ways and involve constant and mutual monitoring by key players. In Putin's *sistema*, state institutions are controlled through his 'core contacts', 'curators' and highly personalized monitoring and reporting practices within Putin's networks.[43] Such control practices penetrate also non-state companies, which are likely to be informally supervised by 'parachuters' — people appointed over the heads of their formal bosses and personally connected to the political leadership.

Some of the most emblematic cases of enforcement of formal sanctions upon former allies have involved influential union leaders in Mexico. In the 1988 presidential elections, Joaquin Hernández Galicia (also known as *la Quina*), the leader of the powerful oil workers' union, who was known for having amassed a personal fortune exploiting his position, challenged the presidential nomination of Carlos Salinas de Gortari from the PRI by instructing union members to vote for the opposition candidate. As a response, Salinas de Gortari pledged to end all chiefdoms (*cacicazgos*), especially those in which corrupt leaders enriched themselves at the expense of citizens and workers. *La Quina* was convicted for illegal possession of weapons and gangsterism in what came to be known as the *Quinazo* — a symbol for personalized and exemplary punishment of regime traitors.[44]

Indirect control patterns: blackmail and self-censorship
Informal control can be exercised indirectly. This is vividly illustrated by the Russian politics of fear, or 'suspended punishment', which is more preventive than punitive and based on collecting compromising materials

L. Morlino (eds), *Assessing the Quality of Democracy*, Baltimore, MD, 2005, pp. 3–17. Although most commonly associated to Vargas, this phrase has also been attributed to former Peruvian president Oscar Benavide. See 'Knock, Knock', *The Economist*, 21 July 2012 <http://www.economist.com/node/21559384> [accessed 28 July 2016].

[42] S. Guriev and D. Triesman, *How Modern Dictators Survive: An Informational Theory of the New Authoritarianism*, NBER Working Paper 21136, 2015 <http://www.nber.org/papers/w21136>.

[43] Ledeneva, *Can Russia Modernise?*; G. Pavlovsky, *The Russian System: A View from the Inside*, Wilson Center, 9 September 2016 <http://www.wilsoncenter.org/article/the-russian-system-view-the-inside>.

[44] *Sistema* wisdom has it: 'Be ready to accept that you may never understand what has brought you down.'

(*kompromat*) on enemies and protestors, but particularly on friends and allies.[45] Heads of the Soviet state were known to rely on their security services for gathering and keeping sensitive information (*kompromat* files) on their staff and appointees. In Putin's *sistema*, the supervisory role of security services goes beyond assembling information and maintaining the 'safety net' of the regime. The presence of *siloviki*, usually associated with the security services and colloquially known as curators (*kuratory* or *smotryashchie*), has increased since the year 2000 together with the state ownership of large companies and the creation of state corporations,[46] and due to their own appetite for acquiring private wealth. The activities of power ministries (*siloviki*) have become associated with informal control and rent-seeking behaviour (*koshmarit'* or *otzhimat' biznes*); 'authorized' corporate attacks (*sistema* raiding), and acts of depriving business owners of their business using threats of state persecution, often covered with the rhetoric of patriotism.[47]

Informal control and monitoring in the context of 'politics of fear' or 'suspended punishment' generates self-censorship among members of the elites and social networks. Understanding that violating unwritten rules is much more dangerous than that of formal laws ensures self-imposed discipline when it comes to the following of the unwritten rules of the game, which typically demand displaying unconditional loyalty and support for the regime.

As the leader of the main PRI labour confederation once put it, 'he who moves does not get in the picture' (*el que se mueve no sale en la foto*), referring to the imperative of standing still, always acquiescing to one's boss and simply obeying those higher up in rank in order to remain part of the political game. Therefore, according to the unwritten informal criteria that prevailed under the PRI regime, the promise of personal loyalty was the most impressive qualification an individual could offer to a superior.[48]

In Tanzania self-censorship behaviours among political groups come about through internal CCM party discipline mechanisms: the president exercises tight control over the legislature given that by law all cabinet-level ministries are to be held by members of parliament. Since all coveted

---

[45] V. Gelman, 'Politics of Fear', in A. Ledeneva, *The Global Encyclopedia of Informality*, London, forthcoming; V. Gel'man, 'The Vicious Circle of Post-Soviet Neopatrimonialism in Russia', *Post-Soviet Affairs*, 32, 2016, 5, pp. 455–73.

[46] V. Pastukhov, 'Mutnye instituty: "Reforma MVD" i krizis "reguliarnogo gosudarstva" v Rossii', lecture given at St Antony's College, Oxford, 3 February 2010; V. Volkov, *Violent Entrepreneurs: The Use of Force in the Making of Russian Capitalism*, Ithaca, NY, 2012.

[47] Ledeneva, *Can Russia Modernise?*

[48] M. Grindle, 'Patrons and Clients in the Bureaucracy: Career Networks in Mexico', *Latin American Research Review*, 12, 1977, pp. 37–66 (p. 41).

cabinet-level positions are political appointees, there is an incentive for CCM Members of Parliament to show discipline and loyalty to the Executive in the hope of being awarded a high level position.

At the grassroots level, our work in low-income rural areas in Mexico revealed a strong belief among community members that benefits from the government's social programmes can be taken away as a means to punish 'bad' behaviours such as criticizing public officials, complaining against the quality of public services or voting for the 'wrong' party in an election.[49] The observable result of such beliefs are actions adopted by community members, which are consistent with the self-censorship pattern; namely never criticizing public officials or the quality of public services and voting for the ruling party in elections.

Reciprocal control: peer pressure

Reciprocal mechanisms of informal control are exercised through peer pressure within closed networks and based on peer control, mutual watch and collective responsibility. The emphasis is on the group, rather than individuals, although they may be held together by shared individual interests, often hidden behind the rhetoric of kin, communal, ethnic or national patriotism.

In our three cases, peer pressure is associated with conformity about how things should be done and a degree of collective (ir)responsibility, where one is responsible for all and all are responsible for one. Peer pressure is inherently ambivalent as peer groups provide protection against external danger and access to resources, while at the same time exercising control and consolidating cohesion within the group.

We find that the reliance on peer pressure mechanisms for monitoring and enforcement of controls is universally observable, but particularly functional in extra-legal contexts. These can be associated with rural or distant areas, closed communities (army, prisons, schools, youth gangs, socially excluded groups) or within weak legal frameworks, but also within political groups.

With regard to the latter, indicative are the internal control mechanisms within political groups or cliques in Mexico (also known as *camarillas*).[50] Such control mechanisms follow the peer pressure pattern and were seen as highly efficient in upholding internal regimes of discipline, responsibility and supervision. Clique members would be aware that mistakes made by them or their fellow group members could be extremely detrimental to

---

[49] Baez-Camargo and Megchún, 'Old Regime Habits Die Hard'.
[50] Grindle, 'Patrons and Clients in the Bureaucracy', p. 42.

the careers of all of them because the camarillas competed amongst each other for favours and for the trust of the incumbent president, who had the last word on the sensitive matter of presidential succession. Hence strict camarilla discipline reaped stages of rewards as the group's political trajectory advanced, hopefully culminating in 'the big one' (la grande): the presidency of the republic.

At the grassroots level, our fieldwork took place in areas of rural Mexico, where communitarian values and practices are remarkably strong. This means that decisions are taken collectively and community members are subsequently vigilant of each other's behaviours to ensure adherence, which results in rapid communication and enforcement of sanctions relative to individual members deviating from the 'official' position adopted by the community. In these cases, community-level mechanisms of social control are enforced to ensure alignment with collective decisions, which are perceived to protect the community from potentially detrimental actions on the part of outsiders.

Historians point out that the Russian state legalized the informal governance observed within peasant communities — the principle of collective responsibility (krugovaya poruka) — for the purposes of tax collection, army conscription and crime control. The law on collective responsibility was only abolished in 1905. Mechanisms of mutual dependence vis-à-vis the state have generated practices of vigilance, informal monitoring, in-group surveillance, peer pressure as well as collective punishments to ensure the survival of the community vis-à-vis external pressure.[51] In Stalin's time, regional elites used the principle of collective responsibility for resisting control and orders from above — covering up for power excesses by regional officials; protecting an official when compromising information about him was leaked to the centre; and punishing the whistle-blowers leaking such information.[52] The immunity and protection provided by the community for its members were intrinsically linked to the limited property rights and inter-group dependence, surfacing prominently again in the post-Communist transition of the 1990s in the contexts of organized crime and regional elites.

[51] See Ledeneva, How Russia Really Works; Geoffrey Hosking, 'Forms of Social Solidarity in Russia and the Soviet Union', in I. Marková (ed.), Trust and Democratic Transition in Post-Communist Europe, Oxford and New York, 2004, pp. 47–62.

[52] Y. Gorlizki, 'Too Much Trust: Regional Party Leaders and Local Political Networks under Brezhnev', Slavic Review, 69, 2010, 3, pp. 676–700; O. V. Khlevnyuk, Master of the House: Stalin and His Inner Circle, Newhaven, CT, 2009; S. Fitzpatrick, On Stalin's Team: The Years of Living Dangerously in Soviet Politics, Princeton, NJ, 2015.

The peer pressure control pattern implies that group members protect each other and feel responsible for their mutual well-being, but will also share shame, should it come to the revealing of corrupt practices. Therefore, Tanzanians use the expression *kujipendekeza*, which means flattering or 'looking nice to somebody', referring to the need to lie and do all that is necessary to protect one's peers; in order to maintain a good standing within the group and to uphold loyalty as a highly valued quality, one often needs to 'make others look good'.

Bottom-up control: social sanctions

Bottom up, the obligations of the public official who must deliver back to his or her particular constituencies are also enforced through informal control mechanisms that go hand in hand with the bottom-up co-optation pattern. Thus, whereas the bottom-up co-optation is effected on the basis of group ascription (considerations such as kinship, ethnicity or exchanged favours) the relationship is maintained on the basis of an expectation of reciprocity or amity, and the control is exercised on the basis of shame and reputation damage.[53]

Accepting that individual needs are also extensive to each member of the group, group-belonging in Tanzania generates a strong sense of responsibility and duty among public officials that may directly be linked to the behaviours of public officials, who are expected to 'eat' on behalf of their extended group. This extended group reciprocity is also enforced through social sanctions, where the role of shame and shaming is significant. 'Giving back' to their community is a key motivation for public office holders who are intent on maintaining and ensuring loyalty, respect and status. Contrarily, failing to deliver the spoils of public office to those who feel entitled to a part of it is socially understood as an omission, entails deep shame on the part of the culprit and is considered offensive and disgraceful.[54]

Camouflage

The institutional façades covering the realities of political co-optation and control represent the third modality of informal governance. Whether covering up the distance between formal procedures and real power or creating it where it is not there, façades are only partially façades. In fact,

---

[53] Hyden, *Beyond Ujamaa in Tanzania*, and 'The Economy of Affection Revisited'; P. P. Ekeh, 'Colonialism and the Two Publics in Africa: A Theoretical Statement', *Comparative Studies in Society and History*, 17, 1975, pp. 91–112.

[54] L. Koechlin, *Corruption as an Empty Signifier: Politics and Political Order in Africa*, Basel, 2010, p. 100.

formal constraints are essential for the effectiveness of informal practices. In other words, the formal rules and institutions of the public sector (the façade) are sustained in order to manipulate, undercut, divert or exploit for the sake of informal interests. The camouflage patterns of informal governance serve in a functionally ambivalent way: they support the formal façades of the regime but only to subvert them, thus allowing the regime to reproduce according to its declared goals, while also subverting them in practice. However, this ambivalence in camouflage practices is unavoidable as they are needed for protection of both the regime and the networks that redistribute resources informally.

Creative façades

Creative façades are in place where an acceptable exterior disguises non-acceptable practices inside.

A telling illustration of the meaning of creative façades comes from Russia, where the colloquial term for façades is 'Potemkin villages', deriving from a historical legend of creative accounting by Count Potemkin, who built façades of fake villages made of cardboard, along the journeying path of Catherine the Great in order to account for the embezzled budget funds designated for building those villages. In the Soviet planned economy, the term was linked to practices of mis- and over-reporting on planned performance targets (*pripiski*), essential for the legitimacy of the old Soviet regime, but unable to persist according to its own declared rules.[55]

Historically, regime survival strategies in Mexico also relied on maintaining a façade of elite consensus among members of the Revolutionary Family. During the PRI era conflict and disagreements were channelled through specific, covert and highly coded political rituals. The media, heavily dependent on bribes and official funds, played a key role in conveying encoded messages between political elites and in building up the public images of potential presidential candidates. The importance of symbolic gestures hidden underneath official protocols was captured by the expression 'in politics, form is the content' (*en política, la forma es el fondo*) as minted by PRI insider and intellectual Jesús Reyes Heroles. This is illustrated by a picture of a Mexican governor greeting a municipal president who had fallen out of grace while placing his hand across his chest to prevent the subordinate from giving him the mandatory hug

---

[55] In contemporary Russia, Potemkin villages are associated with hiding real owners' assets.

common among politicians who were on good terms.[56] This emphasis on encoded messages stands in sharp contrast with the irrelevance of official speeches, public statements and government events where the official line was strictly to maintain an image of elite consensus.

One indicator for the pervasiveness of camouflage is the implementation gap, a reflection of which is a declared commitment to anti-corruption in discourse, but not in practice in our three case studies. There are many examples of leaders' impassioned proclamations against corruption and the adoption of significant legal and institutional reforms to that effect, followed by very little substantive actions. Anti-corruption campaigns have often come about during electoral campaigns, at times of crisis or with increased pressure from international donors, and are therefore symptomatic of the manipulation of the discourse on corruption and anti-corruption as window dressing in the pursuit of narrow political interests.

A significant dimension of camouflage emerges out of the intense international donor intervention and its impact on Tanzanian anti-corruption legislation. As a major aid recipient globally,[57] Tanzania has given in to international donors' demands to significantly strengthen oversight and regulatory agencies. In addition to enacting numerous laws relating to public finance management, audits and anti-corruption, specialized agencies such as the Prevention and Control of Corruption Bureau (PCCB) the Public Procurement Regulatory Authority (PPRA), and the National Audit Office (NAO) have been created. The resulting legal framework adjusts perfectly to Western expectations of best practices, thus providing a politically acceptable façade to cover up the predominance of redistributive practices associated with co-optation. In practice, implementation of the anti-corruption legal framework is impeded by the lack of enforcement powers and virtual impotence of the newly founded agencies (PCCB, PPRA), which remain politically compromised by being under the auspices of the Presidential Office.

Very often, creative façades are put forward by way of euphemisms and references to local norms and practices. Thus, bribing in Tanzania is often given different names like '*takrima*' (which translates as favour or hospitality from Swahili) that would eventually cover up and make it look like it is a normal and legal act. Other common local terms that frame

[56] J. Araujo López, 'En Política, La Forma es Fondo', in Jesús Reyes Heroles (ed.), *Mitos y Otros Cuentos*, Mexico City, 2012.

[57] Since 2007 Tanzania has been receiving approximately 2.7 billion USD per year. See also, Barak D. Hoffman, 'Political Economy Analysis of Tanzania', Center for Democracy and Civil Society, Georgetown College, Washington, D.C., March 2013, p. 22.

bribing as a normal practice include '*kutoa kitu kidogo/chochote*' (meaning giving out something small in return for something), '*kujiongeza*' (doing something to achieve what you want), or '*kueleweka*' (to make oneself understood).[58]

Hidden constitutions

The expression 'hidden constitutions' refers to situations where formal constitutional powers do not necessarily reflect how real power is exercised. The complex relationship between the formal façades and the informal backstage of power is best encapsulated by the metaphor of a puppet theatre. Playing on the distance between front and back stage, manipulating identities, using intermediaries or front persons and creating virtual realities, it provides a contextual model by which to examine presentation of self, virtual reality in the postmodernist age, virtual politics and (in theory) post-Communist privatization.[59]

The gap between formal and informal power is often related to blurred boundaries, as has been the case between the ruling party and the Tanzanian state. Although a formal separation exists between the two, 'almost all civil servants are indirectly accountable to the CCM and the party leadership determines almost all material policy choices'.[60] An illustration of this is how District Executive Directors, while formally the most powerful public servants in the districts, are in reality superseded in effective power and influence by the District Commissioners, who are presidential appointees and CCM representatives, and are known to play a significant role in mobilizing votes for the ruling party during elections.

Fluid identities

Camouflage also can be associated with a blurring of the public/private interests and associated roles taken up by influential individuals. Thus, the more extreme form of camouflage and ultimate case of ambivalence is the complete role reversal, whereby holders of a public office not only pursue their business interests or skim financial benefits, but turn into

---

[58] Baez-Camargo and Sambaiga, 'Between Condemnation and Resignation'.

[59] E. Goffman, *The Presentation of Self in Everyday Life*, New York, 1959; D. Holmes, *Virtual Politics: Identity and Community in Cyberspace*, London 1997; A. Wilson, *Virtual Politics: Faking Democracy in the Post-Soviet World*, New Haven, CT, 2005; J. Allina-Pisano, *The Post-Soviet Potemkin Village: Politics and Property Rights in the Black Earth*, Cambridge and New York, 2008; S. Newton, *The Constitutional Systems of the Independent Central Asian States: A Contextual Analysis*, London, 2017.

[60] Hoffman, 'Political Economy Analysis of Tanzania', p. 11.

'werewolves in epaulets' or 'werewolves in uniforms' — as expressed in this post-Soviet phrase. It reflects the appetites of the law enforcement and intelligence officers to clandestinely acquire personal wealth and in doing so, their capacity to transgress all human norms. It is when the job turns into its opposite,[61] and those charged with defending the public are widely perceived as abusing the public and engaging in illegal raids on private businesses, that vernacular knowledge such as 'werewolves in epaulets' emerge.[62] Russia's 'werewolves' are associated with 'moonlighting' by law enforcement officials, routinely crossing the boundaries between their public duties and private (or informally affiliated) businesses.

A very similar pattern is mirrored in the Mexican expression 'to bite' (*mordida*), which refers to the subtle request by 'biters', such as police officers (*mordelones*), to be paid a bribe. Nowadays, the power and influence of drug cartels has added a new dimension to nebulous boundaries between outlaws and officials: deserters from the army and police forces, trained in tactical operations and the handling of weapons, are allegedly merging into one often indistinguishable group of security officials and cartel members.[63] A former associate of an influential drug baron described in a published statement how 'everyone' in the organization had either military or police affiliation. Confusing images thus arise out of the drug war in Mexico, where killings in broad daylight may be carried out by men in police uniforms and it is not always clear whether the perpetrators were thugs masquerading as policemen or actual policemen providing paid assistance to thugs.[64]

The intrinsic ambivalence of multiple or fluid identities means that Tanzanian leaders delivering informally accrued benefits to their groups are cherished as '*Wakwetu*' (local sons or leaders who care about their own people), whereas the same leaders are denounced as '*Mafisadi*' (a common derogatory Swahili expression) by those excluded from special treatment.

[61] G. Mars, *Cheats at Work: An Anthropology of Workplace Crime*, London, 1983.

[62] Ledeneva, *Can Russia Modernise?*, p. 195.

[63] John Bailey and Matthew M. Taylor, 'Evade, Corrupt, or Confront? Organized Crime and the State in Brazil and Mexico', *Journal of Politics in Latin America*, 1, 2009, pp. 3–29 (p. 19).

[64] P. R. Keefe, 'Cocaine Incorporated', *The New York Times Magazine*, 15 June 2012 <www.nytimes.com/2012/06/17/magazine/how-a-mexican-drug-cartel-makes-its-billions.html?_r=0> [accessed 12 October 2016].

Conclusion: ambivalence and the public/private cross-over

So far we have identified three modalities of informal governance observed in our three cases. For analytical purposes we discuss them separately, but in practice they are highly interdependent. In order to manage and protect the informal redistribution of state resources enacted through practices of co-optation and control, camouflage measures are part and parcel. Our distinction of informal governance modalities has at least two important implications.

First, the informal re-distribution of state resources among exclusive networks entails the collapse of a public/private divide. This leads us to question some of the underlying assumptions of the prevailing, global corruption paradigm. Most mainstream definitions of corruption hinge upon a notion that something public is subverted into something private (misuse of funds, abuse of office, betrayal of trust). Thus, the analytical distinction between the public and private spheres is often taken for granted. However, neither the empirical evidence nor theoretical considerations seem to support such an a priori assumption.[65] Such a discrepancy has been a major obstacle for conventional anti-corruption prescriptions. Founded upon a principal-agent model, these prescriptions rely on the existence of widely accepted rules about the boundaries between the public and the private spheres. Rather, by underplaying the analytical distinction between the public and the private and focusing on the grey zones created by their overlap and interplay, we highlight the implications and impact of informal governance norms in contexts where corruption is endemic.

The informal governance patterns reveal networks of 'insiders' that, in pursuing their interests, affect an informal redistribution of state resources at the expense of excluded groups of 'outsiders'. The borderline between insiders and outsiders within networks is much more indeterminate than

[65] J. Weintraub and K. Kumar, *Public and Private in Thought and Practice: Perspectives on a Grand Dichotomy*, Chicago, IL, 1997; D. M. L. Kennedy, 'Stages of the Decline of the Private/Public Distinction', *University of Pennsylvania Law Review*, 6 1982, pp. 1349–57; R. Sennett, *The Fall of the Public Man*, New York, 1977; A. M. Orum and Z. P. O'Neal (eds), *Common Ground? Reading and Reflections on Public Space*, London, 2010; L. Wacquant, *Punishing the Poor: The Neoliberal Government of Social Insecurity*, Durham, NC and London, 2009; H. Lefebvre, *The Production of Spaces*, Oxford, 1991, and *Writing on Cities*, Malden, MA, 1996; G. Blundo and J. P. Olivier de Sardan (with N. B. Arifari and M. Tidjani Alou), *Everyday Corruption and the State: Citizens and Public Officials in Africa*, London, 2006; A. Ledeneva, 'Corruption in Postcommunist States in Europe: A Re-examination', *Perspectives on European Politics and Society*, 10, 2009, 1, pp. 69–86; A. Persson, B. Rothstein and J. Teorell, 'Why Anticorruption Reforms Fail: Systematic Corruption as a Collective Action Problem', *Governance*, 26, 2013, pp. 449–71.

implied by the public/private distinction, yet its shifting nature is not taken into account in policy making. In the light of these conclusions, the mere differentiation between the public and private spheres as the basis for common corruption paradigms becomes problematic, if not obsolete.

Second, the interrelationship between the three informal governance modalities where co-optation may only be sustained with adequate control mechanisms and the extent that it needs to be camouflaged entails that the practices involved in the informal governance regimes are inevitably ambivalent. In other words, we find that the tensions arising from multiple normative frameworks are resolved in practice by virtue of the ambivalent meanings and elusiveness attached to informal norms and practices.

Recognizing the inherent ambivalent nature of informal practices contributes to a better understanding of the entrenchment and resilience of corrupt behaviours. Exchange of favours can be imbued with a multiplicity of meanings, implications, values and expectations — all simultaneously implied and yet not made explicit.[66] For instance, what is given as a reward for loyalty can be taken away and punishment can ensue, informal understandings may be overturned by the application of the formal normative framework and the reward effectively turns into a trap.

The ambivalence of informal practices also places contradictory demands upon the occupants of a status in a particular social relation. Therefore, a public official may be expected simultaneously to execute public policy, protect collaborators and provide preferential access to resources to his or her kinship group. Since competing norms and obligations cannot be simultaneously complied with, they come to be expressed in an 'oscillation of behaviors', in the form of 'detachment and compassion, of discipline and permissiveness, of personal and impersonal treatment'.[67] Such motivational ambivalence is linked to norms of reciprocity, which is in turn linked to social stability.[68] As an illustration, where the public office is prebendal, or ridden with substantive ambivalence (partly public, partly privatized) we also observe 'normative ambivalence' or double standards displayed by the public. Thus, practices of 'receiving a bone', 'feeding' and 'eating' are not only associated with

[66] A. Ledeneva, 'The Ambivalence of Favour: Paradoxes of Russia's Economy of Favours', in D. Henig and N. Makovicky (eds), *Economies of Favour after Socialism*, Oxford, 2017, pp. 21–49, and 'The Ambivalence of Blurred Boundaries: Where Informality Stops and Corruption Begins', *Perspectives*, 12, Winter 2014–15, pp. 19–22.

[67] R. K. Merton, *Sociological Ambivalence and Other Essays*, New York, 1976, p. 8.

[68] A. W. Gouldner, 'The Norm of Reciprocity: A Preliminary Statement', *American Sociological Review*, 25, 1960, 2, pp. 161–78.

corruption but also accepted; corruption is condemned as morally wrong but at the same time tolerated. The seeming contradictions are resolved in the so-called 'misrecognition game': receiving privileges, rewards and competitive advantages is acceptable in one's own case, but are viewed as corrupt when given to others.

Furthermore, the fluidity of meanings and identities emanating from the ambivalent nature of informal norms is often manipulated by insiders of the system, for whom mastery of this hidden language is often an indispensable requisite for political survival. Across our three cases — Mexico, Russia, Tanzania — this ambivalent nature of informal norms and practices is a key to understanding how and why the same mechanisms that may be used to reward supporters and co-opt dissenters also can be utilized to enforce discipline and good governance.

To the extent that a regime is defined as 'the ensemble of patterns, explicit or not, that determines the forms and channels of access to principal governmental positions, the characteristics of the actors who are admitted and excluded from such access, and the resources [and] strategies that they can use to gain access',[69] we can claim that the modalities that we have identified amount to nothing less than effective instruments of informal governance, actively used for sustaining political regimes.

We believe that a next step in the direction of exploring the potential of harnessing informal practices to improve development outcomes and decrease corruption necessitates more research that continues to decode the various manners in which informal governance practices usurp the functions attributed to formal political regimes. Thus, co-optation practices serve to ensure regime survival because they play a role in addressing the essential problems faced by political elites of avoiding intra-elite splits, constructing loyalties and preventing the strengthening of groups that may contest power.[70] Whereas in formal frameworks associated with good governance and anti-corruption, enforcement typically involves elements such as transparency, informal groups are bound together by considerations such as reciprocity, loyalty, amity, reputation and coercion.[71]

[69] G. O'Donnell and P. Schmitter, *Transitions from Authoritarian Rule: Tentative Conclusions about Uncertain Democracies*, Baltimore, MD, 1986, p. 73.

[70] B. B. de Mesquita, A. Smith, R. M. Siverson and J. D. Morrow, *The Logic of Political Survival*, Cambridge, MA, 2005; B. B. De Mesquita and A. Smith, 'Leader Survival, Revolutions, and the Nature of Government Finance', *American Journal of Political Science*, 54, 2010, pp. 936–50; M. W. Svolik, *The Politics of Authoritarian Rule*, Cambridge and New York, 2012.

[71] Banuri and Eckel point out that researchers have identified four main informal enforcement mechanisms that reinforce adherence to informal contracts: trust, reputation,

Following this logic, we need to focus not only on the informal practices that work but also on how to make them work for promoting positive change. For instance, corruption created by bottom up co-optation could be targeted by generating incentives for social networks to discourage demands made on the basis of amity and by harnessing the collective action potential of social ties and informal practices for the reform.

hostage-taking and reciprocity. See S. Banuri and C. Eckel, 'Experiments in Culture and Corruption: A Review', *Research in Experimental Economics*, 15, 2012, pp. 51–76.

3

Breaking the Cycle?
How (Not) to Use Political Finance Regulations to Counter Public Procurement Corruption

MIHÁLY FAZEKAS & LUCIANA CINGOLANI

1. Introduction

> [...] under the cover of irregular funding to the parties, cases of corruption and extortion have flourished and become intertwined [...] What needs to be said, and which in any case everyone knows, is that the greater part of political funding is irregular or illegal. The parties and those who rely on a party machine [...] have had, or have, recourse to irregular or illegal additional resources. If the greater part of this is to be considered criminal pure and simple then the greater part of the political system is a criminal system. I do not believe there is anybody in this hall who has had a responsibility for a large organisation who can stand up and deny what I have just said.[1]

There are presumably very few more succinct and honest descriptions about the corrupting potential of political party finances ever made by a political leader than this speech by Bettino Craxi, long-term leader of the Italian Socialist Party, made in the Chamber of Deputies in 1992 shortly after he won the national election. The phenomenon he describes is of global reach, affecting high as well as low income countries' democratic representation and quality of institutions.[2]

The authors would like to express their gratitude to two EC funded projects: ANTICORRP (Grant agreement no: 290529) and DIGIWHIST (Grant agreement no: 645852). In addition, the insightful comments at the UCL SSEES ANTICORRP seminar greatly improved this article. The authors are grateful in particular to Allan Sikk and Fiona Harrison.

[1] D. della Porta and A. Vannucci, *Corrupt Exchanges: Actors, Resources, Mechanisms of Political Corruption*, New York, 1999, p. 2.
[2] OECD, *Money in Politics: Sound Political Competition and Trust in Government*, Paris, 2013.

Legal and illegal money in politics has the potential to corrupt the party system and democratic institutions whenever it is used to support candidates in exchange for preferential treatment in the allocation of public funds. Donors can be paid back through a range of channels such as favourable regulation, sale of public property or preferential access to government contracts. Among these, donating to election campaigns[3] in return for public procurement contracts is a corrupt exchange that is widely considered as one of the most frequently used mechanisms which has, in turn, received the highest scrutiny. It has been uncovered in diverse countries such as the Czech Republic, Brazil, Italy, the USA, Romania and Russia, even though evidence in many cases is only suggestive and indirect.[4] It is hardly a surprise that allocating government contracts to favoured companies is a prime method for returning campaign donations. As it accounts for large amounts of public spending, it can be easily centralized in the hands of a few, and political office holders enjoy considerable discretion in awarding contracts.

However, evidence on what works for breaking or curbing this mutual flow of legal or illegal political financing and government contracts to favoured companies is scant. Political financing regulations represent a key set of anticorruption instruments which have received some academic attention and considerable support from international organizations such as GRECO or the OECD. They are attractive as they seem to tackle directly the root of the problem. However, no systematic study exists which establishes whether and under which conditions such regulations are effective in reducing public procurement corruption linked to campaign finances. The only comparable study to ours looks at the variation across states within the USA, taking corruption-related convictions as a measure of corruption, which implies an arguably much less specific impact mechanism.[5]

---

[3] The terms political financing, party financing, campaign finances, campaign financing are used interchangeably throughout this article as they are by and large related to the same set of transactions.

[4] T. C. Boas, F. D. Hidalgo and N. P. Richardson, 'The Spoils of Victory: Campaign Donations and Government Contracts in Brazil', *Journal of Politics*, 76, 2014, 2, pp. 415–29; D. Bromberg, 'Can Vendors Buy Influence? The Relationship Between Campaign Contributions and Government Contracts', *International Journal of Public Administration*, 37, 2014, 9, pp. 556–67; I. M. Doroftei and V. Dimulescu, 'Corruption Risks in the Romanian Infrastructure Sector', in A. Mungiu-Pippidi (ed.), *ANTICORRP Policy Report*, Berlin, 2015, pp. 19–34; M. Mironov and E. V. Zhuravskaya, 'Corruption in Procurement and Shadow Campaign Financing: Evidence from Russia', presented at ISNIE Annual Conference, 2011, and J. Počarovský, *Political Connections in Public Procurement: A Supply Side Analysis*, Prague, 2014.

[5] J. Milyo and A. Cordis, *Do State Campaign Finance Reforms Reduce Public*

It may well be that tackling the corrupting effect of political financing in public procurement directly by party financing regulations is not the most effective strategy, or that it requires a minimum amount of effective tools to lead to any discernible effect. Alternative policies in public procurement or broader 'indirect anticorruption policies' such as meritocratic bureaucracies could play an enabling role or be more effective tools.[6]

In order to start unpacking these issues and provide the first direct evidence of political financing regulations' impact on corruption and favouritism in government contracting, we set out to explore the following research question:

Do political financing regulations contribute to controlling high-level institutionalized corruption in government contracting and, if so, under what conditions?

Although we only provide evidence on the macro patterns of this relationship across Europe, the innovative data and research design provide initial suggestions on what works, and they lay the foundations for further research, teasing out the details of each causal chain and promising tools. Our approach is based solely on 'objective' administrative data on both sides of the regression models. Corruption in public procurement is measured over time in twenty-nine European countries by two 'objective' corruption risk indicators: single bidding on competitive markets and a composite score labelled as the 'Corruption Risk Index'. Political party financing regulations are measured using data from the new large-scale European research project DIGIWHIST[7] and following a methodology pioneered by the International Institute for Democracy and Electoral Assistance (IDEA).[8] By directly measuring changes in legislative constraints on political party financing such as bans on donations from corporations, we can begin to identify the causal impact such regulations have.

The article is structured as follows: first, the theoretical framework is set out, which conceptualizes the link between political party finances and government contracts as a cycle of corrupt exchanges. Second, the

Corruption?, Washington, D.C., 2013.

[6] OECD, *Integrity in Public Procurement. Good Practice from A to Z*, Paris, 2007, and B. Rothstein, 'Anti-Corruption: The Indirect "Big-Bang" Approach', *Review of International Political Economy*, 18, 2011, 2, pp. 228–50.

[7] <digiwhist.eu>.

[8] <http://www.idea.int/political-finance/>.

administrative datasets used and innovative indicators of both theoretical concepts — political financing regulations and public procurement corruption — are described. Third, the results are presented, which indicate that political financing regulations are generally ineffective in curbing public procurement corruption. Finally, a set of further research avenues is proposed, which could build on the proposed data and methodology, and address some of the limitations we had to face.

2. Theoretical framework

There are two key terms playing a central role in our theoretical framework: political financing and high-level institutionalized corruption in government contracting. Each is defined briefly before the introduction of the theoretical framework. Political financing in electoral democracies refers to the '(legal and illegal) financing of ongoing political party activities and electoral campaigns (in particular, campaigns by candidates and political parties, but also by third parties)'.[9] Hence, the regulation of political financing encompasses diverse regulatory tools aiming, among other things, to set limits on donations (e.g. bans on some types of donors or donation amounts), party spending (e.g. an upper ceiling of how much a party can spend on an election) and public funding (e.g. bans on using government funds for party purposes). Political financing regulations often also contain provisions for fines and punishment for misconduct.

High-level institutionalized corruption is a distinct phenomenon from other diverse forms of corruption which have been discussed in the literature such as bribery or bureaucratic corruption.[10] Given the narrow focus of the empirical analysis of public procurement data, it is sufficient to develop a corruption definition which closely fits this context.[11] By implication, the corruption definition focuses exclusively on high-level institutionalized corruption or government favouritism, as isolated instances of low-level bribery are relatively uncommon in public procurement.[12] In public procurement, institutionalized grand corruption

[9] E. Falguera, S. Jones and M. Ohman (eds), *Funding of Political Parties and Election Campaigns: A Handbook on Political Finance*, Stockholm, 2014, p. 2.

[10] A. J. Heidenheimer and M. Johnston (eds), *Political Corruption: Concepts and Context*, New Brunswick, NJ, 2001, and M. Johnston, 'The Search for Definitions: The Vitality of Politics and the Issue of Corruption', *International Social Science Journal*, 48, 1996, 149, pp. 321–35.

[11] OECD, *Integrity in Public Procurement. Good Practice from A to Z.*

[12] M. Fazekas, I. J. Tóth and L. P. King, *Corruption Manual for Beginners: Inventory of Elementary 'Corruption Techniques' in Public Procurement Using the Case of Hungary*, Budapest, 2013.

refers to the allocation and performance of public procurement contracts by bending prior explicit rules and principles of good public procurement in order to benefit a closed network while denying access to all others.[13] The goal of such corruption is to steer the contract to the favoured bidder without detection, often recurrently and in an institutionalized fashion.[14] This can be done in a number of ways, including avoiding competition (e.g. unjustified sole sourcing or direct contract awards), favouring a certain bidder (e.g. tailoring specifications to a particular company) and sharing insider information.[15] Such corruption may involve bribery and transfers of large cash amounts as kickbacks, but it is more typically conducted through broker firms, subcontracts, offshore companies and bogus consultancy contracts. By implication, not everything designated as corruption in this article represents illegal activity.

2.1 The cycle of corruption, government contracts and party funding
The cycle of high-level institutionalized corruption in government contracting and legal or illegal political financing is best conceptualized as an exchange of favours between private and public actors on a regular, highly institutionalized basis (the discussion extensively builds on della Porta and Vannucci).[16] It consists of a stable flow of mutual favours — private money and public contracts — among the high-level members of the corrupt network.

The exchange at the heart of this corrupt cycle involves a favour from private to public actors, such as money or in-kind benefits, in return for preferential treatment in public procurement tenders provided by public actors. In order to grant access to government contracts, public actors (i.e. candidates), must win elections, which is a risky endeavour requiring considerable financial resources. Hence, political party and campaign donations represent a major form of private to public favours supporting a corrupt network. To make the whole enterprise worthwhile, i.e. lucrative, private actors (companies, etc.) need to extract rents from government contracts: they should be productive enough to benefit from higher than

---

[13] A. Mungiu-Pippidi, 'Corruption: Diagnosis and Treatment', *Journal of Democracy*, 17, 2006, 3, pp. 86–99; D. C. North, J. J. Wallis and B. R. Weingast, *Violence and Social Orders: A Conceptual Framework for Interpreting Recorded Human History*, Cambridge, 2009, and B. Rothstein and J. Teorell, 'What Is Quality of Government? A Theory of Impartial Government Institutions', *Governance*, 21, 2008, 2, pp. 165–90.
[14] World Bank, *Fraud and Corruption: Awareness Handbook*, Washington, D.C., 2009.
[15] M. Fazekas, I. J. Tóth & L. P. King, *Anatomy of Grand Corruption: A Composite Corruption Risk Index Based on Objective Data*, Budapest, 2013.
[16] della Porta and Vannucci, *Corrupt Exchanges*.

standard competitive prices or lower than standard competitive quality. The desire to keep such money flows secret makes the use of high secrecy jurisdictions for policy capture and rent extraction commonplace.[17] As courts are typically not available to enforce agreements and contracts among members of a corrupt group, they have to develop private and informal means for controlling each other's actions.[18] Trust among key individuals and mutual blackmail are central to collective action of captor groups.[19] Corrupt groups achieving intra-group trust and the effective means of enforcing agreements have the capacity to broker deals over many months, even years, making the exchange of campaign donations and government contracts only approximate (i.e. not necessarily 100 EUR of donation for 200 EUR of contracts) with payments belonging to a broader scheme rather than a narrow one-to-one exchange.

In the cycle of high-level institutionalized corruption, public procurement and political financing, actors are typically numerous, span across the public-private divide, and control multiple key decision-making positions in both spheres. In a typical case, there are four different types of actors involved:[20] i) politicians, ii) bureaucrats and law enforcement agents, iii) entrepreneurs, and iv) brokers. Politicians, bureaucrats and members of law enforcement agencies (e.g. prosecutors, judges) are the ones who can influence the content of government contracts and the procedures regulating their award. As long as they command sufficient discretion in public decision-making (both in specific tenders and the rules governing contract award) they can maintain the flow of public favours to private actors. As they have to compete for key decision-making positions, they need substantial private resources to gain those positions, in particular campaign donations.[21] Entrepreneurs manage the companies through

---

[17] Tax Justice Network, *Financial Secrecy Index 2013: Methodology*, Chesham, 2013.

[18] Å. B. Grødeland, 'Bulgaria, Czech Republic, Romania and Slovenia: The Use Of Contacts and Informal Networks in Public Procurement', in OECD (ed.), *Fighting Corruption and Promoting Integrity in Public Procurement*, Paris, 2005, pp. 59–76.

[19] D. Gambetta, *Codes of the Underworld: How Criminals Communicate*, Princeton, NJ, 2009, and J. G. Lambsdorff, 'Making Corrupt Deals: Contracting in the Shadow of the Law', *Journal of Economic Behavior & Organization*, 48, 2002, 3, pp. 221–41.

[20] della Porta and Vannucci, *Corrupt Exchanges*; P. Gounev and T. Bezlov, *Examining the Links Between Organised Crime and Corruption*, Sofia, 2010; Z. Szántó, I. J. Tóth & S. Varga, 'The Social and Institutional Structure of Corruption: Some Typical Network Configurations of Corruption Transactions in Hungary', in B. Vedres and M. Scotti (eds), *Networks in Social Policy Problems*, Cambridge, 2012, and J. R. Wedel, 'Rethinking Corruption in an Age of Ambiguity', *Annual Review of Law and Social Science*, 8, 2012, pp. 453–98.

[21] OECD, *Financing Democracy: Supporting Better Public Policies and Preventing Policy Capture*, Paris, 2014.

which the corrupt network extracts rents from government contracts and they finance political party machinery and campaigns.[22] Companies benefiting from favouritist government contracts have to be sufficiently well-managed and productive to be able to earn rents on top of the real cost of contractual delivery. The extracted rents have to be channelled back to political parties and candidates or used for private consumption by corrupt actors. Distributing rents through cash transfers, offshore accounts and company networks without detection requires a great deal of complexity and opacity, which also implies a formidable management problem from the viewpoint of the corrupt network (i.e. who got which amount, when and how). Various types of brokers may play a crucial role in the cycle of corruption, contracts and political finances by providing expert technical knowledge and facilitating inter-personal trust in the absence of formal institutions for enforcing contracts.[23] Expert technical knowledge concerns the technologies of corruption and related activities, such as how to hide large money flows behind offshore accounts or run open public procurement procedures in a biased fashion guaranteeing the success of the pre-selected bidder. Facilitating within-corrupt group trust is done, for example, by serving as a bridge between individuals lacking any prior personal connection or establishing intra-corrupt group accounts and financial controls. Such a diverse set and large number of actors can be assembled in a multitude of organizational forms ranging from decentralized, loose networks to highly hierarchical organizations following a top-down chain of command.

The central characteristic of the cycle of corruption, contracts and political financing is that it trespasses the classic and, in most cases, legally well-established public-private divide. On the one hand, private actors get influence over government decisions on contracts while, on the other hand, political actors get influence over private companies' decisions on finances, profit allocation, hiring or subcontracting.[24] Private actors achieve access and influence over public procurement tenders through their political

[22] M. Levi and P. Reuter, 'Money Laundering', *Crime and Justice*, 34, 2006, 1, pp. 289–375.

[23] D. Jancsics and I. Jávor, 'Corrupt Governmental Networks', *International Public Management Journal*, 15, 2012, 1, pp. 62–99, and Wedel, 'Rethinking Corruption'.

[24] J. S. Hellman, G. Jones and D. Kaufmann, 'Seize the State, Seize the Day: State Capture and Influence in Transition Economies', *Journal of Comparative Economics*, 21, 2003, 4, pp. 751–73, and B. Rothstein and D. Torsello, 'Is Corruption Understood Differently in Different Cultures? Anthropology Meets Political Science', *QoG Working Paper Series*, 2013, 5.

party or campaign contributions,[25] which sometimes even take the form of a payment for political position and decisions. See, for example, the campaign contributions of shell companies in Russia delayed until just after election results are known, suggesting a sort of bonus for successful politicians.[26] It is certainly not the only way to secure access and influence, in fact many companies are likely to use a combination of strategies.[27] Public actors achieve access and influence over private decisions through their informal ties to entrepreneurs by using the 'revolving door' or even by simultaneously holding public and private offices. In addition, the public buyer's post-award power of withholding contract signature, delaying payments or demanding extra-contractual payments all represent effective tools to influence private actors.

The cycle of corruption, contracts and party financing relies on the capacity of each of the participating actors to deliver on corrupt promises. Regarding private to public favours, delivering according to corrupt deals requires the unchecked capacity of private actors to provide campaign contributions to political actors. Regarding public to private favours, keeping corrupt promises requires candidates (i.e. political actors) to win elections and control key decision-making positions in the bureaucracy, which is the function of their own resources as well as that of their opponents. Due to the circular logic of such corrupt exchanges, it is sufficient to disrupt the flow of favours at only one point to disintegrate the whole corrupt network. Nevertheless, any effective disruption has to be systemic,[28] cutting the flow of mutual favours completely, as most corrupt networks tend to be wealthy and adaptive to changing environmental conditions. The two sets of exchanges give rise to two distinct anticorruption strategies each of which on its own is sufficient to break the whole cycle if implemented effectively:

1. Controlling private favours

This means limiting the capacity of private actors to use political financing to create informal, particularistic relationships with selected political actors. This set of strategies encompasses by and large all political financing

---

[25] OECD, *Financing Democracy*.

[26] Mironov and Zhuravskaya, 'Corruption in Procurement and Shadow Campaign Financing'.

[27] T. Rajwani and T. A. Liedong, 'Political Activity and Firm Performance Within Nonmarket Research: A Review and International Comparative Assessment', *Journal of World Business*, 50, 2015, pp. 273–83.

[28] B. Rothstein, 'Anti-Corruption: The Indirect "Big-Bang" Approach'.

regulations[29] such as disallowing some types of private contributions to political parties and candidates, providing public funding to political parties so that they are less dependent on private contributions, curbing spending by political parties so that the need for money in elections is lessened, and strengthening oversight to enforce existing rules.

2. Controlling public favours

This implies limiting the capacity of public actors to return particularistic favours, in particular by increasing the uncertainty of acquiring and holding on to political power and bureaucratic position. While a wide set of tools may contribute to this goal, creating and sustaining an increasing competition among political parties and candidates is prominent.[30] Healthy electoral competition, among other things, depends on allowing new entrants to challenge established parties and making sure that no party commands resources making competition unfair.

2.2 Political financing regulations as a double-edged sword

Political financing regulations influence both sets of exchanges, hence can be part of both types of anticorruption strategies. However, the same sets of instruments may act in contradictory directions depending on the dominant mechanism. The discussion of each mechanism and its empirical support underpins the hypotheses tested in this article.

First, tightening political financing regulations can make it harder for companies to donate to political parties in return for government contracts and also can render political parties more independent of such donations by, for example, increasing formula-based public funding. The anticorruption potential of this mechanism is demonstrated by a range of empirical studies documenting the link between corporate donations and public procurement success. For example, in Brazil, companies' campaign contributions translate into additional contracts won worth fourteen times more than the contributions;[31] the same figure in the USA is only two-and-a-half times.[32] Unfortunately, neither of these studies could establish how much actual performance is expected in return for these contracts from suppliers, making the true amount of corrupt rents earned

---

[29] A. Etzioni, 'The Capture Theory of Regulations — Revisited', *Society*, 46, 2009, 4, pp. 319–23.

[30] A. C. Eggers, 'Partisanship and Electoral Accountability: Evidence from the UK Expenses Scandal', *Quarterly Journal of Political Science*, 9, 2014, 4, pp. 441–72.

[31] Boas et al., 'The Spoils of Victory'.

[32] Bromberg, 'Can Vendors Buy Influence?'.

unknown. Much more direct evidence on the benefits of political party donations in the US (outside of procurement) comes from the sentencing practice of the Securities and Exchange Commission which handed out considerably softer judgements for the CEOs of companies donating to political parties: prison sentences for such CEOs were on average six years shorter.[33] In Russia, companies with at least 5 per cent revenue from procurement contracts increase their illicit political party financing transfers by about 50 per cent a few weeks before elections and gain substantially more procurement contracts than their non-donating peers afterwards.[34] In Latvia, companies whose campaign contributions were not diversified, i.e. they only contributed to the governing party which unexpectedly lost office in 2002, lost roughly 30 per cent of their revenues compared to the control group (arguably to a large degree due to lost procurement income).[35] Emerging micro-level tendering evidence from the Czech Republic and Romania suggests that red flags, such as single bidder contracts, more typically accompany firms donating to political parties than their comparable peers.[36] Such evidence of the particularistic link and the theoretical argument under a corrupt exchange point at the following testable hypothesis:

H_1: Tightening political financing regulations contributes to curbing high-level institutionalized corruption in government contracting.

The mechanism underpinning this hypothesis can come in a number of forms, whereby the timing of reform and its effect is of crucial importance. Electoral campaign donations from private actors are designed to help candidates for political position gain office. These donations are made to electoral campaigns before the voting outcome is known, while payback is only possible if the candidate wins. This particular sequencing of the corrupt cycle suggests that political financing regulations may not be able to curb high-level corruption evenly over time. Rather, political party financing regulations introduced before elections can have an effect of corruption in public procurement after elections only.

[33] S. Fulmer and A. M. Knill, 'Political Contributions and the Severity of Government Enforcement', *AFA 2013 San Diego Meetings Paper*, San Diego, CA, 2013.

[34] Mironov and Zhuravskaya, 'Corruption in Procurement and Shadow Campaign Financing'.

[35] V. Dombrovsky, *Do Political Connections Matter? Firm-Level Evidence from Latvia*, 2008, Riga.

[36] Doroftei and Dimulescu, 'Corruption Risks in the Romanian Infrastructure Sector', and Počarovský, *Political Connections in Public Procurement*.

Second, tightened political finance regulations can influence the resources political parties and candidates have for competing against each other, hence the nature and intensity of electoral competition. One more widely tested relationship in this respect is the effect of public funding on party competition and structure with the overwhelming conclusion that the effect is negligible, although in some cases it might have helped selected parties to consolidate their organizations.[37] More generally, the amount of party finance regulations, such as payout thresholds across Europe, has been shown to have no impact on the emergence of new parties and the permeability of the party system, but has a negative impact on the rate of entry of new parties into national parliaments.[38] Such lack of effect comes as no surprise given the evidence on the lack of relationship between money and electoral success, for example in the USA.[39] However, when the financial resources available for competing parties and candidates are greatly unequal, political competition can be distorted, which can be achieved by restrictions on the kinds of funds parties and candidates can collect.[40] Disparity in funding can be regulated through political finance laws enacted by incumbent parties, as was the case, for example, in Romania.[41] The relationship between deficient electoral competition and public procurement corruption in countries like Italy and Romania provides further support for claims of the potentially damaging effect of political finance regulations.[42] Taken together, the possibility that political finance regulations are strategically modified by incumbents to deprive their political opponents of crucial resources suggests the following counter-hypothesis:

---

[37] J. Pieera, L. Svåsand and A. Widfeldt, 'State Subsidies to Political Parties: Confronting Rhetoric with Reality', *West European Politics*, 23, 2000, 3, pp. 1–24, and S. E. Scarrow, 'Party Subsidies and the Freezing of Party Competition: Do Cartel Mechanisms Work?', *West European Politics*, 29, 2006, 4, pp. 619–39.

[38] I. van Biezen and E. R. Rashkova, 'Deterring New Party Entry? The Impact of State Regulation on the Permeability of Party Systems', *Party Politics*, 20, 2014, 6, pp. 890–903.

[39] Milyo and Cordis, *Do State Campaign Finance Reforms Reduce Public Corruption?*

[40] J. D. Potter and M. Travits, 'The Impact of Campaign Finance Laws on Party Competition', *British Journal of Political Science*, 45, 2015, 1, pp. 73–95.

[41] S. D. Roper, 'The Influence of Romanian Campaign Finance Laws on Party System Development and Corruption', *Party Politics*, 8, 2002, 2, pp. 175–92.

[42] D. Coviello and S. Gagliarducci, *Building Political Collusion: Evidence from Procurement Auctions*, IZA DP No. 4939, Bonn, 2010; M. Fazekas, *The Cost of One-Party Councils: Lack of Electoral Accountability and Public Procurement Corruption*, London, 2015, and M. Klasnja, 'Corruption and the Incumbency Disadvantage: Theory and Evidence', *Journal of Politics*, 77, 2016, 4, pp. 928–42.

H_2: Tightening political financing regulations increases high-level institutionalized corruption in government contracting.

Interestingly, when corrupt governments pretend to reform party finances to hide their increasingly corrupt activities, the empirical patterns are equivalent, at least on the macro level, but imply a different mechanism.

Third, both of these hypotheses, however, can be confronted with a counter-hypothesis: that there is no impact because the above described mechanisms might not work effectively, or other impacts may even override them. This argument is supported by the only comparable study which finds no relationship.[43] There are many indications that political financing regulations have little bearing on actual practices, especially in countries where effective anti-corruption tools are in great need.[44] If regulations are not implemented or only selectively implemented they are unlikely to influence corruption risks in public procurement. For example, a ban on corporate donations can be easily bypassed by organizing private donations by corporations or donating to NGOs linked to parties rather than parties directly.[45] In addition, looking at the whole repertoire of establishing particularistic links between private and public decision-makers, political party donations can be replaced by alternative strategies, such as companies hiring ex-politicians. Moreover, if party finances are truly only marginally important for party success, regulating them would achieve little in the way of influencing electoral results and corruption. If any of these mechanisms play a major role in linking political financing regulations to procurement corruption, we can expect that:

H_3: Tightening political financing regulations has no impact on high-level institutionalized corruption in government contracting.

[43] Milyo and Cordis, *Do State Campaign Finance Reforms Reduce Public Corruption?*
[44] Global Integrity, *The Money, Politics, and Transparency Campaign Finance Indicators: Assessing Regulation and Practice in 54 Countries across the World in 2014*, Washington, D.C., 2015.
[45] Bromberg, 'Can Vendors Buy Influence?'.

3. Data and indicators

3.1 Public procurement tender data

The database derives from public procurement announcements from 2009 to 2014 in the EU27 (EU28 minus Malta)[46] plus Norway and Switzerland (European Economic Area). Announcements appear in the so-called Tenders Electronic Daily (TED), which is the online version of the 'Supplement to the Official Journal of the EU', dedicated to European public procurement.[47] The data represent a complete database of all public procurement procedures conducted under the EU Public Procurement Directive by member states or the European Commission regardless of the funding source (e.g. national, EU funded). All contracts must be awarded according to the procedural rules set out in the Directive if the contract value is above pre-set uniform thresholds: roughly €125,000 for service and goods contracts, and €4,000,000 for construction contracts.[48] The database was released by the European Commission–DG Market which also has conducted a series of data quality checks and enhancements. TED contains variables appearing in 1) calls for tenders and 2) contract award notices. All the countries' public procurement legislation is within the framework of the EU Public Procurement Directive and is therefore directly comparable.[49] The source, TED database, contains over 2.8 million contracts of which 2.3 million are used in the analysis due to exclusions: 1) countries with too few observations such as Malta, 2) contracts below mandatory reporting thresholds[50] and 3) contracts on non-competitive markets.[51] The full Europe-wide contract-level public procurement database can be downloaded at <digiwhist.eu/resources/data>.

3.2 Measuring risks of high-level institutionalized corruption in public procurement

Developing comparative indicators of institutionalized grand corruption in public procurement for all European countries represents a key

---

[46] Malta is excluded as it has too few contracts awarded in this period to run the regression analysis.

[47] DG GROWTH, *TED Structured Dataset (2009–2014)*, Tenders Electronic Daily, Supplement to the Official Journal of the European Union, Brussels, 2015. Source data can be downloaded from <https://open-data.europa.eu/en/data/dataset/ted-csv>.

[48] There are also a few exceptions from these rules: contracts of national security concern and a closed list of specialized services such as some types of legal advice.

[49] European Commission, *Public Procurement Indicators 2012*, Brussels, 2014.

[50] <http://www.ojec.com/threshholds.aspx>.

[51] That is markets with fewer than ten contracts in the observation period suggesting too little spending for sustaining multiple competing firms. Here, markets are defined by product market and geographical location.

methodological innovation of this article. The approach follows closely the corruption risk indicator building methodology developed by the authors making use of a wide range of public procurement 'red flags'.[52]

The measurement approach exploits the fact that for institutionalized grand corruption to work, procurement contracts have to be awarded recurrently to companies belonging to the corrupt network. This can only be achieved if legally prescribed rules of open, fair and transparent competition are circumvented. By implication, it is possible to identify the input side of the corruption process, that is fixing the procedural rules for limiting competition, and also the output side of corruption, that is signs of limited competition. By measuring the degree of unfair restriction of competition in public procurement by modelling such input-output relations, proxy indicators of corruption can be obtained. Full details of the measurement approach and the resulting indicators can be found in Appendix A.

3.3 Political financing legislation in Europe

For the purpose of our analysis we collected yearly information on the existence and scope of political finance regulations in all twenty-nine countries between 2009 and 2014. The primary source of information is the openly available database EuroPAM, a component of the project DIGIWHIST on fiscal transparency and anti-corruption tools.[53] EuroPAM largely relies on the political finance coding framework included in the Political Finance Database published by International IDEA.

EuroPAM presents a series of thematic categories, along which information on more specific regulatory tools is mapped. The four general categories include: bans and limits on private income, public funding, regulations on spending, and reporting, oversight and sanctions. Each of these categories has sub-categories within it, for example in the first category, bans and limits to private income, the sub-categories include: a) bans on foreign donations, b) bans on corporate donations, c) bans on

---

[52] N. Charron, C. Dahlström, M. Fazekas and V. Lapuente, *Careers, Connections and Corruption Risks in Europe*, QOG Working Paper Series 2015:6, Gothenburg, 2015 <http://qog.pol.gu.se/digitalAssets/1526/1526038_2015_6_charron_dahlstr--m_fazekas_lapuente. pdf>; M. Fazekas, J. Chvalkovská, J. Skuhrovec, I. J. Tóth and L. P. King, 'Are EU Funds a Corruption Risk? The Impact of EU Funds on Grand Corruption in Central and Eastern Europe', in A. Mungiu-Pippidi (ed.), *The Anticorruption Frontline: The Anticorruption Report*, *Vol. 2*, Opladen, Berlin and Toronto, 2014, pp. 68–89; M. Fazekas, I. J. Tóth and L. P King, 'An Objective Corruption Risk Index Using Public Procurement Data', *European Journal of Criminal Policy and Research*, 22, 2016, 3, pp. 369–97.
[53] <www.europam.eu>.

donations from trade unions, d) bans on anonymous donations, e) other bans on donations and f) donation limits. Finally, within these categories there are individual questions registering the existence of a particular tool. For example, within bans on foreign donations, the database registers separately bans for political parties and bans for individual candidates. The database contains a total of thirty-seven individual items. A full list of items and their categories and sub-categories is provided in Appendix C.

For the years 2012 and 2015, EuroPAM offers a matrix of all items and registers the existence of each item with a 1, and its absence with 0. We take a simple average of all items per year per country in order to build a continuous measure of political finance regulation score, ranging from 0 to 1. The change of this score by year will capture any increase or decrease in the extensiveness of political finance regulations.

In order to count on a full panel, we manually coded the existence of each individual item per country for the years 2013 and 2014, as well as 2009 to 2011. EuroPAM does not record the specific year in which a regulatory item is introduced, but rather the existing stock of regulations in the years 2012 and 2015. By implication, the authors manually coded laws to create a country-year panel database based on the information provided by EuroPAM on the legislation that contains each particular item.[54]

4. Descriptive statistics and trends
Figure 1 shows the general trends in the average ratio of our two measures of corruption risk: single bidders and CRI (Corruption Risks Index) by year and region. Although the two measures capture slightly different phenomena, their behaviours over region and time resemble greatly. They both show a stark difference between corruption risks in Eastern and Western Europe, with the former registering between 1.5 and 5 times higher levels. Additionally, both measures show a slight upward trend for Western Europe, and in the case of the single bidder a slight downward trend for Eastern Europe, suggesting convergence over time.

---

[54] As EuroPAM is still in a pilot stage, both EuroPAM data and our own coding may be subject to minor changes in the future.

Figure 1. Corruption risk trends, 2009–2014

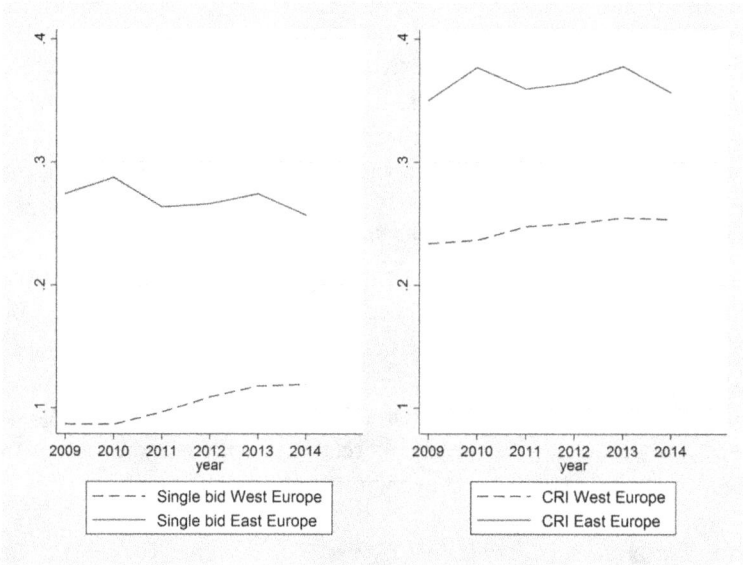

Figure 2. Distribution of political finance regulations scores, 2009–2015

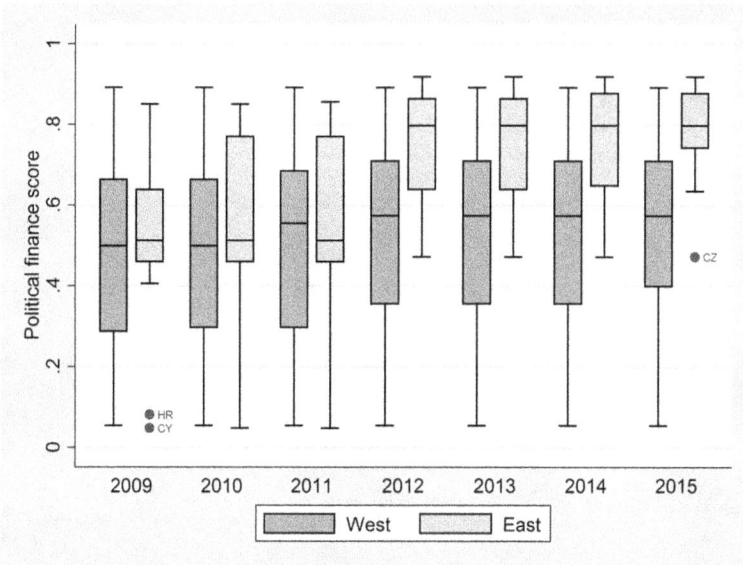

The boxplots in Figure 2 show the summary of the distribution of our main explanatory variable, the score of political finance regulations by year and region. It can be noted that while the median in both regions remains similar until 2011, Eastern Europe experiences a stark jump in regulation for the following years. It can also be observed that while the spread of the distribution is rather large throughout the period for Western Europe, Eastern countries cluster around similar values of political finance score towards the end of the period. Appendix B includes more detailed descriptive statistics of the political finance score.

Finally, Figure 3 shows a simple scatterplot with the bivariate relationships between our two corruption risk indicators and the political finance scores for all twenty-nine countries. It suggests a strong negative relationship by which countries with higher risks of corruption have introduced more political finance regulation. Our estimations in the next section will seek to unravel this relationship further and capture the isolated impact of regulation on corruption levels.

Figure 3. Scatter plots with bivariate regression line comparing political finance regulation scores and corruption risk indicators: single bidding and Corruption Risk Index, country-year observations, 2009–2015

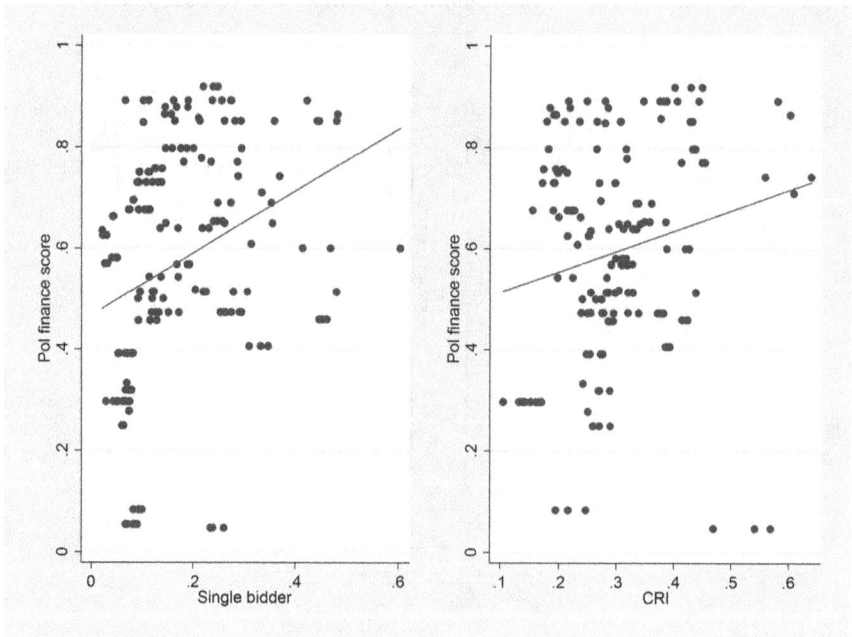

5. Results

In order to test the effects of a series of political finance anti-corruption mechanisms on corruption risk, we conduct a series of panel data regressions in our twenty-nine European countries between 2009 and 2014. In particular the following model is estimated:

$$CorrRisk_{i,t} = a_i + ßPolFin_{i,t} + ßX'_{i,t} + \varepsilon_{i,t}$$

Where *CorrRisk* is a measure of corruption risk in country *i* in year *t*, which will take two alternative forms in our estimations: the average of the ratio of tenders for which only one bidder submitted an offer (Single Bidder), and the more comprehensive corruption risks measure also incorporating tendering red flags (CRI). The main explanatory variable that we put to test is *PolFin*, a continuous score reflecting the level of political finance regulations existing in country *i* in year *t*, ranging from 0 (no political finance regulations) to 1 (highest possible level of financial regulations). The aspects of regulations that are considered in this analysis follow the thematic structured proposed by the EuroPAM database, where the main fields of regulation comprise: a) bans of foreign donations to parties and candidates; b) bans on trade union donations; c) bans on anonymous donations; d) other bans on donations; e) reporting standards from parties and candidates and f) political finance oversight institutions. Our indicator is a simple average of the existence of all items belonging to all thematic categories, as listed in Appendix A. In addition, *X* represents a vector of covariates that will differ by the type of estimation carried out, but in its fullest form include, per country *i* and year *t*: a measure of annual GDP growth, a measure of GDP per capita, an approximate measure capturing regulatory burden by the cost of starting up a business, a proxy measure of technological progress and citizen engagement capturing the number of internet users; a dummy for Eastern European countries and a final proxy measure capturing the level of industrial development of the economy by computing the value added of the industrial sector as a percentage of national GDP. All these covariates are in theoretical terms potential additional explanatory factors for corruption risks in a country. Overlooking them could easily lead to omitted variable bias where changes in both the explanatory and dependent variable may be driven by these omitted aspects. Finally, ε is the random error measure by country *i* in year *t*. As previously mentioned, our period of analysis spans from 2009 to 2014.

Table 1 presents the results of the baseline estimations adapted to three different multivariate regression analyses: a pooled OLS regression with country-clustered standard errors, a first-differenced estimation and a fixed effects panel data regression. The pooled OLS estimations (models 1 and 2) treats every observation as independent, even if the same subjects are observed for different time periods. It therefore only represents a first approximation to the association between our political finance score and the risk of corruption, as it allows us to maximize the number of observations. Although we estimate the pooled OLS regressions by clustering the standard errors by country, this measure does not fully take into account the fact that the same subjects — in this case countries — might behave similarly over time. In order to account uniquely for changes over time, a second alternative we report is the first-differenced estimation (models 3 and 4), in which only yearly changes in the explanatory factors are regressed on yearly changes on our corruption risk indicator. A final and preferred estimation type is fixed effects (models 5 and 6) where the singularity of countries is taken into account by adding a country-specific constant term to the baseline estimation and therefore any potential time-invariant significant explanatory variables (such as legal tradition, cultural norms or religious composition) are not biasing the results. Moreover, fixed effects is a more efficient estimator than first-differences whenever the time periods observed are more than two. Random effects estimations were disregarded as we had indication that they did not pass the random-versus-fixed effects Hausman test.[55]

The overall results in Table 1 suggest an interesting puzzle, already suggested by our scatterplots in the previous section: the impact of increasing the institutional tools against corruption in the area of political finance is positive. In other words, a higher political finance regulation score is associated with higher risk of corruption. For example, in model 5, moving from no regulation to a fully regulated setting increases the proportion of single bidding by 10 percentage points.

These counterintuitive results may be driven by contemporaneous variation around the time the new regulations are introduced rather than an actual causal relationship. In order to account for such bias and allow for a delay in the effect of political finance reform, Table 2 reports similar estimations as in Table 1, but replacing the contemporaneous indicator of our political finance regulations score with its lagged measure.

---

[55] For a gentle explanation of the three methodologies followed, see James H. Stock and Mark W. Watson, *Introduction to Econometrics*, Harlow, 2003.

Table 1. Baseline estimations of the effect of political finance regulations on corruption risk

	(1)	(2)	(3)	(4)	(5)	(6)
	Pooled OLS	Pooled OLS	First Diff	First Diff	Fixed Effects	Fixed Effects
VARIABLES	Single bidder	CRI	Single bidder	CRI	Single bidder	CRI
Political finance score	0.06*	0.01	0.04	0.04**	0.10**	0.10***
	(0.03)	(0.07)	(0.05)	(0.02)	(0.04)	(0.03)
GDP growth	0.00	0.00			0.00	0.00
	(0.00)	(0.00)			(0.00)	(0.00)
GDPpc	-0.00	-0.00	-0.00**	-0.00	-0.00***	-0.00**
	(0.00)	(0.00)	(0.00)	(0.00)	(0.00)	(0.00)
Setup buss cost	0.01**	0.00	0.00	-0.00	-0.00	-0.00
	(0.00)	(0.00)	(0.00)	(0.00)	(0.00)	(0.00)
Internet	-0.00	-0.00*	0.00	0.00	0.00	-0.00
	(0.00)	(0.00)	(0.01)	(0.01)	(0.00)	(0.00)
Eastern	0.12***	0.07*				
	(0.02)	(0.04)				
Industry	0.00	0.00	0.00	0.00	0.00	-0.00
	(0.00)	(0.00)	(0.00)	(0.00)	(0.00)	(0.00)
Observations	163	158	133	129	163	158
R-squared	0.62	0.43	0.07	0.02		
R-squared (overall)					0.32	0.23

Robust standard errors in parentheses. Constant terms are omitted. *** $p<0.01$, ** $p<0.05$, * $p<0.1$. Numbers are rounded to the second decimal.

The results in Table 2 reinforce our previous findings: the coefficient of political finance regulation varies from non-significant to positive depending on the model specification. Hence, even considering a one-year lagged effect of political finance regulations, a result which goes against our general hypothesis, persists (H_1). Similar estimations with longer lagged effects report non-significant coefficients for political finance regulation.

Table 2. Lagged effect of political finance regulation on corruption risk

	(1)	(2)	(3)	(4)	(5)	(6)
	Pooled OLS	Pooled OLS	First Diff	First Diff	Fixed Effects	Fixed Effects
VARIABLES	Single bidder	CRI	Single bidder	CRI	Single bidder	CRI
Political finance score = L,	0.07*	-0.01	0.08	0.08**	0.10**	0.04*
	(0.03)	(0.09)	(0.06)	(0.02)	(0.05)	(0.02)
GDP growth	0.00	-0.00				
	(0.00)	(0.01)				
GDPpc	-0.00	-0.00	-0.00	-0.00	-0.00***	-0.00**
	(0.00)	(0.00)	(0.00)	(0.00)	(0.00)	(0.00)
Setup buss cost	0.01***	0.00	0.00	-0.00	-0.00	-0.00
	(0.00)	(0.00)	(0.00)	(0.00)	(0.00)	(0.00)
Internet	-0.00	-0.00**	0.00	-0.00	-0.00	-0.00
	(0.00)	(0.00)	(0.01)	(0.00)	(0.00)	(0.00)
Eastern	0.12***	0.06				
	(0.02)	(0.04)				
Industry	0.00	0.00	0.00*	-0.00	0.00	-0.00
	(0.00)	(0.00)	(0.00)	(0.00)	(0.00)	(0.00)
Observations	135	131	105	102	135	131
R-squared	0.625	0.43	0.09	0.06		
R-squared (overall)					0.33	0.24

Robust standard errors in parentheses. Constant terms are omitted. *** $p<0.01$, ** $p<0.05$, * $p<0.1$. Numbers are rounded to the second decimal.

Given how counterintuitive these results are, we continue to explore alternative ideas affecting the nature of the link between political finance regulations and corruption risks. Along these lines, we first test the idea that political finance instruments might only have an impact when reforms to political finance regulation have been of high magnitude. For this, we transform our continuous measure of political finance regulations score into a categorical variable with three categories, none to small change, moderate change and large change.

Table 3. Impacts of political finance regulation on corruption risk: Categorical explanatory variable

	(1)	(2)	(3)	(4)
	OLS	OLS	OLS	OLS
VARIABLES	D5 Single bidder	D5CRI	D5 Single bidder	D5 CRI
Polfin reform level = 2	0.05	0.02	0.07*	0.02
	(0.06)	(0.02)	(0.05)	(0.02)
Polfin reform level = 3	0.04	0.09***	0.13*	0.15****
	(0.03)	(0.01)	(0.07)	(0.04)
GDPpc			-0.00	-0.00
			(0.00)	(0.00)
Setup buss cost			-0.00	-0.00
			(0.01)	(0.00)
Internet			0.01	0.00
			(0.00)	(0.00)
Observations	28	27	25	25
R-squared	0.06	0.12	0.24	0.19

Robust standard errors in parentheses. Constant terms are omitted. *** $p<0.01$, ** $p<0.05$, * $p<0.1$. Numbers are rounded to the second decimal.

Strikingly, we find evidence that in those countries which underwent more profound reforms, the impact of political finance regulatory reform leads to an increase in corruption risk with statistical significance in three of our four estimations. The effect size is very small, varying between a 0.09 and 0.015 point increase in our two corruption risk indicators. This means that in countries which underwent large reforms, a change of about 0.1 points in our political finance score translates into less than a one percentage point increase in single bidding share. Although moderate changes in the political finance score generally have a weaker and mainly insignificant effect on corruption risks across the specifications compared to extensive reforms, the coefficients are nevertheless positive too.

Next, we test whether the impact of political finance regulations depends specifically on the type of reform being implemented. For this, we take a separate measure of the political finance regulation score of components, following the thematic structure proposed by EuroPAM: a) regulation on foreign donations; b) corporate donations; c) trade union donations; d) anonymous donations; e) other bans on donations; f) monetary limits to donations; g) level of reporting standards; h) institutions of political finance oversight.

Table 4a. Individual political finance regulation instruments and corruption risks: Single bidder

VARIABLES	(1)	(2)	(3)	(4)	(5)	(6)	(7)	(8)
Fixed Effects								
Single Bidder								
GDPpc	-0.00***	-0.00***	-0.00***	-0.00***	-0.00***	-0.00***	-0.00***	-0.00***
	(0.00)	(0.00)	(0.00)	(0.00)	(0.00)	(0.00)	(0.00)	(0.00)
Setup buss cost	-0.00	-0.00	-0.00	-0.00	-0.00	-0.00	-0.00	-0.00
	(0.00)	(0.00)	(0.00)	(0.00)	(0.00)	(0.00)	(0.00)	(0.00)
Internet	0.00	0.00	0.00	0.00	0.00	-0.00	0.00	0.00
	(0.00)	(0.00)	(0.00)	(0.00)	(0.00)	(0.00)	(0.00)	(0.00)
Industry	0.00	0.00	0.00	0.00	0.00	0.00	0.00	0.00
	(0.00)	(0.00)	(0.00)	(0.00)	(0.00)	(0.00)	(0.00)	(0.00)
Foreign donations	0.07*							
	(0.02)							
Corporate donations		0.09***						
		(0.03)						
Trade union donations			0.06*					
			(0.03)					
Anonymous donations				0.05*				
				(0.03)				
Other bans					0.05**			
					(0.02)			
Donations limits						0.05*		
						(0.03)		
Reporting standards							0.05**	
							(0.02)	
Political finance oversight								0.03
								(0.03)
Observations	163	163	163	163	163	163	163	163
R-squared	0.28	0.34	0.31	0.31	0.31	0.29	0.29	0.29

Robust standard errors in parentheses. Constant terms are omitted. *** $p<0.01$, ** $p<0.05$, * $p<0.1$. Numbers are rounded to the second decimal.

Table 4b. Individual political finance regulation instruments and corruption risks: CRI

VARIABLES	(1)	(2)	(3)	(4)	(5)	(6)	(7)	(8)
Fixed Effects								
CRI								
GDPpc	-0.00*	-0.00**	-0.00*	-0.00*	-0.00*	-0.00	-0.00	-0.00
	(0.00)	(0.00)	(0.00)	(0.00)	(0.00)	(0.00)	(0.00)	(0.00)
Setup buss cost	-0.00	-0.00	-0.00	-0.00	-0.00	-0.00	-0.00	-0.00
	(0.00)	(0.00)	(0.00)	(0.00)	(0.00)	(0.00)	(0.00)	(0.00)
Internet	0.00	-0.00	0.00	0.00	0.00	0.00	-0.00	-0.00
	(0.00)	(0.00)	(0.00)	(0.00)	(0.00)	(0.00)	(0.00)	(0.00)
Industry	-0.00	-0.00	-0.00	-0.00	0.00	-0.00	0.00	-0.00
	(0.00)	(0.00)	(0.00)	(0.00)	(0.00)	(0.00)	(0.00)	(0.00)
Bans on foreign donations	0.05***							
	(0.02)							
Bans on corporate donations		0.06***						
		(0.02)						
Bans on trade union donations			-0.01					
			(0.02)					
Bans on anonymous donations				0.04**				
				(0.02)				
Other bans on donations					0.04***			
					(0.01)			
Donations limits						0.04**		
						(0.02)		
Reporting standards							0.07***	
							(0.02)	
Political finance oversight								0.05**
								(0.02)
Observations	158	158	158	158	158	158	158	158
R-squared (overall)	0.19	0.19	0.16	0.17	0.22	0.18	0.17	0.18

Robust standard errors in parentheses. Constant terms are omitted. *** p<0.01, ** p<0.05, * p<0.1. Numbers are rounded to the second decimal.

We consistently find that none of the specific instruments taken separately have a significant effect in lowering corruption. On the contrary, most of the estimations show again a positive and significant relationship.

After finding evidence refuting H_1 general hypothesis, but supporting H_2 and to a much lesser extent H_3, we further aim to test H_1 also taking into account the sequencing of reform, elections and politicians' ability to pay back with contracts. Hence, we only expect an impact of political finance reform if it was a major reform preceding national elections. This more specific formulation of the hypothesis receives no support from regression models either. When we allow for multiple years for the effects to show up in the measurement of procurement corruption risks (Table 5), all coefficients are insignificant.

Furthermore, difference-in-difference estimation results are also found in Appendix D, pointing once again at the invalidity of H_1.

Table 5. Political finance regulation and elections, impacts on corruption risk

	(1)	(2)	(3)	(4)
	Fixed effects	Fixed effects	Fixed effects	Fixed effects
VARIABLES	Single bidder	CRI	Single bidder	CRI
Elections with prior major polfin reform			0.00	0.01
			(0.02)	(0.01)
Elections with prior major polfin reform = L	-0.02	0.01	-0.02	0.01
	(0.017)	(0.01)	(0.02)	(0.01)
GDPpc	-0.000***	-0.00**	-0.00**	-0.000*
	(0.00)	(0.00)	(0.00)	(0.00)
Setup buss cost	0.00	-0.00	0.00	-0.00
	(0.00)	(0.00)	(0.00)	(0.00)
Internet	0.01	0.00	0.00	0.00
	(0.00)	(0.00)	(0.00)	(0.00)
Observations	135	131	135	131
R-squared	0.30	0.21	0.21	0.23

Robust standard errors in parentheses. Constant terms are omitted. *** $p<0.01$, ** $p<0.05$, * $p<0.1$. Numbers are rounded to the second decimal.

6. Conclusions and future research agenda

In cross-country panel regression and difference-in-difference models, we find that introducing additional political party financing restrictions does not have a measurable negative impact on corruption risks; if anything the effect is positive. The observed relationship remains the same for constitutive components of party financing regulations. In the models investigated, effect sizes, both significant and insignificant ones, are very small, for example ranging between a 1 and 5 per cent point change in single bidder shares. This is at least partially due to the fact that high-level institutionalized corruption in public procurement as measured by our indicators results from a range of factors beyond political party finances. One such other factor is the quality of public bureaucracies: improving public sector meritocracy by one standard deviation (using bureaucrats' self-reported experience with meritocratic promotion as a proxy) results in about a 12 per cent lower single bidder share on the same sample of countries.[56] The positive significant effect of political finance regulations on public procurement corruption risks in some models, unfortunately, does suggest that they may be used strategically by corrupt elites to cover up their increasing particularistic grip on government contracting or strategically modifying the rules of electoral competition to their own advantage.

However, our results are by no means conclusive. Instead, they represent the first imperfect attempt to rigorously test widely held assumptions about the effectiveness of controlling money in politics through regulations. Several challenges remain for a conclusive judgement on political finance regulations' effectiveness to curb corruption, each of which will be possible to thoroughly assess as more data is made available by DIGIWHIST at digiwhist.eu. A few potential extensions to our work include:

- Measuring the implementation of political party financing regulations rather than de jure legislation;
- Allowing for longer time between changes in legislation and expected changes in public procurement corruption risks;
- Considering institutional inter-dependencies such as normative constraints on party financing set by informed and well-organized voters or additional constraints on the pay-back mechanism presented by stringent public procurement legislation; and

[56] The study uses regional differences in corruption risks and meritocracy and instrumental variable methodology to approximate the causal relationship highlighted. See also, Charron et al., *Careers, Connections and Corruption Risks in Europe*, Table 4.

- Comparing findings of European countries with other contexts such as the USA.

The quantitative results delivered by this paper using objective indicators on political financing as well as public procurement corruption should raise concerns about 'best practice' policy advice promoted by multiple actors. The very instruments promoted as effective against corruption may well increase corruption rather than decreasing it. At a minimum, the effects of political financing on political competition as well as directly on public procurement corruption should be investigated, carefully taking into account the political context in any given country.

Appendix A — Measuring corruption risks

Defining 'objective' indicators of corruption risk
The simplest indication of restricted competition in line with our theoretical definition is when only one bid was submitted in a tender on an otherwise competitive market which typically allows for awarding contracts above market prices and extracting corrupt rents (output side). Hence, the percentage of single-bidder contracts awarded in all the awarded contracts is the most straightforward measure we use.

A more complex indication of high-level corruption also incorporates characteristics of the tendering procedure that are in the hands of public officials who conduct the tender and suggests deliberate competition restriction (input side).[57] This composite indicator, which we call the Corruption Risk Index (CRI), represents the probability of corrupt contract award in public procurement defined as follows:

$$CRI^i = \Sigma_j \, w_j * CI_j^{\,i} \qquad (1)$$
$$\Sigma_j \, w_j = 1 \qquad (2)$$
$$0 \leq CRI^i \leq 1 \qquad (3)$$
$$0 \leq CI_j^{\,i} \leq 1 \qquad (4)$$

where CRI^i stands for the corruption risk index of contract i, $CI_j^{\,i}$ represents the jth elementary corruption indicator observed in the tender of contract i, and w_j represents the weight of elementary corruption indicator j. Elementary corruption indicators can be either corruption inputs or outputs. CRI = 0 indicates minimum corruption risk while CRI=1 denotes maximum corruption risk observed. Based on qualitative interviews of corruption in the public procurement process, a review of the literature,[58] and regression analysis, we identified the components of the CRI in addition to single bidding (Table 6).

A simple way to fix tenders is to avoid the publication of the call for tenders in the official public procurement journal as this would make it harder for competitors to prepare a bid. This is only considered in non-open procedures since in open procedures publication is mandatory.

[57] Fazekas et al., *Anatomy of Grand Corruption*.
[58] OECD, *Integrity in Public Procurement: Good Practice from A to Z*; Pricewaterhouse Coopers, *Identifying and Reducing Corruption in Public Procurement in the EU*, Brussels, 2013, and World Bank, *Fraud and Corruption: Awareness Handbook*.

While open competition is relatively hard to avoid in some tendering procedure types such as open tender, others such as invitation tenders are by default much less competitive; hence using less open and transparent procedure types can indicate the deliberate limitation of competition, hence corruption risks.

If the advertisement period, i.e. the number of days between publishing a tender and the submission deadline, is too short for preparing an adequate bid, it can serve corrupt purposes whereby the issuer informally tells the well-connected company about the opportunity well in advance.

Different types of evaluation criteria are prone to fiddling to different degrees: subjective, hard-to-quantify criteria often accompany rigged assessment procedures as a lack of precision creates room for discretion and limits accountability mechanisms.

If the time used for deciding on the submitted bids is excessively short or lengthened by legal challenge, it can also signal a corruption risk. Snap decisions may reflect premediated assessment, while legal challenge and the corresponding long decision period suggests the outright violation of laws.

For continuous variables above such as the length of the advertisement period, thresholds had to be identified in order to reflect the non-linear character of corruption. This is because most values of continuous variables can be considered as reflections of diverse market practices, while some domains of outlier values are more likely associated with corruption. Thresholds were identified using regression analysis, in particular analysing residual distributions.[59] We restricted the sample in two ways:

1. Competitive markets: we only examine tenders in markets with at least ten contracts awarded between 2009 and 2014, where markets are defined by product type (CPV level 3) and location (NUTS level 1) within each country.
2. Regulated tenders: we only used those tenders which are above EU thresholds in order to avoid the noise of too small contracts and voluntary reporting which follows erratic patterns across countries and over time. These together removed 17 per cent of the observations.

---

[59] For more on this, see Fazekas et al., *Anatomy of Grand Corruption*.

Table 6. Summary of elementary corruption risk indicators

Proc. phase	Indicator name	Indicator values
submission	Call for tenders publication (non-open procedures)	0=call for tender published in official journal 1=NO call for tender published in official journal
	Procedure type	0=open 1=non-open (accelerated, restricted, award without publication, negotiated, tender without competition)
	Length of advertisement period	Number of days between the publication of call for tenders and the submission deadline
assessment	Weight on non-price evaluation criteria	Sum of weights for evaluation criteria which are NOT related to prices
	Length of decision period	Number of days between submission deadline and annoucing contract award
outcome	Single bidder contract valid/received	0=more than 1 bid received 1-1 bid received

In addition to the identification of thresholds in continuous variables, regression analysis was also used to identify 'red flags' which are most likely to signal corruption rather than any other phenomenon such as low administrative capacity. Ultimately, the variables and their categories which were selected were those which were large and significant predictors of single bidder contracts. The regression set-up controlled for a number of likely confounders of bidder numbers: 1) institutional endowments measured by type of issuer (e.g. municipal, national); 2) product market and technological specificities measured by CPV division of products procured; 3) contract size (log contract value in EUR); and 4) regulatory changes as proxied by year of contract award.

The logic of regression analysis is the following: if, in a certain country, not publishing the call for tenders in the official journal for open procedures is associated with a higher probability of a single bidder contract award, it is likely that avoiding the transparent and easily accessible publication of a new tender is typically used for limiting competition. This would imply that calls for tender not published in the official journal become part of the analysed country's CRI. Taking another example, if we found that leaving only five or fewer days for bidders to submit their bids is associated with a higher probability of a single bidder contract compared to periods longer than twenty calendar days (a more or less arbitrary benchmark category), this would indicate that extremely short advertisement periods are often used for limiting competition. Then this would provide sufficient grounds to include the 'five or fewer days' category of the decision period variable in the CRI of the country in question. Following this logic, in addition to the outcome variable in these regressions (single bidder) only those variables and variable categories are included in CRI which are in line with a rent extraction logic and proven to be significant and powerful predictors.

Once the list of elementary corruption risk indicators is determined with the help of the above regressions, each of the variables and their categories receive a component weight. As we lack the detailed knowledge of which elementary corruption technique is a necessary or sufficient condition for corruption to occur, we assign equal weight to each variable and the sizes of regression coefficients are only used to determine the weights of categories within variables. For example, if there are four significant categories of a variable, then they would get weights 1, 0.75, 0.5 and 0.25, reflecting category ranking according to coefficient size. The component weights are normed so that the observed CRI falls between 0 and 1.

Each of the two corruption risk indicators has its pros and cons. The strength of the single bidder indicator is that it is very simple and straightforward to interpret. However, it is also more prone to manipulation by corrupt actors due to its simplicity. The strength of the composite indicator approach (CRI) is that while individual strategies for corruption may change as the environment changes, they are likely to be replaced by other techniques. Therefore, the composite indicator is a more robust proxy of corruption over time than a single variable approach. In an international comparative perspective, a further strength of CRI is that it balances national specificities with international comparability by allowing for the exact formulation of the components to vary reflecting differences in local market conditions. The main weakness of CRI is that it can only capture a subset of corruption strategies in public procurement, arguably the simplest ones, hence it misses out on sophisticated types of corruption such as corruption combined with inter-bidder collusion.

Validity of corruption risk indicators
The validity of both the single bidder indicator and the CRI stems from their direct fit with the definition of high-level corruption in public procurement and the theoretical model of corrupt rent extraction. Further analysis of their association with widely used survey-based macro-level corruption indicators, as well as with micro-level objective indicators of

corruption risks underpins their validity, that is, such tests suggest that our corruption risk indicators indicate corruption rather than any other phenomena such as low administrative capacity.

The single bidder indicator and the CRI (as a 2009–2013 average per country using number of contracts) correlate as expected with widely used perception-based corruption indicators, such as the World Governance Indicators' Control of Corruption, Transparency International's Corruption Perception Index and Global Competitiveness Index's Favoritism, in decisions of government officials (Table 7). In addition, a 2013 Eurobarometer survey of bidding companies' experience of corruption across the EU provides the most directly comparable survey-based indicator of corruption in public procurement, which also co-varies with both single bids and the CRI as expected.[60]

Table 7. Bivariate Pearson correlations of % single bidder and the CRI with survey-based corruption indicators, on the country level, 2009–2013

Indicator	Single bidder	CRI	N
WGI – Control of Corruption (2013)	-0.7120*	-0.6933*	28
TI – Corruption Perceptions Index (2013)	-0.6903*	-0.6662*	28
GCI – Favouritism in decisions of government officials (2013)	-0.7003*	-0.6342*	28
Eurobarometer company corruption perceptions (2013)	0.5645*	0.6163*	25

Source: TED[61]
*Note: * = significant at the 5% level*

In order to visually demonstrate the above described correlations, we depict the average 2009–2013 single bidder ratio (Figure 4. Bivariate relationship between WGI-Control of Corruption [2013] and single bidder ratio [period average for 2009–2013], EU-27+Norway, Switzerland) and CRI (Figure 5) scores of EU27 countries and Norway along with their 2013 WGI Control of Corruption scores.

---

[60] While three perception indicators (WGI, TI, and GCI) indicate less corruption with higher values, our indicators and the Eurobarometer indicator are scaled in the opposite direction with higher values implying more corruption.

[61] D. Kaufmann, A. Kraay and M. Mastruzzi, *Governance Matters VIII*, Washington, D.C., 2009; TNS Opinion and Social, *Public Opinion in the European Union-Standard Eurobarometer 79*, Brussels, 2013; Transparency International, *Corruption Perceptions Index 2012*, Berlin, 2012, and World Economic Forum, *The Global Competitiveness Report 2012–2013*, Geneva, 2010.

Figure 4. Bivariate relationship between WGI-Control of Corruption (2013) and single bidder ratio (period average for 2009–2013), EU-27+Norway, Switzerland

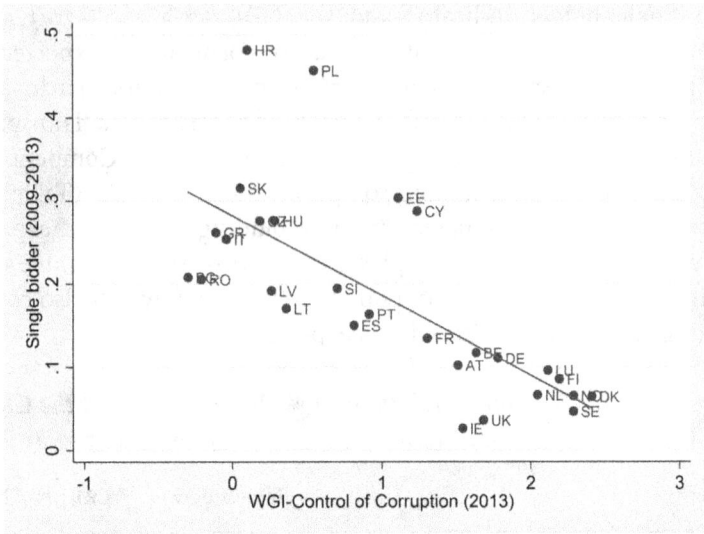

Figure 5. Bivariate relationship between WGI-Control of Corruption (2013) and average CRI (period average for 2009–2013), EU-27+Norway, Switzerland

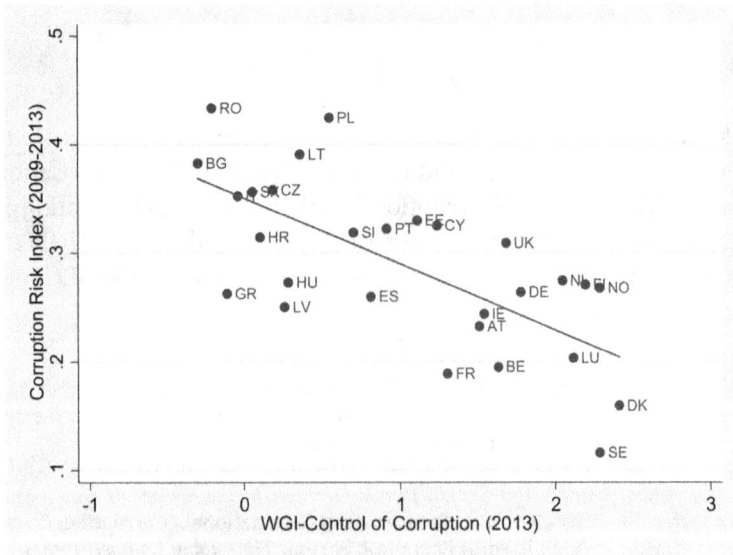

In order to validate our indicators not only on the macro-level, but also on micro-level, we employ two 'objective' risk indicators: procurement suppliers' country of origin and contract prices. It is expected that a contract represents a higher corruption risk if it is awarded to a company registered in a tax haven as its secrecy allows for hiding illicit money flows.[62] In line with our expectations, across the EU27 plus Norway there is a marked and significant difference in the percentage of single bidder contracts won by foreign companies registered in tax havens versus those which are not: 0.28 versus 0.26; similarly for CRI: 0.34 versus 0.31 respectively (Ncontract=28,642).

We also expect corruption to drive prices up. Although reliable unit prices are not available, we can employ a widely used alternative indicator of price, which is the ratio of actual contract value to initially estimated contract value.[63] As expected, both single bidder contracts and a higher CRI are associated with higher prices. Single bidder contracts have between 9–9.6 per cent higher prices than multiple bidder contracts; similarly contracts with one additional red flag (i.e. 0.17 CRI points higher) are 2.5–2.7 per cent more expensive even after controlling for major confounding factors (Table 8).

Table 8. Linear regressions explaining relative contract value, EU27+NO, CH, 2009–2014

Dependent variable	Relative contract value (contract price/estimated price)			
	(1)	(2)	(3)	(4)
Independent variable	CRI	CRI	Single bidder	Single bidder
	0.1484*	0.1607*	0.0963*	00903*
	(0.000)	(0.000)	(0.000)	(0.000)
Sector of contracting entity	N	Y	N	Y
Type of contracting entity	N	Y	N	Y
Year of contract award	N	Y	N	Y
Product market	N	Y	N	Y
Contract value	N	Y	N	Y
Country	Y	Y	Y	Y
N	524441	501783	524442	501784
R-squared	0.0710	0.1248	0.1096	0.1546

*Note: p-value in parentheses; *=significant at 0.1% level; each regression contains constant; relative contract values equal or smaller than 1*

[62] N. Shaxson and J. Christensen, *The Finance Curse: How Oversized Financial Centres Attack Democracy and Corrupt Economies*, Chesham, 2014.

[63] D. Coviello & M. Mariniello, 'Publicity Requirements in Public Procurement: Evidence from a Regression Discontinuity Design', *Journal of Public Economics*, 109, 2014, pp. 76–100.

Appendix B — The political finance regulation score

Table 9. Political finance regulation score: descriptive statistics

Variable/years	N	Mean	St. Dev.	Min	Max
Political Finance Score (all years)	203	0.580	0.238	0.047	0.918
2009	29	0.488	0.241	0.047	0.891
2010	29	0.502	0.248	0.047	0.891
2011	29	0.514	0.249	0.047	0.891
2012	29	0.630	0.220	0.054	0.918
2013	29	0.632	0.221	0.054	0.918
2014	29	0.642	0.221	0.054	0.918
2015	29	0.655	0.215	0.054	0.918

Appendix C — EuroPAM political finance scoring

Table 10. EuroPAM political finance, categories, sub-categories and items

Nr	Category	Sub-category	Item
1	**Bans and limits on private income**		
2		**Bans on donations from foreign interests**	
3			Is there a ban on donations from foreign interests to political parties?
4			Is there a ban on donations from foreign interests to candidates?
5		**Bans on corporate donations**	
6			Is there a ban on corporate donations to political parties?
7			Is there a ban on corporate donations to candidates?
8			Is there a ban on donations from corporations with government contracts to political parties?
9			Is there a ban on donations from corporations of partial government ownership to political parties?
10			Is there a ban on donations from corporations with government contracts to candidates?
11			Is there a ban on donations from corporations of partial government ownership to candidates?
12		**Bans on donations from trade unions**	
13			Is there a ban on donations from trade unions to political parties?
14			Is there a ban on donations from trade unions to candidates?

Nr	Category	Sub-category	Item
15		**Bans on anonymous donations**	
16			Is there a ban on anonymous donations to political parties?
17			Is there a ban on anonymous donations to candidates?
18		**Other bans on donations**	
19			Is there a ban on state resources being given to or received by political parties or candidates (excluding regulated public funding)?
20			Is there a ban on any other form of donation?
21		**Donation limits**	
22			Is there a limit on the amount a donor can contribute to a political party over a time period (not election specific)?
23			Is there a limit on the amount a donor can contribute to a political party in relation to an election?
24			Is there a limit on the amount a donor can contribute to a candidate?
25	**Public funding**	**Public funding**	
26			Eligibility criteria for direct public funding to political parties
37			Allocation calculations for direct public funding to political parties
46			Earmarking provisions for direct public funding to political parties
57			Are there provisions for free or subsidized access to media for candidates?
58			Are there provisions for any other form of indirect public funding?

Nr	Category	Sub-category	Item
65			Is the provision of direct public funding to political parties related to gender equality among candidates?
66			Are there provisions for other financial advantages to encourage gender equality in political parties?
67	**Regulations on spending**	**Regulations on spending**	
68			Is there a ban on vote buying?
69			Are there bans on state resources being used in favour or against a political party or candidate?
70			Are there limits on the amount a political party can spend?
71			Are there limits on the amount a candidate can spend?
72	**Reporting, oversight and sanctions**		
73		**Reporting standards**	
74			Do political parties have to report regularly on their finances?
75			Do political parties have to report on their financies in relation to election campaigns?
76			Do candidates have to report on their campaign finances?
77			Is information in reports from political parties and/or candidates to be made public?
78			Must reports from political parties and/or candidates reveal the identity of donors?
79			Institutions receiving financial reports from political parties and/or candidates

Nr	Category	Sub-categeory	Item
86		**Political finance oversight**	
87			Is it specified that a particular institution(s) is responsible for examining financial reports and/or investigating violations?
94			Other institutions with a formal role in political finance oversight
101			Sanctions for political finance infractions

Appendix D — Difference-in-difference estimations

In order to better isolate the impact of major political finance regulatory reforms, we build on the specific data structure allowing to conduct a quasi-experimental estimation based on the difference-in-difference (DiD) approach. We exploit the quasi exogeneity of political finance reforms taking place in Europe in the last six years (e.g. GRECO recommendations and monitoring), given that they mostly occurred in a single wave in 2012. Because a number of countries did not undertake any political finance reform, we are able to build our two groups for the DiD estimation comprising the years 2011 and 2012: 1) unreformed countries representing the control group; and 2) the reformed countries constituting the treatment group.[64] The wave of reforms taking place in 2012 is naturally our treatment.

The DiD estimation method represents an attempt to further isolate the effects of reforms by focusing on the years of most exogenous change and maximizing the distinction between reformed versus unreformed groups. The lack of significance of the interaction term suggests no effect — positive or negative — of political finance reforms, at least in the short term. The lack of a positive significant impact in contrast to our earlier OLS and panel estimations may be due to the substantial reduction in the amount of observations that arises from reducing the timeframe.

[64] Based on summary statistics, the threshold to define the group of reformed countries was an increase of at least 0.05 points in our political finance regulation score.

Table 11. Political finance reforms and corruption risks, difference-in-difference

	(1)	(2)
	OLS	OLS
VARIABLES	Single bidder	CRI
After reform	0.01	-0.00
	(0.01)	(0.01)
Treatment group	0.04	-0.06
	(0.05)	(0.04)
DiD	0.00	0.02
	(0.02)	(0.01)
Observations	56	56
R-squared	0.04	0.12

Robust standard errors in parentheses. Constant terms are omitted.
*** p<0.01, ** p<0.05, * p<0.1. Numbers are rounded to the second decimal.

4

Through the Lens of Social Constructionism: The Development of Innovative Anti-Corruption Policies and Practices in Bulgaria, Greece and Romania, 2000–2015

ROXANA BRATU, DIMITRI A. SOTIROPOULOS and MAYA STOYANOVA

THE past decade has witnessed two distinct yet interconnected developments in the understanding, policy and practice of corruption studies. On the one hand, corruption has progressively been constructed as a major threat to economic and social development through the use of deceivingly simplistic Western-centric definitions,[1] awareness campaigns and international perception-indexes that create the illusion of measuring real levels of corruption.[2] Such developments have recently been criticized by academic observers[3] and activists alike for presenting corruption as a country-specific issue, closely linked to the public sector. On the other hand, and perhaps counterintuitively, anti-corruption efforts have been decontextualized, focusing on generic fixes that typically involve the public sector. This one-size-fits-all approach[4] has not produced impressive results,[5] and has come under attack for ignoring the historical context and function of contemporary states.[6]

---

[1] For more detail regarding the assumption of public-private divide, see Alena Ledeneva, 'A Critique of the Global Corruption "Paradigm"', in Jan Kubik and Amy Linch (eds), *Postcommunism from Within: Social Justice, Mobilization and Hegemony*, New York and London, 2013, pp. 297–332.

[2] Frederik Galtung, 'Criteria for Sustainable Corruption Control', *The European Journal of Development Research*, 10, 1998, 1, pp. 105–28.

[3] Ledeneva, 'A Critique of the Global Corruption "Paradigm"'.

[4] Bo Rothstein, 'Anti-Corruption: The Indirect "Big Bang" Approach', *Review of International Political Economy*, 18, 2011, 2, pp. 228–50.

[5] Despite massive investments in anti-corruption over the past ten years, there is not a single case of corruption having been tackled successfully in Europe. See the case of anti-corruption in Georgia in Alina Mungiu-Pippidi (ed.), *The Anticorruption Frontline*, The ANTICORRP Project, vol. 2, Oplanden, Berlin, Toronto, 2014.

[6] See Heywood in this volume.

This article examines the construction and development of corruption concerns and anti-corruption practices from a comparative perspective in Bulgaria, Greece and Romania. It poses the question: how do corruption perceptions, policies and assumptions shape anti-corruption practices? Instead of looking at anti-corruption as an analytical category, this article takes the term back to its empirical dimension by contextually examining the emergence, role and practices of anti-corruption from a comparative perspective. Concretely, it focuses on the ways in which corruption in general and 'grand corruption' in particular are conceptualized, institutionalized and tackled. For the purposes of this article, grand corruption is loosely defined as corruption occurring within the highest echelons of power and presenting serious social, political and economic risks. Based on interviews with anti-corruption experts and practitioners from the three countries under discussion and analysis of relevant policy documents and official reports, the article critically examines the role of anti-corruption practices in the production of the contemporary political ethos. The research is based on mixed methods[7] that combine qualitative and quantitative approaches, direct interaction with research subjects and documentary analysis. By combining multiple methods and empirical routes, the researchers have increased the validity of their findings and avoided the intrinsic weaknesses associated with individual methods or research based on single case-studies.

The article proceeds as follows: the first part describes the context of the research with particular reference to (anti)corruption measures. The second part sets out an analytical framework based on a social constructionist approach.[8] The following sections explain step-by-step the evolution, institutionalization, implementation and politicization of anti-corruption in the three countries under examination. In the final section, the three cases are discussed comparatively and wider theoretical implications are drawn.

---

[7] In total, 27 semi-structured interviews were conducted between November 2014 and February 2016 with members of the judiciary (judges and prosecutors), high-ranking administrative officials, experts and journalists. The interviews were conducted in the original languages by the authors, who are native speakers. They lasted between 40 minutes and two hours.

[8] Peter Berger and Thomas Luckmann, *The Social Construction of Reality*, London, 1966.

Why compare Bulgaria, Greece and Romania?

The three cases discussed here are particularly suited for comparison because they are sufficiently similar to permit the emergence of meaningful conclusions, even though the case-study methodology developed in this article is not based on a systematic endeavour. The dimensions of comparison that will be used to highlight differences in outcomes are: perceptions of corruption; local governments' relations with transnational organizations, such as the European Union (EU) and International Monetary Fund (IMF); electoral cycles; government stability; the existence of social or economic crises; entrepreneurial culture; and, in the case of Bulgaria and Romania, the historical Communist background. These analytical dimensions will shed light on key patterns of similarity and difference among the three countries. It is important to note that the three countries are different, most notably in that Greece has undergone neither a transition from Communism to capitalism nor a process of EU accession similar to Romania and Bulgaria. At the same time, the three countries also show strong similarities: high levels of perceived corruption coupled with strong distrust in government, parliament and political parties; harsh economic environments especially following the global financial crisis of 2008; and pressure from the international community to adapt their policies to the required standards (through successive Economic Adjustment Programmes in the case of Greece, and through the Mechanism of Cooperation and Verification [MCV] in the cases of Bulgaria and Romania). These similarities justify the comparative effort undertaken in this article which aims on the one hand to develop a research methodology for more systematic comparison and on the other to unravel the logic behind tackling corruption in a different manner at national level.

There is wide international consensus regarding the prevalence of corruption and the need for tough anti-corruption policies in all three countries. In 2014, for example, the World Bank (WB) assigned some of the lowest scores in the EU regarding control of corruption to Bulgaria (-0.28), Greece (-0.2) and Romania (-0.14).[9] International observers also agree that corruption among high-ranking officials remains a pressing issue in

---

[9]   The index ranges from (-2.5) to (2.5). More details regarding this index at <http://info.worldbank.org/governance/wgi/index.aspx#home>.

Bulgaria,[10] Greece[11] and Romania.[12] These countries have become what Leslie Holmes has called 'rotten states',[13] being perceived not only as highly corrupt, but also as a threat to other EU member-states (given that they might, in the case of Greece, put additional pressure on the EU's already strained budget or, in the cases of Bulgaria and Romania, influence the culture of entrepreneurship and/or restrict access to the market for other European partners).[14]

Such perceptions of corruption were shaped by the contact between national governments and transnational institutions such as the EU and IMF in the context of major financial crises and geopolitical shifts such as EU-enlargement. The global financial crisis of 2008 hit Bulgaria and Romania hard, while Greece came close to the brink of sovereign default and has yet to fully recover.[15] The causes and evolution of the crisis were often mixed with a narrative of blame that traced the roots of the problems to the alleged graft and greed of local elites who had prioritized personal enrichment to the detriment of public well-being. These narratives of blame were strongly supported by the international community — in the case of Greece the troika of the European Commission (EC), European Central Bank (ECB) and IMF and, in the cases of Bulgaria and Romania, the MCV instituted by the EC. These powerful entities, which acted as both international donors and gatekeepers to foreign funding, legitimized popular dissatisfaction with local elites and framed the solution within narratives of anti-corruption and the politics of austerity, putting financial and political pressure on the three countries to 'solve their corruption issue'.[16]

---

[10] European Commission, *Annex Bulgaria to the EU Anti-Corruption Report*, Brussels, 3 February 2014 <http://ec.europa.eu/dgs/home-affairs/what-we-do/policies/organized-crime-and-human-trafficking/corruption/anti-corruption-report/docs/2014_acr_bulgaria_chapter_en.pdf> [accessed 28 September 2015].

[11] Council of Europe, *Third Evaluation Round, Evaluation Report on Greece*, Greco Eval III Rep 2009 (9E), Theme I, Strasbourg, 11 June 2010 (hereafter, Council of Europe 2010).

[12] European Commission, *Annex Romania to the EU Anti-Corruption Report*, Brussels, 3 February 2014 <http://ec.europa.eu/dgs/home-affairs/what-we-do/policies/organized-crime-and-human-trafficking/corruption/anti-corruption-report/docs/2014_acr_romania_chapter_en.pdf> [accessed 28 November 2015] (hereafter, European Commission 2014b).

[13] Leslie Holmes, *Rotten States? Corruption, Post-Communism and Neoliberalism*, Durham, NC, 2006.

[14] It is of course debatable to what extent the labels correspond to reality and how much they shape new perceptions, thereby impacting on real life through self-fulfilling prophecies.

[15] European Commission, 'Financial Assistance to Greece', 11 July 2016 <http://ec.europa.eu/economy_finance/assistance_eu_ms/greek_loan_facility/index_en.htm> [accessed 17 August 2016].

[16] For Bulgaria, European Commission, 'On Progress in Bulgaria under the

Working in crisis mode is certainly familiar to locals, as contemporary international pressure is juxtaposed against a recent history marked by abrupt change and social cacophony (in Greece, the 2008 financial crisis led to street protests and changes in government, while in Bulgaria and Romania the transition from Communism to capitalism was a traumatic process whose social effects are yet to be fully evaluated). Domestic factors such as electoral cycles, government stability and shifts in local elites have had a strong impact, shaping the perception of corruption and the implementation of anti-corruption policies at local level.

Frequent elections have been particularly important for this research because they have put the issue of corruption on the public agenda. Romania is the exception, but parliaments in Bulgaria and Greece have rarely served their full terms and early elections have ushered in new parties and governments. Following its 1989 transition from Communism, Bulgaria underwent a period of political instability, with governments falling before completing their full term in office. As of 1997, Bulgaria's governments became more stable, yet none was re-elected. Governments led by the United Democratic Forces (1997–2001), the National Movement of King Simeon II (2001–05) and the Bulgarian Socialist Party (BSP) led by Sergei Stanishev (2005–09) quickly lost popularity because they failed to deliver on their pre-election promises and to raise living standards. Although a new party, Citizens for the European Development of Bulgaria (GERB), led by Boyko Borisov, won successive elections in 2009, 2013 and 2014, stability remained elusive. Borisov's government was replaced by the short-lived government of Plamen Oresharski (2013–14) and he lost the 2016 presidential election to the BSP candidate, Rumen Radev. Corruption was a recurring theme in the elections of 2009 and 2013.[17]

Cooperation and Verification Mechanism', Brussels, 27 January 2016, pp. 2–9 <http://ec.europa.eu/cvm/docs/com_2016_40_en.pdf> [accessed 16 August 2016]. For Romania, European Commission, 'On Progress in Romania under the Cooperation and Verification Mechanism', Brussels, 27 January 2016, pp. 2, 11, 12 <http://ec.europa.eu/cvm/docs/com_2016_41_en.pdf> [accessed 16 August 2016]. For Greece, European Council. 'Memorandum of Understanding between the European Commission and the Hellenic Republic and the Bank of Greece', 19 August 2015, pp. 31–32 <http://ec.europa.eu/economy_finance/assistance_eu_ms/greek_loan_facility/pdf/01_mou_20150811_en.pdf> [accessed 16 August 2016].

[17] Alexander Stoyanov, Ruslan Stefano and Boryana Velcheva, 'Bulgarian Anti-Corruption Reforms: A Lost Decade?', Working Paper No. 42, April 2014 <http://www.againstcorruption.eu/wp-content/uploads/2012/09/WP-3-Diagnosis-of-Corruption-in-Bulgaria-new.pdf> [accessed 28 September 2015].

Until 2010, Greek governments were by contrast given a second chance. The centre-left Panhellenic Socialist Movement (Pasok) won successive mandates in 1996 and 2000, while the centre-right New Democracy won the 2004 and 2007 elections. This pattern was suspended in 2009, after the victory of Pasok which had to resort to EU rescue mechanisms in 2010 to avoid a sovereign default. Subsequently, the traditional centre-left vs. centre-right cleavage was replaced by pro-austerity vs. anti-austerity. Pasok and New Democracy governed in coalition from 2011–14 but were toppled in January 2015 when the largest anti-austerity party, the radical-left Syriza, won the parliamentary elections. Syriza campaigned on a radical agenda, but subsequently failed to implement it. Cornered by Greece's creditors in July 2015, Syriza called snap elections and won a fresh mandate in September 2015. This time, Syriza took a more balanced approach, promising to follow austerity policies while ensuring that they would not further impoverish middle- and lower-income groups. While there was some academic interest in corruption before the eruption of the financial crisis in 2008, for most of the 2000s Greek politics revolved around economic-policy choices. The pattern was suspended in 2009, after the victory of Pasok which had to resort to EU rescue mechanisms in 2010 in order to avoid a sovereign default.

Romania's transition from Communism to capitalism entailed first and foremost a shift from Eastern/Russian political influence to a Western/EU political affiliation. The political spectrum did not offer a wide array of options, as most parties had similar agendas which were developed top-down, from parliamentary debates, rather than from grassroots constituencies. These agendas were heavily influenced by international constraints regarding the supremacy of the neoliberal market and EU accession. Consequently, political parties had few policy options other than to observe the substantive policy commitments related to EU-entry while seeking at the same time not to destroy their own popularity.[18] The issue of corruption appeared on the political agenda from around 2000 and gained increasing prominence over the coming years, taking centre stage after 2010. In 2000 the Social Democratic Party (PSD) — which relied heavily on the former Communist Party for human resources — won election as a result of popular disappointment provoked by the perceived failure of the outgoing right-wing governing coalition to cope with the deepening economic crisis. Four years later, a liberal-democratic coalition replaced the PSD as the governing entity and maintained this position

[18] Adrian Miroiu and Șerban Cerkez, *Competitia politica in Romania*, Iași, 2013.

over two terms. The new government declared that fighting corruption would be its main priority.[19] Monica Macovei, a prosecutor during the Communist period and a civil society activist during the transition, was appointed Minister of Justice and emerged as leader of the anti-corruption movement. On 1 January 2007 Romania joined the EU.[20] In 2012, the PSD won election again but, amid popular discontent and accusations of corruption, the PSD-led government was replaced by a technocratic one in November 2015.

An important comparative dimension in the present study is the peculiarities of entrepreneurial culture in the three countries. In Bulgaria and Romania, the transition from Communism to capitalism saw the emergence of new elites which aimed to amass both political and economic capital. These new 'business politicians'[21] used their political influence to gain access to formerly state-owned enterprises that were then declared bankrupt and bought at significant discounts. On the one hand, the new 'biznizmen'[22] became 'political investors' by financing individual politicians and political parties; on the other, politicians created their own trusted circles in private companies.[23] Networks of businessmen and politicians also sought to enhance their profits and political influence by engaging in swaps of state-owned land, rigged bids in public procurement, absorption of EU funds and access to state subsidies for targeted business endeavours.[24] In such contexts, the classic public-private divide (on which the definition of corruption is based) loses meaning as there is no clear distinction between state officials and private business interests.

Such practices that favoured the powerful of the day established the patterns of grand corruption which, coupled with popular dissatisfaction with Bulgaria's living standards, led to sustained popular protests against the political influence of big private interests. In June 2013, for example, the Oresharski government's move to appoint media mogul Delyan

[19] European Commission, 'Regular Report on Romania's Progress towards Accession', Brussels, 2005.

[20] Romanian officials were less appreciative of Mrs Macovei's efforts and the Senate voted a motion against her which led to her dismissal. Her successor, Mr Tudor Chiuariu, spent less than a year in office and was dismissed by President Băsescu when charged in a corruption case.

[21] Donatella Della Porta and Alberto Vannucci, *Corrupt Exchanges: Actors, Resources and Mechanisms of Political Corruption*, New York, 1999.

[22] This was typically a male-dominated field.

[23] Stoyanov et al. 'Bulgarian Anti-Corruption Reforms', p. 15.

[24] Ruslan Stefanov, 'Energy and Good Governance in Bulgaria: Trends and Policy Options', Centre for the Study of Democracy, 2011 <http://www.risk.boku.ac.at/download/pub/2011/ENERGY-AND-GOOD-GOVERNANCE-IN-BULGARIA.pdf> [accessed 1 October 2015].

Peevski to head the State Agency for National Security provoked massive public discontent. In November 2015, Romania's Social Democratic prime-minister Victor Ponta resigned in reponse to public protests accusing him of corruption and incompetence. On that occasion, popular discontent was sparked by a fire in a Bucharest night club in which more than sixty young people died.[25]

Anti-corruption through the lens of social constructionism

In order to analyse anti-corruption practices from a comparative perspective, this article employs a distinctively social constructionist approach,[26] arguing that the meaning of corruption is context-contingent, while anti-corruption is a contemporary form of political frame rather than a technical solution to the 'corruption problem'. It examines how claims about corruption have been constructed in the three countries under review, and how such claims affected anti-corruption policies and their implementation at local level. From this perspective, corruption and anti-corruption are not self-evident ideas, but the outcomes of social actions and political interventions. This article considers that (anti)corruption comprises both a set of ideas (knowledge) — as corruption has become a growing, heterogeneous and powerful field of academic inquiry — and a range of practices, actions and interventions (power) since anti-corruption has become a site in which activists work, a field of 'policy expertise'.

Our starting point is the Thomas theorem[27] — a classic sociological theory that states that, if people 'define situations as real, they are real in their consequences'. In other words, reality is a matter of definition since the definition determines the course of action. In the late 1960s, Peter Berger and Thomas Luckman[28] argued that social order is the result of past human activity and exists only insofar as human activity continues to reproduce it. They argued that the process of social construction involves 1) the construction of society as an objective reality through institutionalization (the creation of new rules, laws and customs) and

[25] <http://www.economist.com/news/europe/21678282-protests-about-deadly-nightclub-fire-have-toppled-romanias-government-they-have-yet-change>.

[26] Berger and Luckmann, *The Social Construction of Reality*; Stuart Hall, Chas Critcher, Tony Jefferson, John Clarke and Brian Roberts, *Policing the Crisis: Mugging, the State and Law and Order*, 2nd edn, London, 2013; Dick Hobbs, *Lush Life: Constructing Organized Crime in the UK*, Oxford, 2013; Mark Granovetter, 'The Social Construction of Corruption', in Victor Nee and Richard Swedberg (eds), *On Capitalism*, Stanford, CA, 2007, pp. 152–72.

[27] Formulated in 1928 by W. I. Thomas and D. S. Thomas (1899–1977).

[28] Berger and Luckmann, *The Social Construction of Reality*.

legitimation (ensuring continuity of such rules) and 2) the construction of society as a subjective reality based on internalization (by means of socialization and identity). Through language, new meanings are assigned to old facts, which in turn become 'institutions' through the setup of new rules and laws, thus gaining social recognition as 'permanent' solutions to 'permanent' problems.[29]

Using this approach we argue, in line with Mark Granovetter,[30] that corruption is not a 'natural' but rather a 'social' fact. The very definition of corruption is a site of negotiation between academics and practitioners. Furthermore, over the past two decades the concept of corruption has gradually expanded to include more and more arenas of behaviour. Concomitantly, anti-corruption has also expanded to include a set of practices carried out by various societies seeking to curb corruption. Arnold Heidenheimer[31] argues that three key concepts shape the debate over corruption: public opinion, public interest and public office. Public opinion-centred definitions focus on the public's understanding of corruption, thus turning public opinion into the judge of corruption. Public interest definitions suggest that, through corruption, the public interest is violated in favour of a small group.[32] Criticized for their vagueness,[33] the concepts of public interest and public opinion were deemed unsuitable for policy purposes, rendering corruption 'unmeasurable'. Definitions centred on public office[34] focus on the distinction between public and private and the misuse of public power. This view was quickly adopted by international organizations including the WB, the IMF and Transparency International (TI), which define corruption as the abuse of public power for private gain. This view has been widely legitimized by TI through its Corruption Perceptions Index (CPI), published since 1995.[35]

---

[29] This constructionist view has been instrumentally employed to shed light on contemporary anxieties typically portrayed using vocabularies of crime such as mugging (Hall, *Policing the Crisis*); corruption (Granovetter, 'The Social Construction of Corruption'), organized crime (Hobbs, *Lush Life*).

[30] Granovetter, 'The Social Construction of Corruption'.

[31] Arnold J. Heidenheimer, 'Perspectives on the Perception of Corruption', in Arnold J. Heidenheimer, Michael Johnston, Michael LeVine and Victorio Tanzi (eds), *Political Corruption: A Handbook*, London, 1970, pp. 149–63.

[32] Carl J. Friedrich, 'Corruption Concepts in Historical Perspective', in ibid.

[33] Susan Rose-Ackerman, *Corruption and Government: Causes, Consequences and Reform*, Cambridge, 1999.

[34] Gunnar Myrda, *Asian Drama: An Enquiry into the Povery of Nations*, vol. 2, New York, 1968; Joseph Samuel Nye, 'Corruption and Political Development: A Cost-Benefit Analysis', *The American Political Science Review*, 61, 1967, 2, pp. 417–27.

[35] Frederik Galtung, 'Criteria for Sustainable Corruption Control', *The European Journal of Development Research*, 10, 1998, 1, pp. 105–28.

Corruption interpretations and anti-corruption practices were brought into existence by social events[36] linked to specific contexts and ideologies. The idea that corruption could be measured — that countries could be ranked according to an index — proved so appealing to the international community that TI's CPI became a powerful advocacy tool, despite its methodological shortcomings.[37] By the end of the 1990s, the conventional paradigm of corruption had begun to dominate international debate on the basis of three main assumptions: corruption could be defined, it could be measured and it could be tackled. Recent scholarship[38] describes a massive failure of the conventional paradigm, showing that 1) the present definition of corruption assumes a clear distinction between the public and private spheres which hardly grasps the complexity of everyday activities; 2) contemporary measurement-tools account mostly for the perception of corruption; however, assessments have started to incorporate evidence about experience and several objective measures of corruption have recently been developed;[39] 3) either anti-corruption policies implemented on the basis of current research methodologies have failed, or the present research instruments are incapable of capturing the nature and scope of reforms.[40]

In order to explain this failure, we take a historically informed view to explore the ways in which anti-corruption was sustained by institutional contexts and redefinition of rules, the creation of new forms of 'expertise' and the emergence of new actors, taking into account the relationship between knowledge (experts) and power (practices). In so doing, we move away from the Weberian model of bureaucracy[41] and the Western dichotomist view of public-private/state-society that leaves no room for positive contributions to the understanding of corruption.

Last but not least, we show that anti-corruption is not apolitical. Together with Italo Pardo and Giulianno Prato, we suggest that the state may be an active agent that 'through institutional blindness can allow the

---

[36] Pierre Bourdieu, 'La Force du Droit', *Actes de la Recherche en Sciences Sociales*, 64, 1986, pp. 3-19; Ian Hacking, *The Social Construction of What?*, Cambridge, MA, 2000; Ian Hacking (ed.), *Historical Ontology*, Cambridge, MA, 2002.

[37] See more on CPI methodology and recent changes at <http://www.transparency.org/files/content/pressrelease/2012_CPIUpdatedMethodology_EMBARGO_EN.pdf>.

[38] Ledeneva, 'A Critique of the Global Corruption "Paradigm"'.

[39] Miriam Golden and Lucio Picci, 'Proposal for a New Measure of Corruption, Illustrated with Italian Data', *Economics and Politics*, 17, 2005, pp. 37-75.

[40] Anna Persson, Bo Rothstein and Jan Teorell, 'The Failure of Anticorruption Policies: A Theoretical Mischaracterisation of the Problem', *QoG Working Paper Series*, 2010, 19.

[41] G. Anders and M. Nuijten (eds), *Corruption and the Secret of Law: A Legal Anthropological Perspective*, London, 2009.

interests of the elites'.[42] This approach renders more opaque the borders of legality exploited by power elites who, through law, give significance to and legitimize corruption. Dieter Haller and Chris Shore[43] focus on practices that make corruption a semantic of governance, thereby suggesting that it is a common way to make sense of politics. Davide Torsello[44] has described how environmental movements have used corruption talk (allegations or facts) to frame their protests and communicate with the wider public. This strategy builds on the generalized public talk sustained by media reports and locals' high levels of perceived corruption, enhancing the users' legitimacy through positive associations with an anti-corruption agenda.

To sum up, based on our reading of the literature, we analyse anti-corruption in the three countries under study as a process that involves a series of discrete steps: definition of the problem, institutionalization, legitimation and politicization. Far from being inherent to modernization, anti-corruption processes are the result of social and political manipulation and have been instrumental to various political regimes. We look at our three case-studies with this matrix (Table 1) in mind.

Creating the 'problem': The evolution of corruption and understandings of corruption within the historical context of Bulgaria, Greece and Romania

This section focuses on the first stage of the anti-corruption process (see Table 1). It shows that, over the past fifteen years, corruption has become a recurring theme in the three countries because of popular discontent, civil-society reactions and political usage of the term. Opinion polls have effectively put corruption at the front of public debates, signalling it as a major social problem. At the same time, however, anti-corruption has become a top policy priority only in Romania.

Corruption was installed in the public imagination as a major problem with the use of measuring devices,[45] which created the impression of authenticity regarding the spread and forms of the phenomenon. This not only legitimized the anti-corruption agenda, but transformed it into a powerful narrative of governance. International organizations, such as TI (by means of its CPI, Bribe Payers Index and Global Barometer of Corruption), Freedom House, the WB and the Organisation for Economic

[42] Italo Pardo and Giulianna Prato (eds), *Between Morality and the Law. Corruption, Anthropology and Comparative Society*, London, 2004, p. 6.

[43] Dieter Haller and Chris Shore (eds), *Corruption: Anthropological Perspectives*, London, 2005.

[44] Davide Torsello, *The New Environmentalism? Civil Society and Corruption in the Enlarged EU*, Abingdon and New York, 2012.

[45] Ledeneva, 'A Critique of the Global Corruption "Paradigm"'.

Co-operation and Development (OECD) produce their own composite indexes. Figure 1 shows the trends of corruption in the three countries using the WB's 'control of corruption' index.[46] Despite the index's methodological shortcomings,[47] Figure 1 shows that while corruption is a problem for all three countries under study, it remains a matter of timing and degree.

Table 1. *A social constructionist view of anti-corruption policies and practices*

Anti-corruption as a process: stages	Indicators
The evolution of the understanding of corruption as a social problem and policy priority	• Policy interest vs policy priority • Public concern • Priority for the criminal justice system • Existence and number of anti-corruption strategies
The anti-corruption institutional setting	• Level of institutional development (for example, legislation, number of institutions designated to tackle corruption) • Resources assigned to institutions (for example, human, material, informational, financial)
The implementation of anti-corruption	• Clear measurable progress vs 'implementation gap' • Unintended consequences of anti-corruption policies (for example, new forms of expertise or job specializations in the public and private sectors)
Politicization of anti-corruption	• The frequency of corruption as a narrative in the public space • Political opponents accuse one another of corruption on a regular basis • Anti-corruption institutions are heavily scrutinized by non-state actors (may be accused of political subordination)

[46] The index ranges from -2.5 (weak) to 2.5 (strong) governance performance. See the World Bank website for more details: <http://info.worldbank.org/governance/wgi/index.aspx#home>.

[47] For a thorough critique of composite indexes regarding corruption, see Heywood in this volume. For more methodological details regarding this index, see the World Bank website: <http://info.worldbank.org/governance/wgi/index.aspx#home>.

Figure 1: Control of corruption indicator (World Bank 1998–2014)

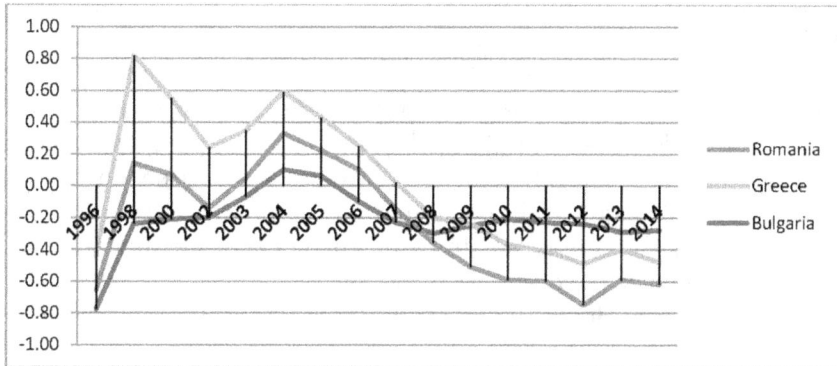

Further to composite indexes, corruption has been objectified through surveys, opinion polls and victimization studies. Regularly conducted (for example, the Romanian Barometer of Opinion is conducted yearly), such instruments began by the end of 2010 to include questions regarding corruption, indicating that it had become seen as a top social problem by then. In Bulgaria, for example, the number of people who considered corruption to be *the most serious* social problem doubled in five years from 31 per cent in 2004 to 65 per cent in 2009.[48]

The ideology of numbers was systematically sustained by the ideology of high-profile corrupt individuals who escaped justice for a long time, thereby increasing popular dissatisfaction. In September 2015, for example, Romanian prime minister Victor Ponta went on trial on charges of fraud, tax evasion and money-laundering allegedly committed in his former career as a lawyer. Earlier that same year the former Romanian Minister of Sports and Youth Affairs, Monica Iacob Ridzi, had received a five-year prison sentence for side-lining funds from her ministry, while Elena Udrea, former Minister of Tourism, was arrested on corruption charges.[49] In April 2008, Bulgarian Interior Minister Rumen Petkov resigned following accusations that he had failed to prevent police officers passing state secrets to organized crime networks. In July 2010, Sergei Stanishev was accused of withholding secret service files with sensitive information regarding organized crime that he had acquired while serving as Bulgarian prime

---

[48] Lyubomir Todorakov, 'A Diagnosis of Corruption in Bulgaria', European Research Centre for Anticorruption and State-building, Working Paper, No. 3, September 2013, p. 2 <http://www.againstcorruption.eu/wp-content/uploads/2012/09/WP-3-Diagnosis-of-Corruption-in-Bulgaria-new.pdf> [accessed 28 September 2015].

[49] Elena Udrea was subsequently released.

minister in 2005–09. More recently, in June 2014, Bulgaria's KTB bank was declared insolvent amid accusations of corruption involving member of parliament Delyan Peevski and businessman Tzvetan Vassilev.[50]

Greece has had its own high-profile corruption cases involving, for example, former deputy prime minister Akis Tsochatzopoulos and Vassilis Papageorgopoulos, mayor of Thessaloniki, the country's second largest city. The former was sentenced to twenty years in prison on charges of money-laundering and bribe-taking; an appeal was ongoing at the time of writing. The latter was initially sentenced to life imprisonment, subsequently reduced to twelve years, on charges of embezzling €18 billion from public funds. He was subsequently released from prison on health grounds.

Civil society was instrumental in projecting corruption as one of the top social problems and a typified model of anti-corruption. More flexible than the public sphere and also more dependent on external funding,[51] the third sector organized coalitions to gain a stronger voice, campaigned for judicial reform, and pressured politicians to meet their electoral commitments. In Bulgaria, for example, civil society (represented by, among other organizations, TI, the Open Society Institute, the Centre for the Study of Democracy and the Centre for Liberal Strategies) played an active role in seeking to prevent corruption and organized crime: during the late 1990s it organized 'Coalition 2000', conducted research on and monitored anti-corruption, and closely monitored judicial reform; after 2007 it used EU structural funding to enable the modernization of public administration.[52]

In Romania, the third sector's concern over corruption spread to the public sphere, especially after the Democratic Liberal Party took power in 2005 and worked to develop a solid partnership with civil society. Between 2005–12, an anti-corruption ethos that aimed to reform the whole of society was translated into awareness campaigns, emergency call-lines, opinion polls, workshops, meetings and training sessions. Using 'Poland and Hungary: Assistance for Restructuring their Economies' (PHARE)

---

[50] This proves once more that public-private division is merely a theoretical abstraction, as in this context entrepreneurs and politicians engage in various transactions undisturbed by definitional issues.

[51] The semantic expansion of corruption was doubled by the development of the anti-corruption market. Michael Bryan estimates that by 2009 the 'fight against corruption', particularly in Eastern Europe and the former Soviet Union, had become a multi-billion dollar industry. For more details see Michael Bryan and Donald Bowser, 'The Evolution of the Anti-Corruption Industry in the Third Wave of Anti-Corruption Work', *Proceedings from the Konstanz Anti-Corruption Conference (2009)* <http://works.bepress.com/bryane_michael/50>.

[52] Todorakov, 'A Diagnosis of Corruption in Bulgaria', pp. 10–16.

funding, the Justice Ministry conducted a €1.8 million anti-corruption campaign from October 2007 to February 2008. The Ministry of European Integration ran an anti-corruption campaign with the slogan, 'I do not give bribes – I do not take bribes' (*E.U. nu dau spaga – E.U. nu iau spaga*). Based on word-play, the message was that EU member-states do not engage in corruption. The General Anti-Corruption Directorate (DGA) and the National Integrity Agency (ANI) popularized the free-of-charge 'Green Line' (TelVerde) telephone system that citizens could use to report crimes committed by officials, while the Fight against Fraud Department (DLAF) focused on preventing fraud related to the EU budget. Partnerships and strategic alliances between civil society and state institutions were established. For example, the DGA cooperated with the Romanian Postal Service to run a publicity campaign called 'No more envelopes!' (*Gata cu plicurile!*) whereby all envelopes and receipts issued to the public were stamped with anti-corruption messages and information about the 'Green Line'.

In Greece, by comparison, civil society was less mobilized on corruption-related issues. Even so, grassroots campaigns were launched to collect information on corruption through social media. One example was the Facebook page 'over and done with' (*teleia kai pavla*)[53] where citizens could anonymously declare where and when they have been asked for bribes. In 2013, TI Greece established an anti-corruption hotline. Another hotline was made available at the Internal Affairs Division of the Greek police, while in autumn 2016 the government announced its intention to establish a new service for reporting corruption.

Campaigns such as these, together with the demands of international financial institutions and the business community, have transformed the fight against corruption into a coordinated campaign, with 'moral entrepreneurs'[54] employing a range of strategies. So far, Romania has had four anti-corruption strategies, each reflecting a change in the 'fight against corruption'. The first anti-corruption strategy (SNA I 2001–04) aimed to align political and penal semiotics by making the legislative framework relating to corruption as comprehensive as possible. The second strategy (SNA II 2005–07) aimed to establish an institutional architecture dedicated to monitoring and preventing corruption. The third strategy (SNA III 2008–11) focused on vulnerable sectors and local administration. The fourth strategy (2012–17)[55] is focused on prevention mechanisms

---

[53] Available at <https://el-gr.facebook.com/teleiakaipavla/>.

[54] Howard Becker, *Outsiders: Studies in the Sociology of Deviance*, New York, 1963.

[55] This Strategy was initially designed to cover the period 2012–15, but on 9 September

such as the implementation of integrity codes and preserving the existing institutional environment.[56]

Bulgaria has also benefited from a number of anti-corruption strategies, the earliest dating from 2001. Bulgaria's latest, five-year national anti-corruption strategy of 2015, contains thirty-three specific measures in six primary areas, but prioritizes the fight against corruption within the highest levels of government.

Since January 2013, Greece has had a national anti-corruption action plan (Ministry of Justice 2013). This is a roadmap drafted with the help of the Task Force for Greece, a technical assistance team made available to the Greek government by the EC to assist in structural reforms. The strategy was upgraded and modified by the government in August 2015, just before the snap elections called for September 2015. Since then, however, government instability has had a negative impact on the design and implementation of the promised anti-corruption measures.

While the fight against corruption has become more substantial in all three countries, their respective societies are marked by strong currents of discontent. Bulgaria, for instance, saw repeated anti-corruption demonstrations in 2013–14, 'revealing an increase in public sensitivity to political corruption'.[57] Citizens were disappointed by the mixed results of Bulgaria's integration into the EU and angry at the austerity measures taken by successive governments. In Romania, November 2015 saw a change in government brought about by massive street protests that coalesced around the issue of corruption.[58] In Greece, elections in 2012 and 2015 focused on the theme of corruption; the New Democracy party won the elections of 2012 by a small margin but was voted out of power in early 2015.

The aim of this section has been to show that corruption has become a sensitive issue over the past fifteen years and remains a recurring theme in local politics. Public pressure to identify those to blame for the deepening

---

2015 the government prolonged its implementation date until 31 December 2017.

[56] Several anti-corruption strategies included as an objective improving on the CPI index, probably assuming that this was an objective measure.

[57] Interview with political analyst, Sofia, 15 March 2015.

[58] The issue here is more complex, as the Romanian demonstrations were sparked by a fire in a nightclub that killed many people. During the investigations, it became apparent that the club had obtained its licences by informal payments or sheer bribery since it did not comply with regulations. Counterintuitively, the protests were less against the private owners of the club, who were seen as 'victims of a corrupt system', and more against the public sphere and the prime minister Victor Ponta, who were perceived as the 'real' perpetrators.

economic crisis combined with pressure from external actors (notably the EU and the IMF) to 'solve their corruption issues' shifted the focus to grand corruption. Table 2 summarizes the key findings. While in Bulgaria anti-corruption remains an important element in the public sphere, only in Romania has anti-corruption become a key policy priority. In Greece, by contrast, anti-corruption has never been a major priority either for political parties campaigning for election or for governments drafting their policy programmes. These different approaches are of vital importance for the next part of our analysis, since they play a key role in the construction of anti-corruption practices at local level.

Table 2. Corruption as a social problem and policy priority: Comparing Bulgaria, Greece and Romania

	Bulgaria	**Greece**	**Romania**
Evolution of the understanding of corruption as a social problem and policy priority	• Policy priority at declaration level, but little action • Public concern • No priority for criminal justice system	• Policy interest, but not enough to secure the necessary resources • Public concern (along with other social issues) • No priority for criminal justice system	• Top policy priority • Public concern • Criminal justice system priority

Creating the 'solution': Institutions and resources made available to tackle corruption in Bulgaria, Greece and Romania

After looking at the ways in which corruption was constructed as an issue in Bulgaria, Greece and Romania, this section analyses the institutional solutions put in place to solve the 'problem of corruption' (referred to in our theoretical model as the second stage — see Table 1). In so doing, we look at two main aspects: 1) the legal codification of corruption in general and of 'grand corruption' in particular and 2) formal institutions with competences in the area of corruption monitoring and prevention. Even though the three countries made use of rather similar tools and strategies, their development and efficiency have been very different. Whereas Romania has a clear legal definition of grand corruption as defined by Law 78/2000, Greece has only a vague approach and Bulgaria is still struggling to find one. Furthermore,

Romania has a strong anti-corruption institution, the National Anti-Corruption Directorate (DNA); this was specially designed to tackle grand corruption and has achieved impressive results over the years. Greece has set up several anti-corruption prosecutorial offices and, since February 2015, a General Secretariat for Anti-Corruption within the Justice Ministry, but both the Ministry and the Secretariat are under-staffed and under-resourced. Bulgaria is still in the process of establishing its first anti-corruption prosecutorial office. Meanwhile, all three countries recognize that both the general public and international organizations are justified in expressing concern over the potential abuse of tailor-made anti-corruption institutions, especially in light of the highly-politicized environment of each country. In Romania, for example, suspicions have been voiced that the DNA might act in accordance with political commands and create files on opponents of those in power.[59]

Formal attempts to define corruption in Romanian legislation are relatively recent. Before the 1989 revolution, the 1969 Criminal Code mentioned corruption only in two distinct cases: corruption of a minor for sexual purposes and corrupting a witness to commit perjury.[60] Neither of these cases had much in common with the present understanding of the concept, which generally refers to 'the abuse of public office for private gain'.[61] In 2000, the Romanian parliament adopted the first law[62] using the modern understanding of corruption. That law also laid the ground for a definition of 'grand corruption', establishing three main conditions: 1) the prejudice resulting from corruption crimes is more than €200,000 or leads to a serious malfunction of the activity of a public institution/authority, or the value of the goods traded through corruption is higher than €10,000; 2) a crime committed by one of the following: a member of parliament, member of the government, state secretary, judge, employee of the National Bank of Romania, military or police officer, mayor, lawyer, member of the

---

[59] <http://www.b1.ro/stiri/eveniment/calin-popescu-tariceanu-atac-la-adresa-lui-klaus-iohannis-si-a-procurorilor-dna-este-instrumentul-institutional-care-initiaza-la-comanda-politica-compromiterea-adversarilor-presedintelui-164940.html>.

[60] Dorinica Ioan, Dan Banciu, Sorin M. Rădulescu (eds), *Corupția în România. Realitate și percepție socială*, Bucharest, 2005. The crimes that incorporated the modern meaning of corruption were instead grouped under 'Crimes in relation to work' and were decoded as bribe giving, bribe taking, trading influence and receiving undue goods (Articles 254 – 57, Criminal Code 1969). However, the concept of corruption was never used in relation to these crimes.

[61] The World Bank, *Helping Countries Combat Corruption: The Role of the World Bank*, Washington, D.C., 1997, p. 8.

[62] Law 78/2000 on preventing, discovering and sanctioning of corruption acts.

Financial Guard, border control officer; 3) a crime against the financial interests of the EU. By 2003, anti-corruption was delivered in packages. For example, Law 161/2003 (labelled, along with Law 52/2003, as the Anti-Corruption Package) criminalized conflicts of interest; prohibited high-ranking public servants (members of the government, state secretaries and sub-secretaries, prefects and sub-prefects) from adopting administrative or judicial acts that would result in benefit for themselves, their partners or a close relative; defined new categories of incompatibility for public servants; modified and clarified other laws regarding corruption (for example, Law 188/1999 and Law 78/2000).

In Greece, the legal definition of grand corruption is vague, covering cases that involve high-ranking officials and crimes of 'considerable social and/or public interest' (Law 4022/2011). The law[63] covers crimes related to the discharge of duties by high-ranking officials including government minsters, members of parliament, general and special secretaries of ministries, presidents, governors and chief executive officers of public bodies, state-owned or state-managed enterprises and mayors (article 1 of Law 4022/2011).[64] As in Romania, anti-corruption policies in Greece were adopted under pressure from international organizations, particularly following the beginning of the 2008 economic crisis. For example, in 2011 the Greek government established a new Authority on Public Tenders and Contracts; in 2013 it strengthened controls on politicians and public officials; and in 2014 Greece adopted legislation on whistle-blowing in the public sector, the financing of political parties, and public procurement. This new codification of corruption was accompanied by a reform of the justice system aimed at ensuring the rigorous application of the new legislation and putting anti-corruption structures at centre stage. This involved two types of institutional reform: 1) setting up new specially designated anti-corruption institutions and 2) reforming the traditional justice and home affairs system to include new anti-corruption departments and/or competences.

In Romania, the main institution dealing with grand corruption is the National Anticorruption Prosecutor's Office (PNA), set up in 2002 at the behest of the EU and with €2 million funding through a PHARE

[63] Voted in September 2011.

[64] Relevant Greek legislation included Law 4013/2011 on the new Authority on Public Tenders and Contracts; Law 4170/2013 on the Anti-corruption prosecutors; Law 4254/2014 on whistle-blowing in the public sector; Law 4281/2014 on public procurement; and Law 4304/2014 on political-party financing. The new Anti-corruption Secretariat was founded by Law 4320/2015.

programme. As the aim of PNA was to target high-level corruption, it focused on cases involving high-ranking officials, and/or sums higher than €100,000. To reflect the importance of this new institution, PNA prosecutors were paid 40 per cent more than their counterparts in the General Prosecutor's Office in recognition of the fact that they were dealing with high-level corruption.[65] This, coupled with a lack of transparency in the selection process, created resentment among employees of the General Prosecutor's Office.[66] Ironically, therefore, Romania's main anti-corruption institution was from its inception suspected of corruption. In 2006, the institution was reformed and renamed the National Anti-Corruption Directorate (DNA). Since then, it has built a strong reputation as a body capable of dealing with grand corruption; as a result of its work, one prime minister, several government ministers and several high-profile entrepreneurs have been investigated and put on trial.

In Bulgaria, tackling grand corruption has long been an objective. Anti-corruption agencies such as the State National Security Agency (DANS) and the advisory agency BORCOR, were established under the Stanishev (2005–09) and Borisov (2009–13) governments. Anti-corruption efforts heightened in June 2015, when Deputy Prime Minister Magdalena Kuneva announced plans to establish a new anti-corruption bureau, independent of the government, which would track corruption among top officials.[67] The new unit was mooted to become operational in 2016, receive asset declarations from top officials, and focus on asset verification.[68] However, the first attempt to establish the bureau was rebuffed by the Bulgarian parliament on the grounds that it had the potential to become too autonomous and thereby exert disproportionate influence over elected officials and civil servants. For example, parliamentarians expressed concern about the bureau's power to open investigations on the basis of anonymous tip-offs.[69] Kuneva tried again in spring 2016, presenting parliament with a new and updated proposal for an anti-corruption

[65] Freedom House, *Politicile anticorupție ale Guvernului României. Raport de evaluare*, Bucharest, 2005.

[66] Ibid., p. 82.

[67] The persons covered by this law are the president, the prime minister, ministers, members of parliament, prosecutors, mayors, municipal councilors and heads of public hospitals and customs offices.

[68] Angel Krasimirov, 'Bulgaria Gives Green Light to Set Anti-Corruption Unit', Reuters, 17 June 2015 <http://www.reuters.com/article/2015/06/17/us-bulgaria-corruption-idUSKBN0OX1LQ20150617> [accessed 30 September 2015].

[69] In other words, Bulgarian parliamentarians questioned the extraordinary mandate given to anti-corruption prosecutors and decided to vote against that.

bureau. This new bill was approved by parliamentary committee but was still being debated by the full parliament in summer 2016.

While grand corruption has not been a top policy priority for the Bulgarian government (see Table 2), Bulgaria does have in place a dedicated anti-corruption institutional framework. All anti-corruption efforts are coordinated by the Commission to Prevent and Combat Corruption (CPCC), which was established in 2006. This Commission coordinates specifically designated anti-corruption committees in the executive, legislative and judicial branches. Furthermore, the judiciary, the ombudsman, the inspectorate services in each ministerial department and the Public Financial Inspection Agency (PFIA, or audit office) are complemented by a host of institutions tasked with fighting corruption; these are larger in number and narrower in terms of competence compared to the corresponding Romanian institutions.[70]

Compared to the situation in Romania and even Bulgaria, anti-corruption cannot be said to have taken centre-stage in Greek politics, where corruption is considered a symptom, rather than a cause, of the general malaise affecting the country. However, in the context of the public outcry related to the 2010 economic crisis of the Greek state, which brought the country to the brink of sovereign default, anti-corruption gained impetus. Several new anti-corruption institutions were created, though the resources made available to them proved mostly insufficient. The post of anti-corruption coordinator was established in 2013 by the coalition government of New Democracy and Pasok. The coordinator was assigned the task of coordinating anti-corruption measures across the state agencies and locating loopholes in Greek criminal law and criminal procedure legislation. The post was abolished in March 2015 by the coalition government of Syriza and the nationalist party Independent Greeks (Anel). The latter coalition created a new General Secretariat for Anti-Corruption and replaced the coordinator with a new, autonomous ministerial post, the Minister for Anti-Corruption. In September 2015 the same coalition government abolished this post and replaced it with the Alternate Minister for Anti-Corruption, a position now subsumed under the Justice Ministry. During the short life-span of the post (2013–15), the Minister for Anti-Corruption concentrated on tackling tax evasion, but evidently lacked the resources or time to carry out the tasks assigned. Two

---

[70] There are six such institutions: Public Financial Inspection Agency, National Audit Office, General Inspectorate, State Agency for National Security, Commission for Prevention and Ascertainment of Conflicts of Interest, Commission for the Establishing of Property Acquired from Criminal Activity.

positions of anti-corruption prosecutors were established in 2013 (serving Athens and Thessaloniki) with the aim of tackling corruption in the public sector and in banking. Other institutions that have more general competences in tackling corruption or crimes associated with corruption are the General Inspector of Public Administration (set up in 2002)[71] and the Financial Intelligence Unit (restructured in 2008).[72]

Table 3 sums up the findings of this section which has looked at the anti-corruption institutional setting, focusing on the legal codification of corruption and the institutional environment with competences in the area of corruption as outlined in Table 1. The findings point to the conclusion that Romania is the most active of the three countries in the area of anti-corruption, having a strong legal framework and institutional establishment. With a similar historical background and in light of recent developments, Bulgaria has an institutional framework to tackle corruption which is not used to its maximum potential. Last, but not least, Greece is only now setting up a proper framework for tackling corruption, struggling to put adequate anti-corruption mechanisms in place.

'The problem' and 'the solution': Comparing the implementation of anti-corruption policies in Bulgaria, Greece and Romania

This section looks at the match between the 'problem of corruption' (which is a continuous work in progress as described in Section 3 and in Tables 1, 2 and 3) and the institutional 'solutions' that have been put in place (as described in Section 4). It focuses on what has changed as a result of anti-corruption policies, what has remained the same (dubbed an 'implementation gap' in corruption literature)[73] and some unintended consequences of anti-corruption policies and practices.

---

[71] It is responsible for preventing and monitoring maladministration (such as undue delays or discrimination affecting citizens) and corruption in the wider public sector, including state-owned enterprises. The GIPA's role is threefold, as it includes inspecting administrative staff, procedures and units, taking disciplinary action against public employees violating the law, and coordinating different bodies of inspectors based in individual ministries. It is an independent public authority and the person who becomes head of the GIPA is selected by the government, but must be approved by the parliament.

[72] It focuses on examining suspicious transactions by natural persons and legal entities, asset declarations of public officials, including ministers, members of parliament, advisors to ministers as well as journalists. It is also in charge of monitoring money-laundering and terrorist financing.

[73] The implementation gap concerns not only anti-corruption but all policy sectors. It has been extensively discussed in public policy studies such as Kevin B. Smith and Christopher W. Larimer, 'How Does It Work? Policy Implementation', in *The Public Policy Theory Primer*, Philadelphia, PA, 2009, pp. 155–56.

Table 3. The anti-corruption institutional setting in Bulgaria, Greece and Romania

	Bulgaria	Greece	Romania
The anti-corruption institutional setting	• Institutions exist, but do not function well • Existence of legal provisions necessary to tackle corruption	• Newly set up institutions • Low level resources • Legislation exists but is vague and recently adopted (after 2010)	• Top EU level institutions that are templates for other countries • Clear legal codification of corruption (since 2000)

Despite the pessimistic view that labels all three countries as 'corrupt', they have undoubtedly made significant progress as a direct result of anti-corruption policies and practices. Putting anti-corruption on the public agenda, either as a policy priority or as a blaming tool to express dissatisfaction with internal affairs or political opponents, has led to positive changes.[74] Such changes tend to be most visible in Romania, due to the specific context that made anti-corruption a priority.[75] These changes included 1) increased salaries for workers in key state sectors (justice, finance, economy) and key roles related to anti-corruption; 2) new jobs in niche sectors; for example, the increased demand for anti-corruption, anti-trust and anti-money laundering compliance by financial institutions has led law firms to make compliance a special and separate service, one that has now become integrated into the traditional practice areas offered to clients; 3) new hiring policies promoted as part of the anti-corruption ethos, which encourage hiring young and inexperienced investigators rather than more experienced practitioners (this is based on the assumption that young equals non-corrupt; for example, it has become a typical strategy for high-profile prosecutorial bodies such as the DNA in Romania to hire young professionals who are aged well under 40);[76] 4) new forms of expertise related to corruption; as new and innovative policies are implemented, local actors are exposed to greater interaction with foreign

---

[74] For the importance of anti-corruption changes in other contexts, see Roxana Bratu, 'The Former Soviet Union', in Alina Mungiu-Pippidi (ed.), *Controlling Corruption in Europe*, vol. 1, Oplanden, Berlin and Toronto, 2013, pp. 55–67.

[75] Ibid.

[76] Roxana Bratu, 'Actors, Practices and Networks of Corruption: The Case of Romania's Accession to European Union Funding', unpublished PhD dissertation, London School of Economics and Political Science, 2014.

experts who are the carriers of new technical languages and practices of governance.

Undoubtedly, a key indicator of the functioning of the new anti-corruption system relates to how well the criminal justice apparatus deals with corruption cases. In all three countries examined here, there is clearly an increasing trend toward the conduct of investigations into grand corruption. Romania, through its DNA, is the absolute champion at investigating and opening grand corruption trials, prosecuting over 1,000 officials in 2015.[77] In Bulgaria, investigations have frequently begun but few cases have so far been tried in court and there have been 'very few convictions in cases involving substantial corruption',[78] while in Greece the grand corruption investigation patterns have so far not been impressive and the results of the new specially dedicated anti-corruption institutional setup are yet to be seen. These differences may be explained by the dimensions explored in the previous sections and outlined in Tables 2 and 3 — they point to the fact that making anti-corruption a top policy priority coupled with designing an adequate legal framework and a strong institutional setup are paramount in increasing the responses of criminal justice to corruption.

Despite these positive changes, experts have noted the existence of an 'implementation gap' in all three counties. This refers to the fact that there are mismatches between the institutional setting, projected functions and actual activities, and between political declarations that declare commitment to 'fight corruption' yet fail to provide practical support for anti-corruption measures. Depending on the context, there is a wide array of explanations for this gap ranging from a lack of monitoring by the international community to a fragmented approach to 'fighting corruption', fluctuating political commitment, lack of expertise, and difficulties in adjusting the new anti-corruption legislation to the vernacular legal narratives.

In Greece, for example, fluctuating government commitment to tackling grand corruption and a dearth of suitable means are the main reasons for the implementation gap. Between 2000 and 2010, there was little political will to focus on grand corruption. The situation changed after the financial crisis when successive governments started to adopt anti-corruption legislation, announcing their readiness to investigate

---

[77] DNA, Activity Report 2015 <http://www.pna.ro/obiect2.jsp?id=249>.
[78] European Commission, 'Report from the Commission to the European Parliament and the Council: On Progress in Bulgaria under the Cooperation and Verification Mechanism (CVM)', Brussels, 2015, p. 8 (hereafter, EC 2015a).

grand corruption in cooperation with foreign authorities. However, this shift in government policy was met with reluctance by the judiciary: 'the higher the degree of politicians' involvement in corruption cases, the more difficulties anti-corruption investigations face, because the outcome of investigations may bear a political cost'.[79] An equally pessimistic view is that 'Greek governments never had a stable commitment to fight corruption. Governments have experimented in short time intervals with the creation and abolition of an anti-corruption coordinator's post, new ministerial posts and a general secretariat of anti-corruption. This shows indecisiveness in fighting corruption'.[80]

Making anti-corruption a government priority was not matched by the mobilization of resources that would allow the practical achievement of policy goals. The judiciary system, if it is to function properly, requires financial resources and technical expertise. In the words of an anti-corruption 'insider' in Greece: 'There are neither skilled anti-corruption civil servants nor are there trained judges specializing in anti-corruption. Even those judges who have acquired relevant experience are overloaded and assigned to try various cases unrelated to corruption'.[81] Furthermore:

> In many cases under investigation the amount of material gathered is unmanageable. The international banking transactions of officials require cooperation between the Greek and foreign authorities, which typically causes unforeseen delays. In view of these obstacles, the number of skilled personnel, such as experienced accountants, at the disposal of the Greek prosecuting authorities, is clearly insufficient. Moreover, the higher salaries which civil servants in the Ministry of Finance enjoy compared to their counterparts in the Ministry of Justice and the Greek courts function as a disincentive for personnel transfer to the latter public services, which remain understaffed.[82]

The 'implementation gap' is also linked to the fact that formal attempts to define corruption in the domestic legislation of each country are rather recent. It is thus difficult to accommodate the new legal codifications in the local criminal legislation. In all three countries, criminal procedure laws still have loopholes which make the investigation, prosecution and trying of grand corruption subject to manipulation and delay given that

---

[79] Interview with middle-ranking prosecutor, Athens, 30 July 2015.

[80] Interview with high-ranking prosecutor, Athens, 20 October 2015.

[81] Interview with former high-level government official of the Ministry of Justice, 24 September 2015.

[82] Interview with high-ranking prosecutor, Athens, 20 October 2015.

the local judiciary systems are overloaded. Furthermore, grand corruption cases require high levels of expertise and extensive time to investigate highly complex economic arrangements.[83] In Bulgaria, investigations into cases of grand corruption have frequently begun but few cases have been tried in court, resulting in few convictions in cases involving substantial corruption.[84] It often happens that cases brought to court are insufficiently substantiated. Evidence is missing, either involuntarily or on purpose. Thus, the hands of judges are tied: 'When in my capacity as a judge I receive incomplete files produced either by prosecutors or the police, how can I condemn the accused of corruption?'[85]

The 'implementation gap' is linked not only to the lack of political will to tackle grand corruption, but also to the strong political will to protect local entrepreneurs, their fortunes and ways of doing things. An example from Greece is the saga with the 'Lagarde list', which contained the names of 2,062 Greek citizens who held HSBC bank accounts in Geneva. They were suspected of tax evasion as their deposits did not correspond to the income declared to the Greek tax authorities. Christine Lagarde, who at that time was French Finance Minister, passed the list to Greek Finance Minister George Papaconstantinou in October 2010 and then to Greek prosecutors in December 2012. Papaconstantinou, accused of deleting the names of three relatives from the list, was convicted in March 2015 to one year in prison suspended for three years. The prosecution of suspects from the Lagarde list remains a work in progress; while false impressions have been created that all those listed had evaded paying taxes, in practice only some are suspected of such unlawful behaviour.

The mismatch between anti-corruption intentions and practices may also have unintended long-term effects. Local resistance to change, compounded by the pressure for reform put on governments by international institutions, can pervert the democratic mechanisms of governance. For example, the 2003 EC country report for Romania noticed an abuse of emergency ordinances, while the 2006 EC country report mentioned 105 emergency ordinances approved between February and July 2006.

---

[83] Like fraud cases, grand corruption cases involve highly-skilled and usually high-profile offenders who had the means to access resources not readily available to ordinary people. Furthermore, such offenders sometimes had the means to exert influence over the top political echelon of each country. In rare cases, they *were* the top political echelon of a country — in for example, in Romania, former prime minister Adrian Nastase and former minister Monica Iacob Ridzi were convicted of corruption. Alina Bica, former organized crime chief prosecutor, was indicted for corruption in 2015.

[84] EC 2015a.

[85] Interview with Bulgarian judge, Higher Administrative Court, Sofia, 13 May 2015.

Often the government has employed a vote of confidence and assumed responsibility for passing particular items of legislation; in 2009 the government wanted to assume responsibility for the adoption of the new Criminal and Civil Codes, invoking the urgency of the matter (eventually, the codes were adopted through ordinary procedure in September 2010).[86] Even though these are extraordinary measures, they have been normalized by overuse. This situation not only creates a perpetual sense of urgency but may, at a more subtle level, subvert the democratic process because these are all mechanisms to *bypass* parliamentary debates.

To sum up, this section has shown that the three countries are at different stages in the process of implementing anti-corruption reforms. Romania has not only designed a strong anti-corruption institutional framework (Table 3), but also made it fully functional. Far from perfect, anti-corruption reforms have taken centre stage in this country. By comparison, Bulgaria has made little use of its specially designed institutional establishment, while Greece has only recently begun to implement an anti-corruption framework.

Politicization of anti-corruption in Bulgaria, Greece and Romania
This section turns to the last row of Table 1. It argues that, in the three countries covered by this research, anti-corruption has become a semantic of governance. As a political exercise, anti-corruption takes different forms, bears various meanings and may have unintended effects ranging from disenchantment with anti-corruption measures as useful tools to counter grand corruption to delegitimization of anti-corruption practices. 'Politics often demands the manufacturing of useful clichés'[87] so, when political elites refer to successful anti-corruption initiatives such as punishment of key corrupt figures, they are seeking to boost their own prestige. Similarly, when political elites employ corruption narratives in their political campaigns to smear their opponents, they are enhancing their own symbolic capital by positioning themselves in antithesis to corrupt individuals. The discursive power of corruption is a recent anthropological theme,[88] which refers to practices that portray political action through corruption talk (allegations or facts). Building on high levels of perceived corruption and media reports, this typical practice becomes a common way to make sense of politics. As a result, political competition is 'reduced

---

[86] Transparency International, *Raportul Naţional asupra Corupţiei Octombrie 2009 – Februarie 2011*, Bucharest, 2011.

[87] Ivan Krastev, 'The Anti-American Century?', *Journal of Democracy*, 15, 2004, 2, p. 10.

[88] Haller and Shore, *Corruption*; Torsello, *The New Environmentalism*.

to a confrontation between a government accused of corruption and an opposition that claims to be slightly less corrupt'.[89] The discursive power of corruption refers to practices that frame political action through development *and* anti-corruption, with the effect of enhancing users' symbolic capital.

In Bulgaria, anti-corruption could always be detected in political party rhetoric, but was rarely followed up on by concrete actions of government officials and the judiciary. The leading political party — GERB — first came to power in 2009 when it won the parliamentary elections on an electoral agenda that focused heavily on the fight against corruption. This was in line with the views of the EC, which had suspended EU structural funding to Bulgaria in the second semester of 2008. However, the issue disappeared from the political agenda until 2013 when popular protests against the nomination of media mogul Delyan Peevski to head the State Agency for National Security returned corruption to the public agenda and made it a major theme in the 2014 electoral campaign. Even so, party representatives refrained from accusing their counterparts of corruption, leaving several doors open for potential post-election alliances.[90]

In Romania, anti-corruption became a political tool mostly after 2004. The elections that year were won by a liberal-democratic coalition and the new government declared that fighting corruption would be its main priority. Macovei was appointed as Minister of Justice and spearheaded an anti-corruption movement. While, as noted above, her efforts were applauded by Brussels, Romanian officials were less appreciative of Macovei's efforts and the Senate supported a motion against her which led to her dismissal. Her successor, Tudor Chiuariu, spent less than a year in office and was dismissed by President Băsescu when charged in a corruption case. Later, former prime minister Adrian Nastase was accused and indicted for corruption and in 2015 Victor Ponta resigned as prime minister amid public discontent that was not unrelated to corruption accusations.

In the context of Greece's polarized party system, consisting of repeated electoral contests between the New Democracy and Pasok parties, accusations of corruption served only the needs of political competition between the two parties. The politicization of anti-corruption dates to 1989

---

[89] Krastev, 'Anti-American Century', p. 10.

[90] For example, the coalition government formed in November 2014, under Prime Minister Boyko Borisov, had three coalition members (GERB, Reformist Block and Alternative for Bulgarian Revival) and also enjoyed parliamentary support from the Patriotic Front.

when opposition parties constructed their parliamentary election campaign by accusing incumbent socialist ministers of corruption. Ever since, parties who won elections threatened to launch criminal investigations against the previous holders of power. Such moves typically hit a dead end due to lack of evidence. For over two decades, no politician was tried for corruption until, in 2015, former Finance Minister Papaconstantinou was convicted. With Greece's economic crisis, accusations of corruption became part of the common narrative used by both left and right. Syriza made use of corruption rhetoric to explain the collapse of state finance. After winning the 2015 January elections, the new Syriza-ANEL coalition further politicized anti-corruption. The newly created Anti-Corruption Ministry divided observers: some saw it as a welcome initiative that showed the government's commitment to anti-corruption efforts. Others were more cautious, arguing that since 'the recent anti-corruption reforms passed in 2015 there is a tendency of establishing political control over the judiciary and independent authorities, which is indicative of the government's aim to use the fight against corruption as a tool of political communication'.[91]

Anti-corruption may indeed be a performance act used to keep up appearances before the international community and domestic population, while in reality serving as a tool to 'look after our own' and provide shelter from prosecution for people from the same social group/business circles/political party. When this is the case, 'fighting corruption' is more a rhetorical device or fashionable trend than an authentic political act. Furthermore, anti-corruption is sometimes used as a negative tool when the justice system is politically influenced by powerful groups keen to discredit their opponents in the lead-up to elections, thereby reducing their electoral chances. In such cases, anti-corruption can end promising political careers. In Romania, for example, former president Traian Băsescu claimed that the attempt to replace him in 2012 was a response to his reformist policies aimed at ending corruption.[92] Last but not least, the impartiality of the justice system is questioned in some cases, as anti-corruption gives an extraordinary mandate to a specific professional category such as prosecution. In Romania, there have been allegations that the DNA is the representative of an abusive justice system that fabricates charges resembling science fiction, making use of 'KGB methods' (a reference to the secret police of the Soviet Union) to create a 'witch hunt'.[93]

[91] Interview with middle-ranking prosecutor, Athens, 27 July 2015.
[92] <http://www.economist.com/news/europe/21605953-traian-basescu-ending-his-presidency-amid-corruption-scandal-oh-brother>.
[93] <http://www2.gandul.info/stiri/protest-ancheta-a-dna-contrata-in-strada-de-

The politicization of anti-corruption is sustained by its spectacularization conducted through mass media. Corruption cases are publicized since they fascinate the public and increase readership/followers. The media market is highly sensitive to such changes so, if a corruption allegation related to a high-profile individual (usually a politician) is considered at least minimally plausible it is likely, regardless of the evidence, to be highlighted by the local press. It is accordingly not uncommon that 'corruption allegations are born in the media and also die in the media'.[94] 'Ideally the publicity around political corruption could have a pedagogical aspect, that is, it could function as a disincentive for politicians prone to engage in corrupt practices while discharging their duties.'[95] More often, however, the media make a spectacle out of criminal investigations, sometimes with the full support of public institutions who hope thereby indirectly to gain legitimacy and public support. It has for example been alleged that the Romanian DNA calls the press when making arrests and subsequently leaks details from the prosecution file to carefully chosen media channels.[96] In Bulgaria, the anti-corruption spectacle has led on the one hand to increased popular sensitivity to corruption and, on the other, to the normalization of expectations:

> The public may have settled for something less than acceptable transparency and accountability of high-ranking officials: corruption has deep roots in society, from the lowest to the highest levels, and is often seen as justifiable, needed or normal in the specific socio-cultural context.[97]

The futility of anti-corruption is sustained by other delegitimization techniques that ironically portray the actors involved as naive fighters against corruption, dreamers, or, in Romania, 'anti-corruption knights'. By using such terms, the media indirectly cast doubt on the institutions and actors involved in anti-corruption, who should be ethical role-models.

This section has analysed the politicization of anti-corruption. It has found that, in all three countries, both corruption and anti-corruption have to varying degrees become part of the semantics of governance.

---

primarul-udemerist-din-sf-gheorghe-conducerea-udmr-vanatoare-de-vrajitoare-si-hartuire-rau-voitoare-impotriva-uniunii-7909654>.

[94] Interview with expert on corruption, Sofia, 08 October 2010.

[95] Interview with former government official of Ministry of Interior, Athens, 24 September 2015.

[96] <www.luju.ro>.

[97] Interview with political analyst, Sofia, 15 March 2015.

Table 4 presents Romania as a context that accommodates the frequent use of corruption narratives with the aim of increasing symbolic capital in everyday political encounters. Simultaneously, anti-corruption institutions, even when strong, are not left unscrutinized by non-state actors. Bulgaria displays high levels of politicization of corruption at the level of political rhetoric, but less focus on the anti-corruption institutional framework, while Greece is only just starting to catch up.

Table 4. Politicization of anti-corruption in Bulgaria, Greece and Romania

	Bulgaria	**Greece**	**Romania**
Politicization of anti-corruption	• Very common narrative • Political opponents accuse each other of corruption on a regular basis	• Common narrative	• Very common narrative • Political opponents accuse each other of corruption on a regular basis • AC institutions are heavily scrutinized by non-state actors (may be accused of political subordination)

Conclusion and theoretical implications

Transnational organizations and governments from various countries have invested heavily in anti-corruption policies and practices with varying degrees of success. In an attempt to explain the variation, we contend that anti-corruption should not be regarded as a technical solution to a technical problem related to the lack of a modernized, watertight legal framework and insufficient resources (funds, personnel and expertise) necessary to tackle corruption. Neither should unsuccessful anti-corruption be interpreted as the result of a prevailing culture of 'particularism'.[98] Without completely rejecting the aforementioned 'political-cultural' and 'technical-organizational' approaches, we have employed a third way that is based on social constructionism. In this view, anti-corruption becomes a contemporary cultural and political form through which modernization is strategized, control is made manifest and history is

---

[98] Alina Mungiu-Pippidi, 'Deconstructing Balkan Particularism: The Ambiguous Social Capital of Southeastern Europe', *Journal of Southeast European and Black Sea Studies*, 5, 2005, 1, pp. 45–65; Stoyanov et al., 'Bulgarian Anti-Corruption Reforms'.

dispersed as old institutions fade so that new institutional layers can be added. Furthermore, anti-corruption is a process, contextually shaped by international and domestic factors that relate to political priorities, organizational development, political party competition and a mass media market that dramatizes corruption. Attempts by political figures to gain and hold power are often legitimized through positive association with an anti-corruption agenda. Conversely, the need to discredit political opponents is negatively associated with corruption scandals.

In comparing our case-studies, we took account of four key elements (see Table 1): the historical evolution of corruption understanding and anti-corruption as a policy priority; the development of the anti-corruption establishment; the implementation of anti-corruption policies; and the politicization of the process. We found that each of our case-studies is at a different stage in the anti-corruption process — see Table 5 for details. We consider Greece as an ideal-type of *unreflective accommodation* with the standard anti-corruption toolkit, a passive receiver of knowledge from international expertise. Despite the fact that anti-corruption has recently been identified by the government as a policy priority, the institutional setting, legal codification and resources assigned to anti-corruption do not show high levels of implementation. This does not however impede the politicization of anti-corruption or its use as a tool in electoral campaigns.

Our second case — Bulgaria — is *reactive legitimation*. In this situation, corruption is a well acknowledged issue and anti-corruption a policy-priority for the government at a discursive level. Anti-corruption institutions do exist, but there is a distinctive implementation gap, as institutions do not function according to their design — for example, there are few corruption investigations, prosecutions and convictions. The levels of scandalization are high, due to the fact that corruption is a matter of serious public concern.

Lastly, Romania represents another ideal type: *proactive assimilation*. In this instance, anti-corruption is a top policy priority. This is reflected not only in government declarations but also in the amount of resources assigned to the anti-corruption establishment and its evolution. While far from perfect, Romania's anti-corruption prosecution has become one of the top criminal justice institutions in the EU. And, even if the match between the size of the problem and the institutional solutions in place is imperfect, there are clear and observable steps towards what could be defined as successful anti-corruption. Such high levels of implementation are matched only by an even higher degree of politicization. On the darker

Table 5. Comparison of anti-corruption practices in Bulgaria, Greece and Romania

	Unreflective accommodation – Greece	Reactive legitimation – Bulgaria	Proactive assimilation – Romania
Evolution of the understanding of corruption as a social problem and policy priority	• Policy interest, but not enough to secure the necessary resources • Public concern (along with other social issues) • No priority for criminal justice system	• Policy priority at declaration level, but little action • Public concern • No priority for criminal justice system	• Top policy • Public concern • Criminal justice system priority
The anti-corruption institutional setting	• Newly set up institutions • Low level resources	• Institutions exist, but do not function well	• Top EU level institutions that are templates for other countries
Implementation of anti-corruption	• Really very little implementation (unsurprising given the newly set up institutions, low resources and policy priorities)	• Implementation gap at its best	• Clear, measurable steps; not perfect, but working fast
Politicization of anti-corruption	• Common narrative	• Very common narrative • Political opponents accuse each other of corruption on a regular basis	• Very common narrative • Political opponents accuse each other of corruption on a regular basis • AC institutions are heavily scrutinized by non-state actors (may be accused of political subordination)

side, accusations of corruption are part and parcel of everyday rhetoric. Anti-corruption institutions themselves are heavily scrutinized and are not infrequently accused of political involvement.

The theoretical implication of this social constructionist approach is that we problematize the feelings of inevitability that surround anti-corruption institutions and practices. The empirical implication is that we investigate anti-corruption episodes as processes that, far from being inherent to transitions, have been instrumental to the legitimation of new regimes and whose creation is the result of social and political manipulation. Without disregarding its moral or social benefits, we argue that anti-corruption has more often than not become a site for the negotiation of political agendas whose results have benefited the initiators and local elites. Unlike more traditional approaches, this article does not assume that anti-corruption is 'good' or 'apolitical' to societies because of its alleged merits. Quite the contrary, this article aims to increase our understanding of how anti-corruption efforts are constructed and shaped by their historical and institutional contexts, social actions and political bargains.

5

Managing Business Corruption: Targeting Non-Compliant Practices in Systemically Corrupt Environments

STANISLAV SHEKSHNIA, ALENA LEDENEVA and
ELENA DENISOVA-SCHMIDT

Introduction

As argued by Paul Heywood in this volume, the effectiveness of the principal-agent model approach to anti-corruption policy-making had been questioned in the light of accumulating evidence for the underperformance of anti-corruption interventions.[1] Recent research has revisited the theoretical underpinnings of these interventions to gain new insights, arguing for a move away from principal-agent based interventions to ones that emphasize collective action, which is more relevant for systemically corrupt environments. The collective action perspective is better equipped to embrace the fact that while corruption is widely perceived as a social bad, it is also widely practised by individuals seeking to find practical solutions to real-life problems. In other words, where outsiders characterize corruption as a 'disease', the causes, conditions and effects of which must be diagnosed, monitored and cured,[2] insiders tend to perceive it as a 'cure' for situations where no better solutions are available. Such ambivalence in perceptions — 'if I do it — it's need, if others do it — it's greed' — has been insufficiently articulated in research.[3] Those involved in corrupt

---

[1]   See also A. Mungiu-Pippidi, *The Quest for Good Governance: How Societies Develop Control of Corruption*, Cambridge, 2015; H. Marquette and C. Pfeiffer, *Corruption and Collective Action*, Anti-Corruption Resource Centre Research Paper 32, Bergen, 2015; A. Persson, B. Rothstein and J. Teorell, 'Why Anticorruption Reforms Fail — Systemic Corruption as a Collective Action Problem', *Governance*, 26, 2013, 3, pp. 449–71.

[2]   S. H. Alatas, *Corruption: Its Nature, Causes and Function*, Aldershot and Brookfield, VT, 1990. See also <www.anticorrp.eu> for the findings of the ANTICORRP Media and Corruption work package.

[3]   For an exception, see M. Bauhr, 'Need or Greed Corruption', in *Good Government: The Relevance of Political Science*, edited by S. Holmberg and B. Rothstein, Cheltenham, 2014.

practices more often than not are conceptually silenced in the analytical frameworks employed to study them. Studies of corporate corruption are based predominantly on normative assumptions about good and bad governance; appropriate organizational behaviour and misbehaviour; bad organizations (bad barrels) and bad individuals (bad apples).[4] These dichotomies, however, limit our understanding of systemically corrupt environments, where principals are not principled, good people do bad things and property rights are not secure and the public/private distinction cannot be made. Anthropologists find that what appear to be instances of corruption from the normative perspective might in fact constitute a hybrid phenomenon, best understood on its own terms.[5] Moreover, even where non-compliant practices that conform to neither official nor social norms (or to both but in a hybrid way) are acknowledged on their own terms, they are 'chronically underestimated' and 'systematic analyses of the practical norms governing these non-compliant practices' are few.[6] Analysing firm-level issues (such as retaining best qualified managers who are likely to leave the firm if their informal income opportunities are streamlined) through normative approaches and prescriptive policies on good governance and integrity in such settings is not sufficient. Focus on practical norms and non-compliant practices is not the same as the

---

[4]   Some scholars call it 'deviant behaviour': R. E. Kidwell, Jr. and C. L. Martin, 'The Prevalence (and Ambiguity) of Deviant Behaviour at Work: An Overview', in Kidwell and Martin (eds), *Managing Organizational Deviance*, Thousand Oaks, CA, 2005, pp. 1–21; S. L. Robinson and R. J. Bennett, 'A Typology of Deviant Workplace Behaviors: A Multidimensional Scaling Study', *Academy of Management Journal*, 38, 1995, pp. 555–72, or 'organizational misbehavior': S. Ackroyd and P. Thompson, 'Why Organizational Misbehavior?', in Ackroyd and Thompson (eds), *Organizational Misbehavior*, London, 1999, pp. 8–30; A. Sagie and S. Stashevsky and M. Koslowsky (eds), *Misbehavior and Dysfunctional Attitudes in Organizations*, New York, 2003; Y. Vardi and E. Weitz, *Misbehavior in Organizations: Theory, Research and Management*, Mahwah, NJ, 2003, but very often just a 'criminal act': Galt de Jong and Hans van Ees, 'Firms and Corruption', *European Management Review*, 11, 2014, 3–4, pp. 187–90.

[5]   M. L. Caldwell, *Not By Bread Alone: Social Support in the New Russia*, Berkeley, CA, 2004; A. Ledeneva, *Russia's Economy of Favours: Blat, Networking and Informal Exchange*, Cambridge, 1998; A. Ledeneva, *How Russia Really Works: the Informal Practices that Shaped Post-Soviet Politics and Business*, Ithaca, NY, 2006; N. Ries, *Russian Talk: Culture and Conversation during Perestroika*, Ithaca, NY, 1997; R. Mandel, and C. Humphrey (eds), *Markets and Moralities: Ethnographies of Postsocialism*, New York and Oxford, 2002; D. Torsello and V. Betrand, 'The Anthropology of Corruption', *Journal of Management Inquiry*, 25, 2016, 1, pp. 34–54.

[6]   J. P. O. de Sardan, 'For an Anthropology of Gaps, Discrepancies and Contradictions', *Antropologia*, 3, March 2016, 1, pp. 111–31 (pp. 114, 117). On informal norms and the interaction with formal systems, see Princeton University Research on innovations for successful societies (for example the Colombia Bogota case and the Philippines cases at <http://successfulsocieties.princeton.edu/research/publications>).

revisionist view of corruption that implies functionality of corruption in coping with overly rigid political and bureaucratic regimes.[7] We find that while the official norms prescribe intolerance and the practical norms prescribe tolerance towards corruption, business leaders solve their problems by 'managing' corruption at the firm level and invent strategies 'that work' to resolve the paradox of official and unofficial constraints.

The problem-solving approach in our study includes assembling bottom-up accounts of non-compliant practices and sustaining the meanings the actors ascribe to their actions in a context-bound way. We use the language of participants in our data collection and in the design of monitoring tools for non-compliant practices. We investigate tensions that exist between the formal compliance with anti-corruption legislation adopted at the national level and the firms' non-compliant practices essential for solving firm-level problems in systemically corrupt environments: where the 'letter' of national anti-corruption regulation is complied with, its 'spirit' is routinely violated to keep businesses competitive — corporate leaders cannot be expected to pioneer anti-corruption campaigns at the firm-level. And yet, some of them do. Thus, we seek to explain the cases of outliers — leaders experimenting with firm-level anti-corruption strategies — and consider these cases of 'individual agency' in the context of the debates on organizational behaviour:

> More recent theoretical developments in organizational research have argued that the realm in which single individuals can impact organizational performance is so limited that there is essentially no reason to worry about whether there are any behaviours or attributes that are unique to leadership. For example, resource dependence research[8] argues that most organizational action can be understood not as an exercise of individual agency but as an organizational response to the demands of external actors upon which organizations depend for resources and support.[9]

In other words, external pressures are so strong that they over-determine organizational reactions to set up a 'template of strategies [...] that organization mimics because they are perceived as legitimate and appropriate'.[10] Such templates in Russia are not so different from

---

[7] J. Girling, *Corruption, Capitalism and Democracy*, London, 1997.
[8] J. Pfeffer and G. R. Salancik, *The External Control of Organizations: A Resource Dependence Approach*, New York, 1978.
[9] N. Nohria and R. Khurana, 'Advancing Leadership in Theory and Practice', in *Handbook of Leadership Theory and Practice*, Cambridge, MA, 2013, pp. 3–26 (p. 9).
[10] Ibid.

establishing 'transparency, accountability, disclosure' elsewhere. Adopting such strategies in systemically corrupt environments, however, results in a de-facto situation of 'over-regulation and under-enforcement' that leaves it to corporate leaders to bridge the gap. Corruption remains one of the main challenges in doing business in many countries.[11] Examining the current initiatives undertaken by companies to manage the risk of corruption, PricewaterhouseCoopers found that only 22 per cent of firms are confident of the effectiveness of the anti-corruption programmes they already have.[12] Fast-developing economies like China, India, Brazil, Indonesia and Russia have all been scoring high in the 2011 Bribery index.[13]

1. Identifying and monitoring non-compliant practices

Our previous research has identified business practices ubiquitous in Russia and introduced specific tools for monitoring non-compliant practices in Russian firms.[14]

[11] R. Fisman and J. Svensson, 'Are Corruption and Taxation Really Harmful to Growth? Firm Level Evidence', *Journal of Development Economics*, 83, 2007, 1, pp. 63–75; R. M. N. Galang, 'Victim or Victimizer: Firm Responses to Government Corruption', *Journal of Management Studies*, 49, 2012, 2, pp. 429–62; S. Knack and P. Keefer, 'Institutions and Economic Performance: Cross-Country Tests Using Alternative Institutional Indicators', *Economics and Politics*, 7, 1995, 3, pp. 207–28; P. Mauro, 'Corruption and Growth', *The Quarterly Journal of Economics*, 110, 1995, 3, pp. 681–712; A. Shleifer and R. W. Vishny, 'Corruption', *The Quarterly Journal of Economics*, 108, 1993, 3, pp. 599–617; S. Globerman and D. Shapiro, 'Governance Infrastructure and US Foreign Direct Investment', *Journal of International Business Studies*, 34, 2003, 1, pp. 19–39; K. A. Getz and R. J. Volkema, 'Culture, Perceived Corruption and Economics: A Model of Predictors and Outcomes', *Business Society*, 40, 2001, 1, pp. 7–30.

[12] The PricewaterhouseCoopers Report, 'Confronting Corruption: The Business Case for an Effective Anti-Corruption Program' is available online at <http://www.pwc.com/gx/en/forensic-accounting-dispute-consulting-services/business-case-anti-corruption-programme.jhtml>. The report is based on a survey of 390 senior executives, supplemented with in-depth interviews with 36 senior executives and experts in anti-corruption efforts. The geography of the survey covers many several countries around the world including Russia: 42% Asia-Pacific, 16% Middle East and Africa, 23% Western Europe, 8% North America, 5% Latin America and 5% Central and Eastern Europe. It examines the current and possible future actions companies perform to manage the risk of corruption.

[13] <http://www.transparency.org/bpi2011>.

[14] S. Shekshnia, A. Ledeneva and E. Denisova-Schmidt, *Reflective Leadership vs. Endemic Corruption in Emerging Markets*, INSEAD Working Paper 2013/121/EFE <http://sites.insead.edu/facultyresearch/research/doc.cfm?did=53474>; S. Shekshnia, A. Ledeneva and E. Denisova-Schmidt, *How to Mitigate Corruption in Emerging Markets: The Case of Russia*, Edmond J. Safra Working Papers No. 36, Cambridge, MA, 2014 <http://discovery.ucl.ac.uk/1451069/1/EDS_SS_AL_SSRN-id2391950.pdf>.

Russia is an interesting case:[15] it is one of the largest emerging economies in the world, yet it is also labelled as one of the most corrupt countries.[16] In 2008–2011, the Russian government undertook significant anti-corruption efforts in line with OECD, WTO and World Bank policy recommendations, but the results of such efforts at the firm level have been far from conclusive. Part of the reason is political. Mungiu-Pippidi observes that many former Communist regimes have attempted to make the transition from a particularistic system to a universalistic one (i.e. from predominantly relations-based to the predominantly rules-based forms of governance), but have so far only reached a stage that she calls 'competitive particularism'. She argues that at this point most countries in the region are hybrids, combining the elements of the two 'ideal types', while the distinction between public and private remains blurred.[17] Theoretical perspectives based on a presumption of the public/private distinction may have misled the policies in the region.[18] Marquette and Pfeiffer argue that anti-corruption initiatives failed not because they are based on inadequate theories, such as principal-agent theory and/or collective action theory, but rather because they do not consider the third perspective — that corruption might be an effective tool that helps people to get things done, especially in weak institutional environments.[19] Replacing corrupt channels by innovative solutions has been an important shift in public policy (e-governance) and among non-governmental organizations (Integrity Action Fix rate).[20] In order to address corruption-related challenges in corporate contexts, we developed a practical tool that allows leadership to identify specific non-compliant practices on the firm level and to devise mitigating strategies.

[15] In spite of the current political situation, many international companies still consider Russia a promising market in the mid- and long-term perspectives. See E. Denisova-Schmidt and O. Kryzhko, 'Managing Informal Business Practices in Russia: The Experience of Foreign Companies', *Mir Rossii*, 24, 2015, 4, pp. 149–74.

[16] Transparency International measures the perception of corruption in the public sector in the aggregate Corruption Perception Index (CPI). In 2015 Russia was placed at 119 out of 168 countries.

[17] See note 1 above.

[18] See articles by Heywood and Camargo-Baez/Ledeneva in this volume and Marquette and Pfeiffer (note 1).

[19] GCB2013 data shows insignificant variation in the use of contacts. In the USA, a person might arrange a job interview as a favour, but that person will not necessarily be hired. In Russia and the other BRIC countries, on the other hand, being hired would be expected. See D. J. McCarthy, S. M. Puffer, D. Dunlap-Hinkler and A. M. Jaeger, 'A Stakeholder Approach to the Ethicality of BRIC-Firm Managers' Use of Favors', *Journal of Business Ethics*, 109, 2012, 1, pp. 27–38.

[20] See <http://integrityaction.org/training-materials/56>.

At the exploratory stage, we examined the existing typologies of corruption in post-Communist societies[21] and conducted a content analysis of the media in order to identify corrupt practices that correspond to these types. In a 2006 World Bank paper, which adopts the Transparency International definition of corruption as 'the misuse of entrusted power for private gain', economist Stephen Knack organizes these variations into six dimensions of corruption: by their level of the political system (central government, provincial, municipal), roughly corresponding to 'petty' and 'grand' corruption; by the purpose of the improper actions: to influence the content of laws and rules ('state capture') or to influence their implementation ('administrative corruption'); by the actors involved in the corrupt transaction: various combinations of firms, households and public officials; by the characteristics of a particular set of actors, such as the bribes that are required for large versus small firms, or for rich versus poor households; by the administrative agency or service: tax and customs, business licenses, inspections, utility connections, courts or public education and health facilities; and by the incidence or magnitude of bribes or by the uncertainty they create for businesses and households.[22] In more than thirty interviews, we asked CEOs and directors of companies operating in Russia to comment on the familiarity of each practice, as well as on its frequency. In the 2010 pilot survey, conducted face-to-face, we reserved a space for respondents to add to our list of practices — yet only two practices have been added.[23] Among the obvious reasons as to why open-choice survey questions remain unanswered, such a low number of additions to the list of informal practices could be interpreted either as a validation of sufficiency of the existing list or a statement of the unarticulated nature of the practices for those who use them routinely (apart from intention to conceal that we did envisage but have

---

[21] V. Tanzi, *Corruption Around the World: Causes, Consequences, Scope, and Cures*, IMF Staff Papers, 45, IMF, Washington, D.C., 1998; R. Karklins, *The System Made Me Do It: Corruption in Post-Communist Societies*, Ithaca, NY, 2005; S. Knack, *Measuring Corruption in Eastern Europe and Central Asia: A Critique of Cross-Country Indicators*, World Bank Policy Research Working Paper 3936, Washington, D.C., 2006; A. Ledeneva, *How Russia Really Works: The Informal Practices that Shaped Post-Soviet Politics and Business*, Ithaca, NY, 2006; A. Ledeneva, 'From Russia with Blat: Can Informal Networks Help Modernize Russia?', *Social Research*, 76, 2009, 1, pp. 257–88; A. Ledeneva, *Can Russia Modernise? Sistema, Power Networks and Informal Governance*, Cambridge, 2013.

[22] Knack, *Measuring Corruption in Eastern Europe and Central Asia*.

[23] A. Ledeneva, and S. Shekshnia, 'Doing Business in Russia: Informal Practices and Anti-Corruption Strategies', *Russie.Nei.Visions*, 58, 2011, IFRI, Paris <https://www.ifri.org/sites/default/files/atoms/files/ifriledenevashekshniafracorruptionmarch2011jn.pdf>.

not encountered).[24] While interpreting the pilot data, we made a decision to allow the list of questions to be long and inclusive, yet also feasible for CEOs to handle in 15–20 minutes. The final questionnaire includes twenty-seven practices and nineteen anti-corruption strategies (Tables 1 and 2).

Inspired by Kay's concept of obliquity, whereby 'goals are best achieved indirectly', we have replaced the negatively connoted 'non-compliant practices' by the more neutral 'informal ways of getting things done' — the practical norms that CEOs and top managers use to achieve results.[25] We ask the respondents to report anonymously the extent to which their firm is engaged in each practice, choosing from three possible answers: 'systematically', 'sometimes' or 'never', and similar assessments are made for strategies.[26] Anonymity has been emphasized and preserved, even where it imposed serious limitations on our analysis. Given the level of our respondents and somewhat sensitive nature of our questions, we had to make an extra effort to ensure that those completing the survey were willing to share their views. Personal assurances were given where possible.

It was not our aim to create a representative sample. Originally we identified 500 businessmen — clients of a top executive search company — and one of the authors approached them directly. At the later stage we added some respondents who attended executive development programmes and business school alumni forums (volunteering). The survey data gave us insights to explore in the in-depth interviews on the role of leadership in systemically corrupt environments, as well as opportunities to explore the potential of using the 'language of participants' recognized by the respondents.

[24] R. M. Groves, D. A. Dillman, J. L. Eltinge and R. J. A. Little, *Survey Nonresponse*, Hoboken, NJ, 2001.

[25] J. Kay, *Obliquity: Why our Goals are Best Achieved Indirectly*, London, 2011.

[26] This instrument was tested in the Ukrainian business environment. See E. Denisova-Schmidt and M. Huber, 'Regional Differences in Perceived Corruption among Ukrainian Firms', *Eurasian Geography and Economics*, 55, 2014, 1, pp. 10–36; E. Denisova-Schmidt, and Y. Prytula, 'Liike-elämän korruptio Ukrainassa' (Business Corruption in Ukraine), *Idäntutkimus: The Finnish Review of East European Studies*, 1, 2016, pp. 94–95; E. Denisova-Schmidt and Y. Prytula, 'The Shadow Economy and Entrepreneurship in Ukraine', in *The Entrepreneurship and Shadow Economy*, edited by A. Sauka, F. Schneider and C. Williams, Cheltenham and Northampton, MA, 2016, pp. 151–68; E. Denisova-Schmidt, M. Huber and Y. Prytula, 'Corruption among Ukrainian Businesses: Do Firm Size, Industry and Region Matter?', in Johannes Leitner and Hannes Meissner, *State Capture, Political Risks and International Business: Cases from the Black Sea Region*, Abingdon and New York, forthcoming 2017; E. Denisova-Schmidt and Y. Prytula, 'Corruption and Trust Among Ukrainian Firms', *Eastern European Economics*, forthcoming.

Table 1. *Informal Practices vs. Corruption*

Forms of corruption in the TI classification	Informal Practices as known to participants	Initiator	Beneficiary
	Extorting bribes by regional regulatory agencies: tax inspectorate, sanitation service, police, etc.	Officials	Officials
	Paying for the services of regional regulatory agencies: tax inspectorate, customs, sanitation service, police, fire inspectorate, standardization agencies, etc.	Executives	Officials
	Paying exorbitant board of directors' fees to cronies	Executives	Executives
	Extorting bribes by regional authorities	Officials	Officials
BRIBERY,	Paying police and the prosecution service to open or close criminal cases	Executives	Officials
ABUSE OF POWER	Paying for favourable court rulings by the regional courts	Executives	Officials
OR OFFICE	Paying for tax audits and other inspections in regional subdivisions with pre-agreed results	Executives	Officials
	Using 'telephone rule' — informal pressure on regional managers and verbal instructions — by representatives of federal regional authorities	Officials	Officials
	Regional authorities; pressure on the company's regional managers to provide funding for their regional programmes and projects	Officials	Officials
	Using informal tools (comprising documents and information, material from security services and *krugovaia poruka*) against competitors	Executives	Executives
	Using informal tools (comprising documents and information, material from security services and *krugovaia poruka*) to manage company staff	Executives	Executives
	Using informal tools (comprising documents and information, material from security services and *krugovaia poruka*) to exert pressure on regional authorities	Executives	Executives

Forms of corruption in the TI classification	Informal Practices as known to participants	Initiator	Beneficiary
	Using company staff to carry out personal assignments for regional managers (assistance to family members, construction and decoration of housing, organization of holidays and entertainment)	Executives	Executives
GIFTS AND HOSPITALITY	Receiving kickbacks or other informal rewards (e.g. expensive gifts) by regional managers from vendors, suppliers and buyers	Vendors	Executives
	Receiving commissions or other material benefits from job candidates by heads of regional subdivisions	Employees	Executives
FRAUD	Paying salaries and bonuses to staff of regional subdivisions in cash without paying social tax	Executives	Executives
	Using company funds by heads of regional subdivisions to buy expensive cars, telephones, to pay for travel, etc.	Executives	Executives
	Leasing of the company's production, office premises or production equipment by regional managers for personal gain	Executives	Executives
	Disregarding 'conflict of interest' of regional managers, e.g. their use of companies affiliated to them, recruitment of relatives, etc.	Executives	Executives
CRONYISM AND NEPOTISM	Selecting vendors/contractors with whom regional managers have informal relationships or arrangements	Executives/Vendors	Executives/Vendors
	Using informal connections and networks to obtain state orders (state procurement) and loans from state banks	Executives	Executives
	Selecting winners of open tenders at the regional level on the basis of informal relationships and arrangements	Executives/Vendors	Executives/Vendors

Forms of corruption in the TI classification	Informal Practices as known to participants	Initiator	Beneficiary
INFLUENCE PEDDLING	Funding of publications in regional press and broadcasts on regional TV and radio	Executives	ALL
	Paying or providing services (foreign trips, medical expenses, etc.) to regional executive authorities	Officials/ Executives	Officials/ Executives
	Paying or providing services (foreign trips, medical expenses, etc.) to regional legislative authorities	Officials/ Executives	Officials/ Executives
	Receiving subsidies and tax benefits from regional authorities	Executives	Executives
COLLUSION	Creating informal alliances with other companies in the region to exert influence on regional authorities	Executives	Executives

Table 2. Anti-Corruption Strategies

Strategy	Target category	Prevention/ Control	Transmission channels
Creation and dissemination of internal policies and procedures setting out detailed rules for working with contractors, such as holding tenders amongst suppliers and contractors	Executives, employees	Prevention	Admin
Use of high-profile campaigns	All	Prevention	Social
Use of the security department to detect and stop internal abuses and theft	Executives, employees, contractors	Prevention/ Control	Admin
Training of managers and regional staff in the internal rules of interaction with their counterparts	Executives, employees	Prevention	Admin
Creation and dissemination of Codes of Corporate Conduct	Executives, employees	Prevention	Admin
Use of internal audit service to identify internal abuses and violations	Executives, employees, contractors	Control	Admin
Pro-active communication of company's rules and standards on working with contractors, government and regulatory agencies and mass media to partners	Officials, contractors	Prevention	Admin
Pro-active proposals to regional authorities and regulatory agencies on cooperation programmes and methods	Officials	Prevention	Admin

Strategy	Target category	Prevention/ Control	Transmission channels
Engaging top management companies-counterparts in countering unscrupulous actions by their regional representatives	Society	Control	Social
'Buffer' strategy — the use of subcontractors, agents and third parties to work with regional authorities and regulatory agencies	Officials	Prevention	Social
Use of courts to counter unscrupulous actions by regional authorities or regulatory agencies	Officials	Prevention	Admin
Allocation of annual budget for developing informal relationships with representative authorities and regulatory agencies	Officials	Prevention	Admin
Exchanging information with other companies about unscrupulous businesses, regional authorities and regulatory agencies	Officials	Prevention	Social
Allocation of annual budget for developing informal relations with representatives of the regional media	Officials	Prevention	Admin
Use of informal contacts ('telephone law' and oral instructions) to put pressure on the representatives of regional authorities to counter unscrupulous actions and to ensure respect of law	Officials	Control	Social
Formal approaches to federal officials to counter unscrupulous actions by regional authorities and regulatory agencies	Officials	Control	Admin
Use of the media to counter unscrupulous actions by regional authorities or regulatory agencies	Officials	Control	Social
Creation of alliances with other companies in the region to counter unscrupulous actions by the representatives of the authorities or the regulatory agencies	Officials	Control	Social

Strategy	Target category	Prevention/ Control	Transmission channels
Engagement of representatives of religious institutions in promoting the company's interests in the regions	All	Prevention	Admin
Additionally reported anti-corruption strategies			
Telephone hot-lines available for employees and external parties to report corrupt acts of company executives	Executives	Control	Admin
Offering commissions to employees uncovering corporate fraud	Executives	Control	Admin
'Buying' an executive position in regional governmnet to protect business from corrupt officials	Officials	Prevention	Social
Gaining a seat in local legislature to protect business from corrupt officials	Officials	Prevention	Social
Video-taping of contract negotiations	Executives, Contractors	Prevention	Admin

2. Conceptualizing 'managing corruption' in systemically corrupt environments

Our data set was collected between 2010 and 2013. The total sample includes 110 questionnaires in addition to thirty in-depth interviews. Appendix 1 provides an overview of the firms' characteristics. Although the list of characteristics looks rather short, it was congruent to our primary goal of reaching out to the firms' leaders and creating a questionnaire that could be completed in 15–20 minutes. It is interesting to note that further studies based on this methodology conducted in Ukraine showed no statistically significant differences in terms of the firms' industry or size or the respondents' experiences with the firm, gender or educational levels.[27]

During our in-depth interviews, we asked executives to speak about their business environment and systemic corruption in Russia. On the basis of the management literature analysis on government corruption, Galang argues that a firm's behaviour in a corrupt environment is determined by two factors: the firm's political resources and the dependence of the industry in which it operates on government regulations. Factors such as a country's institutional development, and the corporate culture and structure of the firm also play a part.[28] Galang identifies four distinct strategic approaches to government corruption:

Alter (high regulatory dependence-high level of political resource) which leads to engagement with the government, institutional change and regulatory capture; this strategy benefits both the firm and the economy.

Avoid (low regulatory dependence-high level of political resource) which leads to self-restraint, non-investment and formation of business groups; this strategy benefits the firm.

Ally (high regulatory dependence-low level of political resource) which leads to networking and forming joint ventures; this strategy benefits both the firm and the economy.

---

[27] Statistically significant differences were found only in terms of the regions (the western part of Ukraine is perceived to be less corrupt) and ownership (foreign companies are more resistant to corruption). Denisova-Schmidt, Huber and Prytula, 'Corruption among Ukrainian Businesses'. See also, E. Denisova-Schmidt and M. Huber, 'Regional Differences in Perceived Corruption among Ukrainian Firms', *Eurasian Geography and Economics*, 55, 2014, 1, pp. 10–36, and Denisova-Schmidt and Prytula, 'Corruption and Trust among Ukrainian Firms'.

[28] R. M. N. Galang, 'Victim or Victimizer: Firm Responses to Government Corruption', *Journal of Management Studies*, 49, 2012, 2, pp. 429–62.

Accede (low regulatory dependence-low level of political resource) which leads to acceptance of the rules of the game proposed by government officials and bribing; this strategy benefits both the firm and the economy.

Based on our qualitative data, we identified four dispositions that executives take up in relation to corruption that are not dissimilar from Galang's findings:

The first — *toleration* — is the most widespread among interviewees: 'Because the whole society is corrupt, and unless systemic changes occur, corruption cannot be effectively dealt with and is widely accepted. It is not up to us to promote anti-corruption changes; the government should take care of it.'
The second — *exploitation* — is expressed openly only by a small minority: 'Since Russian society is deeply corrupt, corruption should not only be accepted but also proactively used to advance business interests.' In other words, the endemic nature of corruption makes it a legitimate instrument for doing business.
The third — *avoidance* — is also articulated by a small minority: 'Even in an endemically corrupt environment, where corruption is generally accepted, it is possible to avoid it and to run a business without it playing a role. Others may suffer from corruption but we can find a way to stay away from it.'
The fourth — *management of corruption* — is shared by a select few: 'Corruption is a problem and we are working on it, even where we are unable to change the environment.' These executives recognize corruption as a major risk and develop specific strategies and mechanisms to mitigate it.

The four positions articulated above can be organized into a matrix demonstrating that the majority of executives do not prioritize a full-scale fight against corruption (percentage estimated by the interviewers) (Table 3). A number of psychological and technical factors prevent them from taking up the anti-corruption challenge.

Table 3. Executives' attitudes to corruption

Attitudes to corruption	Passive attitude	Active attitude
Acceptance of corruption as a significant risk to business	Toleration (60%)	Management (15%)
Non-acceptance of corruption as a significant risk to business	Avoidance (15%)	Exploitation (10%)

Failure to recognize corruption as a threat to business in systemically corrupt environments (often at a subconscious level) or rationalization of personal inability to tackle it prevents executives from managing corruption effectively.[29] Limited applicability of top-down 'template' of government-driven strategies, as well as the lack of knowledge of alternative firm-level methods, reduces executives' capacity to act. As shown above some corporate leaders consider corruption as a way to develop their business (the exploitation disposition). Corporations tend to blame corruption in the public sector and hide internal corruption from the public, while the most important aspect of corruption — the interaction between the state and the firm — remains unscrutinized.

Only a few corporate executives demonstrated what we call 'reflective leadership'. Reflective leaders confront external corruption proactively and deploy anti-corruption instruments to deal with the firm's internal corruption. This is a particularly daunting task in systemically corrupt environments. It boils down to tackling specific corruption risks associated with non-compliant practices where these are widespread in the company, i.e. with a concrete set of objectives in mind. One of the interviewed CEOs framed it as follows:

> We spend hundreds of millions on IT and I knew that we suffered from kickbacks received by our purchasing managers from vendors. I wanted to fight this so I have set three goals: reduction of our IT-related costs by 10 per cent next year; a review of the list of our IT vendors in order to get rid of companies affiliated with our managers in some way, and uncovering a few cases of kickbacks and making them public.

[29] V. Anand, B. E. Ashforth and M. Joshi, 'Business as Usual: The Acceptance and Perpetuation of Corruption in Organizations', *Academy of Management Executive*, 19, 2005, 4, pp. 9–23; P. Fleming and S. C. Zyglidopoulos, *Charting Corporate Corruption: Agency, Structure and Escalation*, Cheltenham and Northampton, MA, 2009.

A combination of both top-down and bottom-up approaches could make a difference at the firm level. However, we found that in the majority of cases executives either do not try or struggle to identify the shortlist of most damaging practices. We propose a simple yet comprehensive four-step approach to identify targets of anticorruption strategies at the firm level.

First, we develop a custom-made list of practices using in-depth interviews with executives and the content analysis of business publications in the national and regional media. It is essential to keep the original formulation of practices — sample of the formulations can be found in Table 1 — while verifying the list against existing classifications.[30]

Second, experts with deep company knowledge (senior executives and business unit managers) are invited to add to the list of practices, especially where these are specific for their own company. It is practical to keep the list manageable so that it can be converted into a simple-to-answer questionnaire. Any omission may lead to failure to identify some of the most widespread practices and those that are taken for granted.

Third, once the final list is determined, company employees are asked to assess whether, in their experience, these practices occur 'systematically', 'occasionally' or 'never'. Since the study takes place in systemically corrupt environments, where informal networks and cultural traditions penetrate corporate organizations, people who know about the practice may be constrained from reporting it, even if they do not directly participate in it. To overcome this limitation, we recommend: a large random sample of firms' employees at all levels, on-line survey, anonymity of respondents and a survey administrator independent of the management. The survey produces a list of the informal practices most frequently recognized and acknowledged by company employees. It will form a foundation for prioritising targets and developing specific anti-corruption measures.

Fourth, the CEO and senior corporate leaders select a limited number of specific practices they want to target, identify concrete goals they aim to achieve with regard to each of them and select monitoring instruments. The proposed instrument allows executives to identify specific corruption risks rather than 'corruption in general', to direct limited resources to most relevant targets, to communicate the anti-corruption strategy effectively and to monitor the change.

---

[30] See Tanzi, *Corruption Around the World*; Karklins, *The System Made Me Do It*; Transparency International typology of corruption in TI 2012 <http://www.transparency.org/cpi2012/results>.

We came across three companies that have successfully implemented a similar approach. The choice of appropriate execution strategies is discussed in the next section.

3. Firm-level strategies

Our research into corruption mitigation strategies adopted by companies operating in Russia has tested Lange's model of organizational controls. In his theoretical attempt to organize existing internal corruption mitigation mechanisms Lange identifies four types (functions) of corruption controls by organizations: 1) autonomy reduction (AR); 2) consequence systems (CS); ensuring reward and punishment; 3) environmental sanctioning, 'in which an organization interprets and transmits external pressures to the member for legal/regulatory compliance and social conformity' (ES); 4) 'intrinsically oriented controls, in which an organization fosters and facilitates the member's own inclination to reject corruption behavior' (IC).[31] In other words, the executives who subscribe to the management of corruption adopt two distinct types of strategies when dealing with it — control and prevention — and use two distinct transmitting channels for their actions — organizational hierarchies and personal networks.

In the control mode, managers deal with non-compliant practices reactively after these practices have already taken place and damaged the business. For example, the CEO of an oil company publicly fired a successful regional manager for selling gasoline at a lower price to a company affiliated with him. In the prevention mode, executives deal with risks which might hurt the business if they occur in the future and proactively look out for practices that may be indicative of those risks. For example, the CEO of a mining company issued an executive order prohibiting sales managers from sponsoring foreign trips for government officials.

Hierarchical strategies imply the use of such institutional instruments as executive orders and procedures, codes of conducts, incentive-based systems (punitive or rewarding), formal agendas, direct campaigns. Network-based channels are used for communicating informal signals, hidden agendas, personalized incentives and other methods of informal governance.[32]

Our interviewees point out that in addition to formal policies, it is crucial to communicate the degree of commitment of the leadership informally. Informal incentives and signals can be more effective in mitigating

---

[31] D. Lange, 'A Multidimensional Conceptualization of Organizational Corruption Control', *Academy of Management Review*, 33, 2008, 3, pp. 710–29.

[32] Ledeneva, *Can Russia Modernise?*, pp. 211–43.

corruption risks and preventing specific informal practices by personal example. One CEO set an example for his regional directors and declared a personal commitment to fight conflicts of interest among managers working with informally affiliated vendors and suppliers. He sent a strong signal about the forthcoming change through his company-wide informal network: he would no longer tolerate any divergence from the new strategy, no matter how close his relationships with a particular manager had been in the past. According to him, that informal warning had a stronger impact than all formal policies and procedures developed to tackle the issue.

The combination of two modes and two types of transmitting channels discussed above creates four ideal types of corruption management at the firm level, as presented in Table 4.

Table 4. Types of corruption management at the firm level

Types of Corruption Management	Control	Prevention
Formal channels (heirarchical, official, written, codified)	Reactive management through formal channels (1)	Proactive management through formal channels (3)
Informal channels (network-based, unofficial, unwritten, non-codified)	Reactive management through informal channels (2)	Proactive management through informal channels (4)

The four types are ideal types. Thus, in the example above, the CEO has applied proactive management through informal channels, yet he has also targeted widespread practices of conflict of interest indicating that his actions may have been reactive. Below, we illustrate the ideal types with examples that featured in our qualitative database:

1. *Reactive-formal.* An internal audit investigation of acquisition of assets in a new region results in identifying a conflict of interest on the part of the responsible manager. The CEO fires the manager for abuse of corporate office.
2. *Reactive-informal.* With the help of the founder-CEO's network, a bank employee caught stealing $200,000 from a bank client is not only sacked, but a criminal case against him is opened and a five-year

sentence handed down. Reactive in one case, the sentence is a powerful deterrent for other employees.

3. *Proactive-formal*. Rotating membership in a tender committee every two years as a matter of policy prevents long-term informal affiliations of its members, bias in decisions and inflated contracts for affiliated vendor and suppliers of large oil and gas companies.

4. *Proactive-informal*. Before introducing a new policy with regard to purchasing managers' expenses, a Russian energy company CEO attends a number of meetings with them and discusses the proposed policy off the record. These meetings allow the managers to share concerns, raise important questions and create awareness, thus giving them a chance to adjust their routines in advance of publication of the formal policy.

None of the described types of strategies is superior in delivering effective management of corruption. The choice depends on such contingencies as the nature and prioritization of specific corruption risks, the initiators, beneficiaries and cost bearers of the specific non-compliant practice, the resources available to the CEO, and the corporate culture of the firm. CEOs of companies operating in a systemically corrupt environment need to master all four types and to develop the largest possible arsenal of anti-corruption strategies.[33]

The example of one leading Russian energy company demonstrates how it can be done. In 2010, the CEO's team initiated a thorough investigation of corruption risks in the company and identified two targets: vendors' kickbacks and managers' conflicts of interest. With an aim to fully eradicate cases of undeclared and unauthorized conflict of interest in relation to vendors' contracts in excess of US $20 million and to reduce total corporate purchasing costs by 15 per cent in three years. They identified the initiators (owners and managers of suppliers related to corporate executives and corporate executives), the beneficiaries (corporate executives and related parties, owners of vendor companies) and the cost bearers (five individuals, including the CEO, who owned the company). After that the CEO and his team outlined a set of specific strategies with regard to each identified stakeholder group, as presented below in Table 5.

---

[33] A simulation game was developed by Stanislav Shekshnia and Alena Ledeneva as an INSEAD tool of training leaders for handling high-risk environment and uncertainty.

Table 5. Corruption mitigation strategies

	Stakeholders	
	Owners and CEOs of vendors	**Corporate executives with conflict of interest**
Control/Informal	Collecting rumours about vendors/executives' relations through informal networks.	Sending informal signals to specific executives to fix their conflict of interest or to be publicly ostracized.
Control/Formal	Breaking contracts with vendors suspected to be in affiliation with corporate executives. Instructing internal audit and internal security to conduct investigations of potential cases of conflict of interest.	Amnesty (3 months) for all reported cases of conflict of interest. Firing people with conflict of interest after 3 months. Opening criminal cases against some executives.
Prevention/ Informal	Informal CEO meetings with key suppliers to communicate the new policy and advise on disengaging corporate executives and their relatives from shareholders/ beneficiaries of their businesses.	Sending a strong signal through the company grapevine about the seriousness of the new strategy.
Prevention/Formal	Updating vendors' management rules. Communicating new procedures of vendors' management at vendors' conference. Establishing conflict commissions for vendors' complaints.	Replacing committee principle with individual general manager's responsibility in purchasing management.

After three years these anti-corruption initiatives have achieved some tangible results: the cost of purchasing decreased by 15 per cent, more than twenty companies were excluded from the suppliers' list, twenty-seven corrupt managers lost their jobs, and five received jail terms.

Conclusion

We would like to conclude by summarizing key action points for senior business leaders to effectively manage corruption in systemically corrupt environments such as Russia:

1. Make corruption management one of the CEO's top priorities. Start by recognizing corruption as a major risk for the company and its stakeholders, overcome blind spots and lack of recognition with regard to corruption risks.
2. Channel the priority status of the anti-corruption management through both the organizational hierarchy and informal networks.
3. Use a bottom-up, ethnographic approach to identify specific practices that are particularly problematic. Spend time and resources investigating which specific informal practices inflict most systematic damage on the corporation. 'Slice' the corruption 'elephant' into smaller pieces that can be more easily tackled in endemically corrupt environments.
4. Target specific non-compliant practices, not corruption in general.
5. Combine formal tools and informal influence. Effective anti-corruption strategies are based both on formal tools (such as hotlines, codes of conduct, open tender competition and standard policies and procedures) and informal influence (role modelling, peer pressure and other instruments of informal governance).
6. Provide training to employees to develop skills to identify, articulate, measure and mitigate non-compliant practices. Most CEOs seeking to mitigate the risks of business corruption in Russian companies agree that making key employees at every level of the organization active participants in the anti-corruption strategy is critical for its success. Conducting detailed surveys on informal practices and providing a platform for discussion of the elephant-in-the-room in systemically corrupt environments is an important addition to anti-corruption legal training and integrity education. A leader's will to control the risks associated with corruption, to go beyond general programmes of anti-corruption compliance and to offer specific skills to identify, articulate, measure and manage corrupt practices can and does work in endemically corrupt environments.

Appendix 1 — Descriptive Statistics

	Frequency	Per cent	Cumulative per cent
Firm size: number of employees			
no response	8	7.27	7.27
> 50,000	4	3.64	10.91
10,000 – 49,999	10	9.09	20.00
1,0000 – 9,999	21	19.09	39.09
100 – 999	33	30.00	69.09
50 – 99	14	12.73	81.82
> 50	20	18.18	100.00
Industry			
no response	5	4.55	4.55
extractive industry	3	2.73	7.27
energy, oil & gas	7	6.36	13.64
manufacturing	13	11.82	25.45
telecommunications & IT	16	14.55	40.00
financial services	12	10.91	50.91
retail	5	4.55	55.45
services	25	22.73	78.18
other	24	21.82	100.00
Firm ownership			
no response	5	4.55	4.55
foreign company	13	11.82	16.36
joint venture	9	8.18	24.55
public company	5	4.55	29.09
government-controlled public company	2	1.82	30.91
state-owned company	6	5.45	36.36
private company	70	63.64	100.00
Firm: present in number of regions			
no response	5	4.55	4.55
> 10	28	25.45	30.00
5 – 9	17	15.45	45.45
2 – 4	41	37.27	82.73
1	19	17.27	100.00

	Frequency	Per cent	Cumulative per cent
Firm: age			
no response	6	5.45	5.45
> 20	16	14.55	20.00
11 – 20	46	41.82	61.82
6 – 10	25	22.73	84.55
2 – 5	12	10.91	95.45
< 5	5	4.55	100.00
Respondent: position in firm			
no response	5	4.55	4.55
supervisory board	12	10.91	15.45
vice-president	6	5.45	20.91
CEO	40	36.36	57.27
board of directors	13	11.82	69.09
shareholder	10	9.09	78.18
other	24	21.82	100.00
Respondent: years within firm			
no response	5	4.55	4.55
11 – 20	25	22.73	27.27
6 – 10	31	28.18	55.45
2 – 5	36	32.73	88.18
< 5	13	11.82	100.00
TOTAL	110	100.00	

NOTES ON CONTRIBUTORS

Claudia Baez-Camargo is Head of Governance Research at the Basel Institute on Governance, University of Basel.

Roxana Bratu is an ANTICORRP Postdoctoral Research Associate in Global and European Anti-Corruption Policies at UCL SSEES (2012–17).

Luciana Cingolani is a Post-Doctoral Researcher at the Hertie School of Governance, Berlin.

Elena Denisova-Schmidt is Lecturer for Russian Culture and Society at the University of St. Gallen.

Mihály Fazekas is a Research Associate at the University of Cambridge and Corvinus University of Budapest.

Paul M. Heywood is Sir Francis Hill Professor of European Politics at the University of Nottingham and Programme Leader of the British Academy-Department for International Development Anti-Corruption Evidence (ACE) partnership, 2015–18. He is a Trustee of Transparency International-UK.

Philipp Köker is a Senior Research Fellow in Politics and International Relations in the School of Psychology, Politics and Sociology at Canterbury Christ Church University, and ANTICORRP Fellow at UCL SSEES from 2012 to 2016.

Alena Ledeneva is Professor of Politics and Society at UCL SSEES.

Stanislav Shekshnia is Senior Affiliate Professor of Entrepreneurship and Family Enterprise at INSEAD, Fontainebleau.

Dimitri A. Sotiropoulos is Associate Professor in the Department of Political Science and Public Administration, University of Athens.

Maya Stoyanova is researcher in the Department of Political Science and Public Administration, University of Athens.

www.ingramcontent.com/pod-product-compliance
Lightning Source LLC
Chambersburg PA
CBHW072144270326
41931CB00010B/1879